THE GOVERNMENT OF NORTHERN IRELAND

Oxford University Press, Amen House, London E.C.4

GLASGOW NEW YORK TORONTO MELBOURNE WELLINGTON
BOMBAY CALCUTTA MADRAS KARACHI LAHORE DACCA
CAPE TOWN SALISBURY NAIROBI IBADAN ACCRA
KUALA LUMPUR HONG KONG

THE GOVERNMENT OF NORTHERN IRELAND

Public Finance and Public Services 1921–1964

R. J. LAWRENCE

Lecturer in Political Science
The Queen's University of Belfast

CLARENDON PRESS · OXFORD
1965

MADE AND PRINTED IN GREAT BRITAIN BY
WILLIAM CLOWES AND SONS, LIMITED, LONDON AND BECCLES

TO MY WIFE

Preface

THE primary aim of this book is to provide evidence for the formulation of definite conclusions about the system of government known as parliamentary devolution, which since 1921 has given Northern Ireland a status that is unique in the British Commonwealth. Neither a dominion nor a colony, Northern Ireland is an integral part of the United Kingdom, yet it possesses a written constitution and a separate legislature and executive. Why was devolution devised? Has it succeeded? Could it be extended with advantage to Great Britain? These in the main are the questions I have tried to answer.

The scope of the work is therefore limited. It is not a detailed account of every aspect of government in Northern Ireland. The emphasis, as the sub-title indicates, is on the evolution of public finance and public services, for it is principally in these directions that one must look to appreciate the difficulties and assess the achievements of regional self-government. However, in order to make the volume more useful, I have outlined the constitution of Northern Ireland and the structure and functions of the central government and other public authorities. The narrative has been carried up to 1964 and it incorporates statistical material that was published by the end of that year, but some events of unusual importance at the beginning of 1965 have also been noted.

As the work took shape, it became necessary to lengthen the perspective. The fortunes of Northern Ireland were linked with those of the rest of Ireland until 1920, and many problems dealt with in this study have their roots in the earlier period. It would, however, be disproportionate to devote much space to the affairs of the whole island before 1920 as a prelude to examining later developments in a small part of it. I have met this difficulty by sketching in those events that seem to have been of special significance for Northern Ireland. I am prepared to believe that, in my desire to be clear as well as short, I have made statements that do not accommodate all the subtleties of Irish affairs and Anglo-Irish relations.

In Northern Ireland itself after 1921 virtually every activity of government was the subject of bitter controversy. A scholar has therefore a special duty to present evidence fully and fairly, to distinguish matters of fact from matters of opinion, and to make judgments only after careful and dispassionate examination. These are the ideals I have set before myself. But the most acute controversies arose because the aims of different groups were irreconcilable, and I could not conceal my own views even if I had wished to do so. I have, however, tried to inform rather than to persuade; and the rather voluminous footnotes are designed, not only to anchor the narrative to the facts, but to direct the reader's attention to sources that may help him to make up his own mind.

In preparing this work, which is based upon a thesis that was accepted for the degree of Ph.D. by the Queen's University of Belfast, I have received much generous assistance. Professor J. H. Warrender read the whole of the typescript, made many suggestions for improving it, and gave me much counsel and encouragement. I wish to express the warmest gratitude for all the help he has given me. Professor R. D. C. Black and Dr. W. Black read through early drafts, and I thank them for their helpful comments. I am indebted to Miss E. M. Harrison for advice on particular points, and to my son Richard for help in checking the statistics. Mr. T. B. Graham, formerly Town Clerk of Bangor, co. Down, and Mr. R. J. Lynn, Superintendent of Rate of the City of Belfast, read portions of the typescript and kindly gave me the benefit of their special knowledge. My other friends in various branches of the public services must remain anonymous, but I offer them sincere thanks for helping me to avoid errors of fact and of emphasis. Most of my work was done in the Library of the Queen's University of Belfast and in the Linen Hall Library, Belfast, and I am grateful for the ready help given me by the librarians and their assistants.

Some material in the book has previously been published in the form of articles. For permission to use these I am indebted to the editor of *Public Administration* and to the editor of *Political Studies* and the publishers of that journal, the Clarendon Press, Oxford. Her Majesty's Stationery Office has kindly given me permission to reproduce extracts from Parliamentary Debates and to make use of other Official publications.

Queen's University, Belfast R. J. L.
July 1965

Contents

List of Statistical Tables

Note on the Citation of Official Documents

IN the notes references to United Kingdom statutes and parliamentary papers are distinguished from references to corresponding Northern Ireland documents in the following manner:

Education Act, 1944	United Kingdom statutes
Education Act (N.I.), 1923	Northern Ireland statutes
127 H.C. Deb., 5 s., 1125	United Kingdom House of Commons Debates, 5th series, vol. 127, col. 1125
H.C. Deb. (N.I.), 10, c. 25	Northern Ireland House of Commons Debates, vol. 10, col. 25
Senate Deb., 4, c. 32	Northern Ireland Senate Debates, vol. 4, col. 32
U.K. C., Cd., Cmd.	United Kingdom Command Papers
Cmd.	Northern Ireland Command Papers
H.C.	Northern Ireland House of Commons Papers
P.A.C.	Reports from the Select Committee on Public Accounts, Northern Ireland
C.A.G.	Reports of the Northern Ireland Comptroller and Auditor General on the Appropriation, Consolidated Fund Services and Revenue Accounts

The title, year, class and number of a document are given when it is cited for the first time in each chapter. For example: P.A.C. 1947–48, H.C. 873. In subsequent references only the class and number are given.

PART ONE
Perspective

CHAPTER ONE
The Debate on Home Rule

THE creation of the United Kingdom of Great Britain and Ireland extended over three centuries. The political assimilation of Wales with England dating from 1536, of Scotland with England and Wales from 1707, and of Ireland with Great Britain from 1801, subjected all the peoples of the two islands to laws made by a single Parliament.

Why single? Could not the unity of the realm be reconciled with, or even strengthened by, a plurality of parliaments? London is geographically remote from Edinburgh, Cardiff and Dublin; Englishmen know little and care less about Scottish, Welsh and Irish affairs; yet England has always had a large and permanent majority in the House of Commons. Members of purely local legislatures, on the other hand, would be acquainted with local conditions, sensitive to the wishes of local electors, personally interested in resisting the erosion of local culture and traditions; and the wider their powers, the more they would contribute to reduce congestion and delay at Westminster.

So runs an argument that ever since the 1880's has impressed some Scottish and Welsh patriots and a handful of British parliamentarians. It has, however, never been put to the test of experience—except in an area where it held little appeal. Northern Ireland, generally known today as Ulster, was obliged in 1920 to accept a Parliament that her people did not ask for; and the self-government imposed upon them was the outcome, not of discussion on the abstract merits and demerits of parliamentary devolution, but of the debate on Irish Home Rule.

What, it may be asked, is the significance of these statements?

The attitudes of a bygone generation and the origins of an institution are irrelevant to assessments of its present value. If we wish to reach conclusions about the merits of parliamentary devolution, as distinct from studying the forces that produced it in one particular area, should we not confine our attention to its actual working in Northern Ireland today?

The answer will become apparent as the narrative unfolds. We shall show that Northern Ireland after 1920 was caught in a predicament which is incomprehensible if torn from its historical context. Ulster has overcome this predicament. For many years she has apparently been a successful working model of regional self-government. Our examination will suggest that this is due, not to the intrinsic excellence of devolution, but rather to the fact that the attitudes of Ulstermen were moulded by historical influences that have no counterpart in Britain.

Through the social structure of Ireland there ran a fissure caused by English policy and widened by tension between the Roman Catholic and Protestant conceptions of life. For centuries before the Union of 1801 the Celtic Irish and the Anglo-Normans who mingled with them suffered from English rule. Their language, laws, property rights, culture and religion were undermined, at times indirectly and subtly, more often with the directness and ferocity of a crusade. This policy was worse than a crime. Its authors made the mistake of being, not savage enough permanently to enforce their will, but sufficiently barbarous to sow seeds of hatred. 'To have exterminated the Catholics by the sword,' says Hallam, 'or expelled them, like the Moriscoes of Spain, would have been little more repugnant to justice and humanity, but incomparably more politic.'[1] Even after the Union and Roman Catholic emancipation in 1829, the mass of the Irish peasantry were still victims of sickening misfortune—above all, the famine of 1845–47. To them, with their long memories of English misrule and their distinctive way of life which no government had been able wholly to obliterate, the United Kingdom of Great Britain and Ireland was a symbol, not of union, but coercive power. As British politicians during the nineteenth century gradually weakened their Protestant landlords and masters and gave them the right to send their own representatives to Westminster, so the

[1] H. Hallam, *Constitutional History of England* (Everyman edn., 1936), vol. iii, p. 351.

repeal or amendment of the Union and a measure of self-government seemed an increasingly attractive panacea for every remaining frustration.

Protestants by natural reaction clung the more tightly to the British connexion. In southern Ireland the landed gentry in particular looked to England to preserve their privileges against the Catholic majority, though there were exceptions. Parnell, effective leader of the Irish parliamentary party from 1877 to 1890, was a Protestant landlord.

In the north-east, however, history had left a different stamp. Of the nine counties that formed the province of Ulster (Antrim, Down, Armagh, Cavan, Donegal, Fermanagh, Londonderry, Tyrone and Monaghan), the first two were already in part in Protestant ownership when, at the beginning of the seventeenth century, all the others except Monaghan were declared forfeit by the Crown and large areas were turned over to English and Scots settlers.[1] In consequence of this plantation in Ulster, there gradually arose a relatively compact community which, swollen by natural increase and spontaneous migration from England and Scotland, gave much of the province its distinctive characteristics —Protestantism and devotion to the Crown.

In Ulster itself society was not, indeed, wholly coherent. Protestants often clashed and rarely mixed with Roman Catholics, who were especially numerous in the south and west. The Orange Order, an anti-Catholic society with the professed object of maintaining religious and civil liberty, was founded in 1795, not in the mainly Protestant county of Antrim, but in Armagh. Then, too, the lines between episcopacy and dissent were sharply drawn. The Church of Ireland, buttress of the establishment and the landlords, enjoyed privileges that were not finally extinguished until Gladstone disestablished it in 1869. By contrast, Scots Presbyterians and other dissenters suffered disabilities and were debarred from all public offices in the late eighteenth century. This antagonism—between church and dissent, English and Scots, conformity and independence of mind—retained its vitality long into the nineteenth century. It was especially in evidence in the sensitive field of educational policy. Britain's attempt in 1831 to promote unity in Ireland by creating national schools was frustrated by resistance, not only or even mainly from Roman Catholics,

[1] J. C. Beckett, *A Short History of Ireland* (London, 1952), p. 71.

but also from Presbyterians and adherents of the established Church.[1]

Nevertheless, this antipathy gradually ceased to excite men's minds after the Union. Considerations of material interest powerfully reinforced the ties of racial stock and religion that already bound most people in northern Ireland to Britain. Always the wealthiest of the four Irish provinces, Ulster prospered under British commercial policy. The Belfast area, in particular, became an integral part of the British industrial complex, sharing the same markets, the same sources of materials and to a large extent the same manpower.[2] In southern Ireland, however, free trade proved disastrous both to the host of small farmers and to the handful of manufacturers. On the one side, therefore, the Nationalist demand for repeal of the Union and for protective tariffs became more strident. On the other, Protestant Ulstermen closed their ranks to resist the establishment in Dublin of a legislature that would certainly tax the north for the benefit of the south and possibly raise barriers against trade with Britain and the outside world.

Despite these divisions, the Liberal Party, committed by Gladstone to Home Rule, persisted in trying to create a single Irish Parliament by their Home Rule Bills of 1886, 1893 and 1912. The first was rejected by the Commons, the second was thrown out by the Lords, and when the third finally reached the statute book in 1914 (the Lords' veto having been overridden by the Commons' use of powers conferred by the Parliament Act, 1911), it was suspended because war had broken out. So the only practical outcome was to sharpen the Nationalist appetite for self-government, drive more Protestant Ulstermen to seek political and social solidarity within the Orange Order and the Ulster Unionist Council set up in 1905, and fuse together the disparate elements bent on maintaining British rule—Irish Unionists, Liberal Unionists and—most powerful in numbers and influence—the Conservative and Unionist Party, which finally absorbed its allies.

Yet in 1920 a predominantly Conservative Parliament sanctioned a solution that differed from Gladstone's in only one material respect: instead of one Parliament in Ireland there were to be two, in Dublin and Belfast. By that time, however, conditions in Ireland

[1] See Chapter Six (Education).

[2] At the end of the nineteenth century more than half the trade unionists of Belfast were members of British-based unions, and labour flowed freely between industrial areas in England, Scotland and Ulster. E. Strauss, *Irish Nationalism and British Democracy* (London, 1951), p. 234.

were transformed. Moderate Nationalists in the Irish parliamentary party had been superseded by the revolutionary Sinn Féin (Ourselves) organization. Southern Ireland repudiated the limited scheme of self-government and after a bitter struggle seceded first from the United Kingdom and later from the Commonwealth.

So much for the bare facts. What construction are we to put on them? The accepted view today is that Anglo-Irish relations after the Union constitute a tragedy of errors. If Ireland had not become a bone in the English party dog-fight, Home Rule with effective safeguards for Ulster might have been successfully imposed at any time before extreme nationalism became rampant.[1] Northern Ireland herself has shown that Home Rule is practicable.[2] Gladstone may have been precipitate, but he was at least acting on realistic (and, some would say, equitable) principles. Conservative Unionists, however, were governed by greed and fear. Their attitude was moulded, so it is argued, by their determination to maintain in Ireland the great Protestant landowners and by their imperialist resolution to preserve inviolate the United Kingdom as the hub of Empire. Ulster, to the majority of English Unionists, was simply an excuse, an Orange card to be played in a game for higher stakes.[3]

The trouble with this argument for our present purpose is that it ignores the hard, practical problems of Home Rule. It makes Anglo-Irish relations coherent, but only because it does not correspond wholly with the facts. This can readily be seen if we consider two points.

First, Conservatives played a part in destroying the Protestant ascendancy in Ireland. A Tory Administration first weakened the supremacy of the Protestant faith. By forcing Roman Catholic emancipation through Parliament in 1829, Peel and Wellington cleared the ground for Irish representation at Westminster and wove Irish grievances into the texture of British politics. One of the deepest of those grievances—the government of Irish counties by unrepresentative grand juries—was ended by Gerald Balfour's Local Government (Ireland) Act of 1898, a measure which (in the words of John Redmond, Irish Nationalist leader from 1900 to

[1] G. M. Trevelyan, *British History in the Nineteenth Century and After* (2nd edn., London, 1946), p. 457.

[2] R. C. K. Ensor, *England, 1870–1914* (Oxford, 1936), p. 450.

[3] See e.g. R. Blake, *The Unknown Prime Minister* (London, 1955), pp. 122–3, 149–50, 157.

1918) 'completely disestablished the old ascendancy class from its position of power and made the mass of the Irish people masters of all the finance and all the local affairs of Ireland'.[1] Another Conservative Chief Secretary (George Wyndham) introduced the Land Act of 1903, which enabled really large numbers of Irish peasant farmers to buy out their landlords. These measures probably did more to break the grip of the ascendancy than Gladstone's land reforms or his disestablishment of the episcopal Church. Yet by the beginning of the twentieth century, when the Protestant ascendancy was in an advanced stage of decay, Unionist resistance to Home Rule was as strong as, if not stronger than, ever before.

Secondly, to say that Unionists were imperialist conveys little information about their attitude to Ireland. The only aspect of their policy after, say, 1886 that could be called 'imperialist' was their determination to maintain the political unity of the United Kingdom and the supremacy of Parliament. On this issue, though, there was no difference whatever between them and Liberal Home Rulers. Gladstone himself, after the general election of 1885 had routed his party in Ireland and convinced him of the need for an Irish legislature, stipulated that the first condition of any admissible plan for Home Rule was 'union of the Empire and due supremacy of Parliament'.[2] From that he never deviated, nor did Mr. Asquith as long as he was Prime Minister.[3]

There was, however, one clear issue that divided the parties. They differed profoundly in their estimate of the consequences of conceding to Ireland limited self-government. Liberal Home Rulers believed with Gladstone that the surest way to strengthen the ties between Britain and Ireland was to loosen them: the thread of liberty would prove stronger than the chains of coercion.[4] Their opponents regarded this as rhetoric. They, whether Tories, dissident Liberals or Irish Unionists, held that the alternatives lay between maintaining the Union and giving Ireland complete independence. Short of a wholesale reconstruction of the British

[1] D. Gwynn, *The Life of John Redmond* (London, 1932), p. 90.

[2] J. Morley, *The Life of William Ewart Gladstone* (London, 1903), vol. iii, p. 263.

[3] In 1920, when no longer in power, Mr. Asquith declared his readiness to give Ireland to all intents and purposes the status of a dominion. 127 H.C. Deb., 5 s., 1116.

[4] See e.g. Gladstone's speech introducing the Bill of 1893. 8 Parl. Deb., 4 s., 1241 et seq.

constitution on federal principles—which no party seriously contemplated—there was no half-way house between union and separation. That was a distinctive and abiding feature of the Unionist argument.

In order to explain that argument and show how Northern Ireland became entangled by it, we must sketch in the relevant features of the Union which, as from 1 January 1801, abolished the Irish Parliament and inaugurated changes (broadly on the model of the Scottish Union of 1707) designed to weld the Kingdom into a fiscal and economic as well as a political unit. Ireland lost the power to tax, to spend and to protect her industries, and her financial affairs were no longer segregated. She was not, indeed, subject at once to British rates of taxation, but fiscal equality was gradually introduced (principally by Gladstone) until by the end of the century taxation throughout the United Kingdom was virtually uniform. British and Irish national accounts were kept separate only until 1817, when the two Exchequers were amalgamated, all receipts henceforth being paid into the Consolidated Fund of the United Kingdom. The cost of imperial services (e.g. the national debt and defence) was initially divided between Britain and Ireland in the proportion of fifteen to two—a ratio taken to express their relative wealth—but after the amalgamation of the Exchequers this arrangement was abolished. Finally, all restrictions on trade between Britain and Ireland were removed, and after 1825 no accounts were kept of the quantity or value of merchandise shipped from one country to the other.[1]

Parliament at Westminster therefore imposed all taxes; taxpayers paid at the same rates into one Exchequer; and the Exchequer financed all central government services. It was no longer possible to measure Ireland's true revenue (mainly because she had no custom-house), nor her true contribution to imperial services, and there was not much point in making estimates.[2] For the conception of a geographical area was no longer relevant. Ireland was not taxed as a country. Irishmen, like Englishmen,

[1] For extended summaries of financial developments under the Union see *Royal Commission on the Financial Relations between Great Britain and Ireland*, Minutes of Evidence, vol. i, U.K. C. 7720–I (1895), App. I and *Committee on Irish Finance*, Minutes of Evidence, U.K. Cd. 6799 (1913), App. IX B.

[2] A number of estimates were made, mainly in connexion with Home Rule proposals. The Royal Commission on Financial Relations concluded in 1896 that Ireland was over-taxed. U.K. C. 8262 (1896). The Committee on Irish Finance found in 1911 that Ireland was not paying her way. U.K. Cd. 6153 (1912).

were taxed as individuals. It was not necessary to set local expenditure against local taxation, and British governments on the whole did not try to do this in Ireland any more than in Scotland or England and Wales. The system was indiscriminate and on the whole equitable.[1] What was unjust was its application. There can be little doubt that less public money was spent in Ireland than was warranted by her people's needs. As we shall see, Northern Ireland inherited services that were inferior to the general standard in Great Britain.

However, if Ireland was to be given self-government—if the notion of a distinct political unit was to have reality—it was necessary to revise the whole system. An Irish Parliament that was more than a façade would need powers to raise money. Now, the greater part (as much as 80 per cent. at the turn of the century)[2] of the revenue imputed to Ireland came from customs and related excise duties; and all experience of government in modern times, from the American Union in 1787 to the German Zollverein of 1834 and the Commonwealth of Australia in 1900, went to show that political union could not be secured without centralized control of customs. An Irish legislature with power to tax imports would not only be able to raise a customs barrier against Britain, but would also be tempted to conclude open or covert commercial treaties with foreign countries. That would mean separate Irish representation abroad and pressure for a distinct foreign policy. In such circumstances friction between Britain and Ireland was certain and the eventual disruption of the Union highly probable.

For these reasons most Home Rulers and all Unionists agreed that the United Kingdom must retain customs duties and those excise duties that could be used as protective devices.[3] Britain

[1] It is probable that the structure of taxation was unfavourable to a greater proportion of the people of Ireland than of Great Britain. On the whole question see A. E. Murray, *A History of the Commercial and Financial Relations between England and Ireland* (London, 1907), chap. xviii.

[2] The amount of revenue that Ireland could fairly claim raised highly controversial questions. The General Council of Irish County Councils reckoned that revenue during the five years 1905–9 averaged £10·3 m., of which customs and excise accounted for £8·1 m. (U.K. Cd. 6799, App. VI).

[3] Gladstone in 1886 originally intended to give Ireland complete control of taxation, a course logically linked with his intention to exclude Irish members from Westminster. On these and other issues he accepted the resignation of Joseph Chamberlain. Morley, op. cit., vol. iii, pp. 295 ff. When Hugh Childers, then Home Secretary, also threatened to resign if customs and excise were handed over, Gladstone gave way. S. Childers, *The Life and Correspondence of Hugh C. E. Childers* (London, 1901), vol. ii, pp. 248–9. Thereafter Gladstone

would levy and collect the greater part of Irish taxation. What, then, of Irish self-government? L. S. Amery wrote in 1912:

> The idea that an Irish Chancellor of the Exchequer can carry on in dependence on a British Budget which may at any moment upset all his calculations of revenue is absurd. So is the idea that there can be separate tariffs with mutual free trade or a common tariff without a common government to frame it.[1]

Austen Chamberlain made a similar point:

> Whether customs and excise are handed over to the Irish Parliament or retained by the imperial Parliament, the consequences are equally embarrassing. In the one case Ireland would be deprived of the control of some sixty per cent. of her present revenue and of all power of expansion; on the other, British trade with Ireland might be gravely injured by hostile legislation and the union of the three kingdoms in financial and commercial policy would be destroyed. But this is not federation, nor is it a step towards it. It is separation pure and simple. Unless we are prepared to accept separation as the end of our policy the control of customs and therefore of excise must remain an imperial affair.[2]

Confronted by this dilemma, Liberal governments decided to retain customs and excise. Indeed, in their last pre-war Bill (that of 1912) the Liberals proposed to withhold from Ireland the power to vary income tax, so as to avoid administrative confusion.[3] The leaders of a victorious party in Ireland would thus find themselves saddled with responsibility but little power. Unable to inaugurate with confidence those social reforms on which Irishmen set great store, forbidden to protect local industries, and in general constrained from trying to evade the repercussions of policies shaped mainly by England and directed mainly to her interest—in these

---

himself always took the view that fiscal unity must be maintained. Speaking on the Government of Ireland Bill on 8 April 1886, he said, 'To give up the fiscal unity of the Empire would be a great public inconvenience and a very great public misfortune—a very great public misfortune for Great Britain; and I believe it would be a still greater misfortune for Ireland were the fiscal unity of the Empire to be put to hazard and practically abandoned.' 304 Parl. Deb., 3 s., 1057. He continued to hold this view in 1893, though it plunged him into the difficulty that Ireland could not be taxed by the United Kingdom if she had no representation in its Parliament. 8 Parl. Deb., 4 s., 1260 et seq. In 1912 Mr. Asquith's Government incorporated in their Bill the most careful safeguards against any possibility of discrimination by Ireland against British goods. 46 H.C. Deb., 5 s., 2201.

[1] S. Rosenbaum (ed.), *Against Home Rule* (London, 1912), p. 287.

[2] ibid., pp. 115–16.

[3] 46 H.C. Deb., 5 s., 1252.

conditions Irish politicians, though formally in possession of political authority, would be reduced to near impotence. They, their opponents in other parties, the Press and the electorate would soon realize that the Chancellor of the Exchequer in effect dominated their Parliament, and political pressures would inevitably find their chief outlet in renewed protests against British ascendancy.

That was not all. The Liberal attempt to create a separate Irish Exchequer raised two further problems. The first concerned charges for imperial services. Ireland under Home Rule would not only enjoy internal self-government; she would also benefit from, and through her representatives at Westminster share control of, such common or imperial services as defence and relations with other countries. So it was taken for granted that she ought to contribute to their cost. This at once made it essential to segregate Irish revenue from British revenue.

It should be noted that neither of these points was necessary to maintain the Union. The British Government could have paid for common services from common taxes and remitted to Ireland a sum equal to the difference between Irish domestic expenditure and Irish revenue. Such an expedient was bound to give rise to contentious questions. How much should Ireland spend? How much ought she to raise by local taxes? These problems, however, were not wholly novel. Parliament had already made workable though not frictionless arrangements for financing federal and regional services in Canada and Australia. The British North America Act, 1867 (s. 118) required the Dominion to pay specific sums to the Canadian provinces. The Commonwealth of Australia Constitution Act, 1900 (s. 87) provided that for ten years the Commonwealth should pay to the states three-fourths of the revenue from federal customs and excise duties and (s. 96) empowered it to grant financial assistance to any state. In both cases federal services were paid for from federal taxes. It is true that the constitutions in question were largely the work of Canadians and Australians themselves; but at the end of 1919, when the Government of Ireland Bill had already taken shape, the Speaker's Conference on Devolution appointed a Committee under Lord Chalmers to frame a financial scheme for devolution within Great Britain itself.[1] Neither the Conference nor the Committee

[1] Following a Resolution of the House of Commons on 4 June 1919, the Conference was constituted in October with terms of reference extending to the

contemplated arrangements for imperial contributions. Imperial and other non-transferred services were to be financed by the central Exchequer. Local parliaments would have limited powers of taxation: the Committee dismissed the 'facile plan' of financing them entirely by lump-sum grants-in-aid. They also dismissed the 'equally facile but infinitely more fatal plan of leaving each nationality with the revenue assumed to arise within its borders'.[1]

That such a plan would be equally fatal in Ireland seems never to have occurred to Gladstone and his followers. A fundamental object of the Home Rule Bills was to create a distinct and self-sufficient fiscal unit that would both pay for its own services and help to pay for imperial services. Although (as we shall presently explain) British politicians did not confine Irish revenue to sums actually collected in Ireland, they evidently intended to prevent that unhappy country from enjoying self-government at Britain's expense. They therefore revived the arrangements that had applied during the early years of the Union. Of the public income attributable to Ireland, part was to be kept within the United Kingdom Exchequer as a contribution to imperial expenditure.[2] Hence, there were two claims on Irish revenue, for domestic services and imperial services, and the sum spent on one would vary inversely with that spent on the other. In other words, the imperial contribution had either to be a first charge or the residue left after expenditure on Irish services had been allowed for.

A first charge was clearly impracticable. Whether a fixed sum as proposed in 1886[3] or a variable amount such as a third part of Irish revenue as provided for in 1893,[4] it would have prior claim on receipts that might at any time be reduced by a cut in United Kingdom customs and excise duties or by a fall in their yield due to changes in British commercial policy. An Irish Minister of Finance would then be obliged either to economize on domestic

---

whole United Kingdom. Shortly afterwards, however, the Government of Ireland Bill was published and the Conference therefore restricted the scope of their inquiry to Great Britain.

[1] *Conference on Devolution: Letter from Mr. Speaker to the Prime Minister*, U.K. Cmd. 692 (1920), p. 20.

[2] The Government of Ireland Act, 1914 made no provision for an immediate imperial contribution because at that time expenditure on Irish services exceeded Irish revenue. By s. 26, however, arrangements were to be made with a view to securing a contribution when the Irish account showed a surplus.

[3] Government of Ireland Bill, 1886 (Bill 181), cl. 13.

[4] Government of Ireland Bill, 1893 (as amended in Committee, Bill 428), cl. 10 (4).

services or to increase taxation within the very limited field under his control. To expect Irishmen to tolerate either course while the imperial contribution continued to rank as a prior charge was unrealistic. On the other hand, if the imperial contribution were fixed and the United Kingdom were to impose higher taxes, Ireland would get a windfall which she might not need and the relative size of her contribution would diminish. Joseph Chamberlain said in 1893:

> Consider what would be the position of the Irish Chancellor of the Exchequer under these conditions. . . . The British Chancellor of the Exchequer reduces taxation and by so doing sweeps away the Irish surplus and leaves the Irish Chancellor of the Exchequer to find in the best way he can from the only taxes open to him—which are all in the nature of direct taxation on property—the sum he wants for his patriotic undertakings. . . . Look at it from another point of view. I have spoken of a reduction of taxation, but suppose that the imperial Chancellor of the Exchequer had to levy new taxes on account of increase in the imperial expenditure or even of British expenditure. . . . Is it not probable, is it not certain, is it not necessary under these circumstances that the Irish members will have a good deal to say as to your British finance? Can they allow their own finance to be disorganized and upset purely at the will and for the convenience of the British Chancellor of the Exchequer?[1]

The alternative—to make the imperial contribution a residue—was never embodied in any Home Rule Bill, for it was even more unworkable. If Britain was to be sure of a residue she would need power to scrutinize and if necessary prune the Irish Budget each year. A people who aspired to govern themselves were hardly likely to accept that. Even if they were, their Government's plight would be intolerable. With little control of revenue and without sole control of expenditure, and therefore unable to bring the one into relation with the other, they would find the balancing of their Budget to be largely a matter of chance.

The second problem that concerns us was probably the more difficult. What was Ireland's true revenue? It was certainly larger than the sum collected on her soil. For example, duty collected in Britain on goods exported to Ireland was incorporated in the price paid by the Irish consumer and was therefore attributable to Ireland. Again, it could be argued that the Irish Exchequer should be credited with the proceeds of taxes borne by residents of

[1] 15 Parl. Deb., 4 s., 219–21.

Ireland who worked in Britain or who owned taxable assets there. Such questions raised issues of equity and of fact: of equity, because what was at stake was Ireland's fair share of general revenue; of fact, because her share had to be measured. Even on the latter point the financial experts disagreed, and it was impossible to resolve their differences to the satisfaction of all parties because the United Kingdom was a fiscal unit and Ireland neither had nor was to have a custom-house. Liberal governments proposed to remit these and other controversial financial matters to a joint exchequer board (in 1893 a joint committee), of representatives of Great Britain and Ireland. Unionists contended that to do so would only provide a new focus for conflict. In 1912 Bonar Law declared:

> Under your Bill the Exchequer Board will be the most powerful body in Ireland, far superior to any Prime Minister, for they will have to decide, not on matters of fact, but on matters of opinion.[1]

A. V. Dicey, unionist and eminent constitutional lawyer, wrote:

> The financial policy of the Home Rule Bill of itself provides for perpetual disputes between England and Ireland which will mainly be decided by a Board which will exercise powers inconsistent with the real supremacy of the Imperial Parliament and cannot command the confidence at once of England and of Ireland.[2]

To sum up: Unionists and Home Rulers were equally determined to preserve the Union and the supremacy of Parliament, but Unionists did not share the belief that these aims could be reconciled with the creation of an Irish legislature. This was not only because of Irish nationalism (though that sharpened all the issues), but because, within terms of reference accepted without question by both parties, the maintenance of union and local autonomy in finance were mutually exclusive. Sir Edward (later Lord) Carson, leader of the Ulster Unionists, summed up the matter in 1912:

> We see, as Irish Ministers saw in 1800, that there can be no permanent resting place between complete union and total separation. . . . If there were no other objection to the establishment of a separate government in Dublin, it would be impossible because legislative autonomy can only be coupled with financial independence.[3]

[1] 38 H.C. Deb., 5 s., 683.
[2] A. V. Dicey, *A Fool's Paradise* (London, 1913), p. 81.
[3] Rosenbaum, op. cit., pp. 18, 29.

Eight years later, in 1920, he said:

> The truth of the matter is that there is no alternative to the Union unless separation, and anybody who for a moment will think out the circumstances will necessarily come to that conclusion. We have said it for the last thirty years. It has always been one of our main stock arguments which our opponents jeered at.[1]

So much in bare outline for an argument that has been singularly neglected in accounts of Anglo-Irish relations but which may readily be pursued by turning to 'Hansard'.[2] It is not the whole argument against Home Rule: we have selected those questions that are relevant to our purpose. It should not be imagined, either, that reason was the only influence, or even the main influence, within the Conservative and Unionist Party. The Irish question stirred such profound emotions that it would be naïve to overrate the rationality of any of those who were immersed in it. Nevertheless, if we are to treat history as intelligible debate, it is clear that in one form or another the assertion that union and Home Rule were incompatible was central to the Unionist case.[3]

It is equally clear that Liberal Home Rulers could not ignore that case—their Irish supporters saw to that. Between 1886 and 1912 Liberals slid from one difficulty to another, constantly harried by their Irish allies whose demands they were never able to satisfy. Indeed, among all the uncertainties embedded in the tortuous history of Anglo-Irish relations one thing seems certain: none of the Liberal Home Rule Bills would have worked in Ireland. That theme is not our direct concern but Appendix I to this work will show that no prolonged research is needed to establish its credibility.

What is more to the point is this: Unionists in 1920 imposed on Northern Ireland the very predicament which they and their predecessors had analysed.

[1] 127 H.C. Deb., 5 s., 1289.

[2] On the Bill of 1893 see especially speeches by Joseph Chamberlain, Sir M. Hicks-Beach, G. J. Goschen and G. Wyndham in 10 and 11 Parl. Deb., 4 s. and debate on new clause (financial arrangements) in 15 Parl. Deb., 4 s. On the Bill of 1912 see speeches by L. S. Amery, A. J. Balfour, Sir E. Carson, Austen Chamberlain and Bonar Law in 36, 37, 38, 44 and 46 H.C. Deb., 5 s.

[3] It may be observed that the Unionist argument makes Ulster's fanatical resistance to Home Rule more explicable. Her Protestant population and her business and commercial interests could not depend on safeguards in an Act of the United Kingdom Parliament once Ireland was independent. To that extent, Ulster's attitude was a special case of the general Unionist thesis.

Why did they do it? The Bill of 1912 was put on the statute book on 18 September 1914, but on the same day a Suspensory Act postponed its operation until the end of the war. After the general election of December 1918 Mr. Lloyd George and his Government were thus faced with a problem which they could neither solve nor shelve. The Act of 1914 would automatically come into force when the war officially came to an end, yet simply to repeal it was out of the question. The south of Ireland had flared into open rebellion and the Government were as anxious to placate opinion in Britain —and, no less in America—as they were resolved not to force six counties of the province of Ulster (Antrim, Armagh, Down, Fermanagh, Londonderry and Tyrone) to submit to the authority of a Dublin Parliament. They decided to divide Ireland into two parts but to place squarely on Irishmen themselves the responsibility for making partition permanent or temporary.

The Government of Ireland Act, 1920 provided for the creation in southern and northern Ireland of Parliaments with power to unite if they wished. Those Parliaments were not sovereign. Both Mr. Lloyd George and Mr. Bonar Law (then Lord Privy Seal and Leader of the House of Commons) were convinced that the concession of dominion status to southern Ireland would inevitably lead to an Irish republic.[1] The United Kingdom therefore retained control of the armed forces of the Crown, the conduct of foreign affairs and a number of other imperial services, and reserved the power to impose and collect throughout Ireland customs duties, excise duties on manufactured and produced articles, and taxes on incomes and profits.[2] The Irish Parliaments had no power to impose and collect any tax substantially the same in character as any of those duties and taxes, and they were forbidden to impose any general tax on capital. These were sweeping restrictions, but the Government insisted on retaining income tax, both to avoid complications arising from three systems of assessment and collection, and also to preserve collection at source, which provided a substantial and automatic security for payment of an imperial

[1] 127 H.C. Deb., 5 s., 1125; 134 H.C. Deb., 5 s., 1431.

[2] The Act (s. 36) envisaged the possibility, but no more, that customs and excise might be transferred after the date of Irish union. In such an eventuality the method by which an imperial contribution could be secured was also to be considered. The Government refused to accept an amendment providing for the unconditional transfer of taxation to a united Irish legislature. 133 H.C. Deb., 5 s., 2138.

contribution.[1] From the proceeds of these reserved taxes the United Kingdom was to deduct, as an Irish contribution to imperial services, a fixed sum (provisionally £18 m. for the whole of Ireland) for an initial period of two years, and to pay the residue to the Irish Governments. After the initial period the amount of the contribution was to be determined by a Joint Exchequer Board, which was also to decide other financial questions of considerable complexity.

In this way British Conservatives were driven to that middle course between union and separation which on their own logic was impracticable. They pleased neither Irish Unionists nor the handful of Irish Nationalists at Westminster. The most implacable opposition, however, now lay outside Parliament. At the 1918 general election Sinn Féin swept Ireland outside Ulster on a policy of establishing an independent republic. In January of the following year Dáil Éireann, a self-constituted Parliament in Dublin, refused to recognize British authority and issued a declaration of independence. There followed a cruel and savage struggle between British and Irish forces until in July 1921 a truce was declared. Three months later, in October, negotiations between British Ministers and a southern Irish delegation began in London. The outcome was the Treaty of December 1921 by which Sinn Féin secured for the Irish Free State virtual financial autonomy and the constitutional status of the Dominion of Canada. Finally, in 1949, the Republic of Ireland seceded from the Commonwealth.[2]

In these circumstances it may be asked why Ulster also did not repudiate the Act of 1920 in order to revert to the Act of Union. The short answer had already been given by an Ulster Unionist during the debate on the Government of Ireland Bill. A separate Parliament would serve to entrench unionists in Ulster, and Ulster within the United Kingdom.[3]

So it proved. During the Anglo-Irish negotiations referred to

[1] 133 H.C. Deb., 5 s., 2125–9. S. 25 of the Act empowered the Irish Parliaments to grant relief from income tax, but only from their own resources and not at the United Kingdom's expense.

[2] J. L. McCracken, *Representative Government in Ireland* (London, 1958), chaps. i–iv, xiii.

[3] Captain C. C. Craig (a brother of Sir James Craig) said on 29 March 1920 that they were prepared to accept a Parliament which they did not really want because they would then be absolutely sure of staying within the United Kingdom until of their own volition they joined the rest of Ireland. 127 H.C. Deb., 5 s., 989–90.

above, Ulster's status was at once brought into question. The Irish delegates were passionately opposed to partition. Mr. Lloyd George (then Prime Minister) evidently shared their view. In a letter to Sir James Craig (Prime Minister of Northern Ireland) on 10 November 1921 he set out four main principles for a settlement. One of these was recognition of the unity of Ireland by the establishment of an all-Ireland Parliament. In a subsequent letter (on 14 November) he dwelt on the evils of a frontier based 'neither upon natural features nor broad geographical considerations'. He continued, 'Partition on these lines the majority of the Irish people will never accept, nor could we conscientiously attempt to enforce it.'[1]

For Craig, however, the debate on Ulster's status had closed with the Royal assent to the 1920 Act. Lloyd George, for all his wizardry, could not induce him to reopen it; and without Ulster's consent the British Prime Minister could do nothing. Only five months before, in June 1921, King George V in person had opened the Parliament of Northern Ireland. Henceforth Ulster's position as an integral part of the United Kingdom was secure. That any British government would eject her by force was unthinkable. Nor was it realistic for Sinn Féin to make coercion a condition of an Irish settlement.[2] The most they could secure was the Treaty of 1921 which (by Article 1) gave dominion status to Ireland as a whole, but which also (by Article 12) enabled Northern Ireland to vote herself out of the Irish Free State within one month of the Treaty's ratification. Both Houses of the Parliament of Northern Ireland unanimously took this course on 7 December 1922, two days after the statutory date of ratification.[3] The Government of Ireland Act was then modified so as to apply only to Northern Ireland.[4]

So by 1922 the six north-eastern Irish counties had become the

[1] *Correspondence between His Majesty's Government and the Prime Minister of Northern Ireland relating to the Proposals for an Irish Settlement*, U.K. Cmd. 1561 (1921).

[2] Mr. Lloyd George in December 1921 emphasized that he had always relied on persuasion, not coercion, to induce Ulster to join an all-Ireland Parliament. 149 H.C. Deb., 5 s., 38–9.

[3] In the event of Ulster's opting out of the Irish Free State the Treaty provided for the setting up of a Commission to determine the boundary between Northern Ireland and the rest of Ireland. Northern Ireland refused to appoint a representative on the Commission, and the boundary as fixed by the Act of 1920 was subsequently confirmed.

[4] Irish Free State (Consequential Provisions) Act, 1922.

vestigial remnant of the Home Rule struggle. The Protestant population had achieved their dominant aim, to stay in the United Kingdom. Roman Catholics in Ulster (as the six counties came to be called) by and large still cherished the ambition to break the British connexion. Both communities had been obliged to accept a Parliament which they had never demanded and did not really want, and that Parliament's financial powers were ludicrously inadequate. The Northern Ireland Comptroller and Auditor General, in his first Report on the Appropriation Accounts, pointed out that Britain controlled about 88 per cent. of Ulster's revenue and 60 per cent. of her expenditure.[1] Commenting on this in 1924, the Northern Ireland Select Committee on Public Accounts said:

> This position can scarcely be regarded as satisfactory. Northern Ireland has no control over this large portion of its revenue or over this large portion of its expenditure, and its Parliament receives no accounts relating to either.[2]

Sir James Craig was not indulging in empty rhetoric when, in reply to Mr. Lloyd George's letter of 10 November 1921, he wrote 'As a final settlement and supreme sacrifice in the interests of peace the Government of Ireland Act, 1920 was accepted by Northern Ireland, although not asked for by her representatives.'[3]

[1] C.A.G. 1921–22, H.C. 21, p. 20.
[2] P.A.C. 1924, H.C. 60, p. 8.
[3] U.K. Cmd. 1561, p. 5.

PART TWO

Government and Public Finance

CHAPTER TWO

The Constitutional and Social Setting

THE constitution of Northern Ireland, set out in the Government of Ireland Act, 1920, as amended from time to time,[1] is the subject of several studies.[2] We need therefore summarize only its salient features.

Parliament at Stormont (the district near Belfast where the Parliament Buildings are situated) consists of the Queen, the Senate and the House of Commons. The Governor of Northern Ireland summons, prorogues and dissolves Parliament in the Queen's name and gives the Royal assent to Bills. The Senate consists of two *ex-officio* Senators (the Lord Mayor of Belfast and the Mayor of Londonderry) and twenty-four Senators elected for eight years by the House of Commons by proportional representation. It has always been dominated by the Ulster Unionist Party, has never come into conflict with the Commons, and attracts even less attention than a second chamber normally does nowadays in a system of parliamentary (as distinct from presidential) government.[3] There is invariably one Cabinet Minister in the

[1] See *The Constitution of Northern Ireland,* being the Government of Ireland Act, 1920, as amended (H.M.S.O.).

[2] On the law of the constitution see Sir A. S. Quekett, *The Constitution of Northern Ireland* (H.M.S.O., Parts I–III, 1928–46); J. L. Montrose and F. H. Newark, 'Northern Ireland' in *Halsbury's Statutes of England* (2nd edn., 1950), vol. xvii; L. A. Sheridan, 'Northern Ireland' in G. W. Keeton (ed.), *The British Commonwealth* (London, 1955), vol. i. Wider studies of government and politics are N. Mansergh, *The Government of Northern Ireland* (London, 1936); D. G. Neill (ed.), *Devolution of Government* (London, 1953); T. Wilson (ed.), *Ulster Under Home Rule* (London, 1955). See also the *Ulster Year Book,* the Official Year Book of Northern Ireland (H.M.S.O., triennial).

[3] If the Senate reject a public Bill passed by the Commons in two successive sessions, the constitution (s. 17) provides for a joint sitting of both Houses in the

Senate, but any Minister may sit and speak in both Houses, though he can vote only in the House of which he is a member.

The Commons, which has a term not longer than five years, is made up of forty-eight members representing territorial constituencies, together with four members representing the Queen's University of Belfast. The latter are elected by those graduates of the University who are British subjects, by the method of proportional representation (the single transferable vote), which the Act of 1920 prescribed for Northern Ireland as a whole; but for elections outside the University the provincial Parliament in 1929 reverted to the British system of election by simple majorities in single-member constituencies. Unionists have held a majority of seats since 1921. Parliamentary procedure and the system of public finance are based upon the United Kingdom pattern, but Stormont has no Select Committee on Estimates.[1]

Ulster sends twelve members to the House of Commons at Westminster, and for this purpose constituencies and elections are regulated by United Kingdom law. A Boundary Commission presided over by the Speaker of the House of Commons reviews constituencies, as in England, Scotland and Wales.[2] The United Kingdom franchise is virtually the same as in Britain, except that in Ulster there is a qualifying period of three months' residence.[3] The Northern Ireland franchise, prescribed by the local Parliament, is similar with two notable exceptions: (*a*) an elector must have been born in Northern Ireland or resident in the United Kingdom for seven years ending on the qualifying date; (*b*) plural voting (abolished in the United Kingdom in 1948) has been

---

second session to deliberate and vote on the Bill as last proposed by the Commons and on amendments made by one House and not agreed to by the other. A majority of members present determine whether the Bill and any amendments shall be passed. If the Senate reject a Money Bill the joint sitting may be convened during the same session. It has never been necessary to use this procedure because in both Houses the Government has a majority, though sometimes an uncomfortably small one. On the Senate see A. G. Donaldson, 'The Senate of Northern Ireland' in *Public Law*, 1958, pp. 135 ff.

[1] See *Parliament of Northern Ireland: Standing Orders of the House of Commons, Public Business, 1964*, H.C. 1604 and debate on parliamentary practice, H.C. Deb. (N.I.), 54, cc. 206 et seq. The Comptroller and Auditor General's 'Introduction to the work of the Public Accounts Committee (Northern Ireland)' in P.A.C. 1961–62, H.C. 1556, App. III, is useful for students of Ulster's public accounts.

[2] House of Commons (Redistribution of Seats) Act, 1944, s. 1.

[3] Representation of the People Act, 1949, s. 1 (2).

retained.[1] There is no boundary commission, and the forty-eight territorial constituencies have undergone no general adjustment since proportional representation was abolished in 1929.[2]

The Parliament has power to make laws in matters relating exclusively to Northern Ireland; in general, its jurisdiction does not extend beyond its territory, though this has been somewhat relaxed by constitutional amendment. In addition its legislative powers are specifically limited in the following manner. First, the right of citizens to religious freedom and the rights of certain institutions are written into the constitution. The legislature is prohibited from making laws so as to interfere with religious liberty or equality and, except for certain purposes, to acquire compulsorily the property of religious denominations or educational institutions, even on payment of compensation.[3] Laws that purport to do these things, and indeed any law for which no authority can be found in the constitution, can be contested in and nullified by the courts. Secondly, Northern Ireland cannot legislate in respect of excepted services and reserved services. The former include the Crown, defence, external trade and relations and generally matters on which uniformity throughout the realm is essential.[4] Reserved services include the Supreme Court of Northern Ireland, the postal service and the imposition and collection of customs duties, excise duties on articles manufactured or produced, income tax and surtax, purchase tax and any tax on profits. Stormont cannot impose any general tax on capital but can grant relief from income tax and surtax, though only at the expense of the Northern Ireland Exchequer. The United Kingdom provides and controls all these excepted and reserved services, but they must be distinguished because they are financed differently.[5]

[1] An elector may vote in respect of a residence qualification and also in respect of either a business premises or a university qualification, but he can vote only once in one constituency. Electoral Law Act (N.I.), 1962, ss. 1, 29 (3), 31 (2).

[2] In 1963 the number of Northern Ireland parliamentary electors for each territorial constituency averaged 18,348. The range from lowest to highest was from 7,478 (Dock, Belfast) to 40,990 (Mid Down). H.C. Deb. (N.I.), 56, c. 1373.

[3] See below, p. 156, n. (1).

[4] These matters comprise the Crown, the making of peace or war, the royal forces, defence, treaties and external relations, titles of honour, treason, alienage, naturalization, trade with any place out of Northern Ireland, navigation, submarine cables, wireless telegraphy, aerial navigation, lighthouses, buoys or beacons, coinage, legal tender, negotiable instruments, weights and measures, trade marks, copyright, patent rights.

[5] Matters reserved in 1920 (except customs and reserved excise duties as noted on p. 15 above) were to be transferred to the Parliament for the whole of

The constitution (s. 23) requires Northern Ireland to make only a contribution (commonly called the imperial contribution) towards imperial liabilities and expenditure,[1] but the British Government deducts from reserved taxation the whole cost of reserved services except the Post Office, which was split off from the Exchequer in 1961.[2]

Executive power, vested in the sovereign, may be exercised on her behalf by the Governor of Northern Ireland; but the framers of the constitution did not expect, in Ulster any more than Britain, that the monarch or her representative would actually direct the administration. They therefore gave the force of law to several rules which in the United Kingdom are conventions. Thus, Parliament must meet at least once a year,[3] and the Governor's executive powers in transferred matters are to be exercised through departments headed by Ministers who must be members both of the Parliament (within six months of their taking office) and of the Privy Council of Northern Ireland and who, together with any other persons appointed as Ministers, constitute an executive committee of the Privy Council called the Executive Committee of Northern Ireland.[4]

The Executive Committee (or Cabinet, though that word is not used in the Act) therefore includes all the Ministers, of whom there are now nine. They are the Prime Minister, the Minister in the Senate and seven Ministers each in charge of one of the following departments: Finance, Home Affairs, Health and Social Services, Education, Agriculture, Commerce and Development.[5] The

Ireland for which the Act made provision. The United Kingdom has de-reserved some services but retains those mentioned in the text and also the Post Office Savings Bank, Trustee Savings Banks and designs for stamps. The Northern Ireland Act, 1962 enables Northern Ireland to legislate on certain Supreme Court matters.

[1] The Sixth Schedule to the Act lists these as follows: national debt charges; naval, military and air force expenditure; civil expenditure, including that on the civil list and Royal Family, foreign and colonial services and external trade; and other departmental expenditure determined by the Joint Exchequer Board to be imperial expenditure.

[2] The Post Office Act, 1961 established a separate Post Office Fund, and since 1 April 1961 virtually all Post Office revenue and expenditure have been excluded from the Northern Ireland accounts.

[3] Government of Ireland Act, 1920, s. 11.

[4] ibid., s. 8.

[5] The Attorney-General is not in the Cabinet. The Minister of Health and Social Services is responsible for the National Assistance Board. The Comptroller and Auditor General, who is independent of the executive, is head of the Exchequer and Audit Department.

allocation of functions is a matter of some difficulty. Since 1921 the scale of transferred services has been enormously increased and their scope has been widened by constitutional amendment, but the number of departments is limited by the need for economy and by the relatively small size of the legislature. Of the fifty-two members of the House of Commons in March 1964, one was the Speaker, one the Chairman and another the Deputy Chairman of Ways and Means, and twelve held posts in the Government.[1] Administrative expansion has therefore for the most part been effected, not by creating new Ministries, but by enlarging those that already exist. Today there are eight departments, including that of the Prime Minister. In 1921 there were seven. Six of these, namely, the Prime Minister's Department and the Ministries of Finance, Home Affairs, Education, Agriculture and Commerce still exist with the same titles, though their duties are more extensive. The seventh was the Ministry of Labour, later renamed Labour and National Insurance.

Major revisions of the machinery of administration have occurred only twice. In 1944 there was established a new Ministry of Health and Local Government. In 1965 it was restyled the Ministry of Development and given responsibility for roads and public transport, while its former functions relating to public health, health and welfare services and hospitals were transferred to and merged with those of Labour and National Insurance to form a distinct Ministry of Health and Social Services. The timing and character of reconstruction have been determined, generally speaking, by the money available and by the decision of a newly-appointed Prime Minister to concentrate and co-ordinate effort in those directions where improvement was most needed. Thus, the Ministry of Home Affairs in 1921 was given a wide and miscellaneous range of functions, among them public health, though other departments were also answerable for some health services. Partly because responsibility was so diffused, the health of the community suffered in the years between the wars. Lord Brookeborough became Prime Minister in 1943, and the Ministry of Health and Local Government which he created in 1944 revolutionized the health services in Northern Ireland.[2] This success, together with vast but largely haphazard public activity

[1] These were the Prime Minister, seven other Ministers, the Attorney-General and three Parliamentary Secretaries.

[2] See Chapter Seven (Health Services).

in providing houses, hospitals, roads, water and sewerage, schools and factories, and expansion of the private sector of the economy, meant that during post-war years the need to plan the use of land became relatively more urgent. Planning was a duty of the Ministry of Health and Local Government, but it was not its main purpose, and most other departments had functions connected with physical development. For these and other reasons planning was not resolutely pursued.[1] After Lord Brookeborough's resignation in 1963, the new Prime Minister (Captain T. M. O'Neill) brought planning firmly within the ambit of a Ministry of Development and, as already explained, he established a Department of Health and Social Services and redistributed some other functions. This took effect from 1 January 1965.

From that date the chief responsibilities of the eight departments can be summarized as follows. The Prime Minister's Department (in which is included the Cabinet Secretariat) is the official channel of communication between Belfast and London, where the Home Secretary is mainly responsible for Ulster's affairs and for seeing that her interests and constitutional rights are safeguarded. Within the Home Office a member of the Northern Ireland Civil Service acts as liaison officer.[2] In addition there is an extensive and fluid pattern of co-operative arrangements between individual departments in Britain and Ulster.[3] The Ministry of Finance is analogous to the Treasury. It exercises financial control over all other departments, provides for them an advisory service on organization and methods, and deals with the pay, recruitment, conditions of work and training of the Civil Service and other establishment matters. The Ministry of Home Affairs, which corresponds to the Home Office, has a large number of miscellaneous functions, mostly connected with the preservation of peace and the administration of justice. The Ministry of Health and Social Services is responsible for hospitals, health and welfare services (including those administered by local authorities), social security (national insurance, industrial injuries insurance and family allowances) and employment services. The actual provision and administration of hospitals and general health services is the task of separate statutory authorities which operate

[1] See Chapter Eight (Housing and Planning).

[2] Sir Frank Newsam, *The Home Office* (2nd edn., London, 1955), pp. 167–70.

[3] Political and Economic Planning, 'Local Self-Government', *Planning*, vol. xxvi (1960). This is a useful outline of self-government in Northern Ireland and other parts of the United Kingdom and Islands dependent on the Crown.

under the Ministry's general control. These and other *ad hoc* bodies are noted below. The duties of the Ministry of Education include education at all levels and ancillary services. Education outside university, like many other matters, is also the concern of local authorities. Agricultural services and drainage come under the Ministry of Agriculture. The Ministry of Commerce has a wide range of duties, notably to promote trade and industry and regulate commercial activity. On the Ministry of Development rests over-all responsibility for planning. Its other functions include roads, railways and public transport, housing and water supplies, and general control of local government.

Local government in Ireland before 1920 was built on the English pattern with some modifications. Thus, Ireland was not given parish councils, and the central government kept education and police (the Royal Irish Constabulary) in its own hands. The categories of local authorities evolved in this manner still remain in Ulster and no new ones have been created. There are two county boroughs (Belfast and Londonderry), six administrative counties (Antrim, Armagh, Down, Fermanagh, Londonderry and Tyrone), ten boroughs, twenty-four urban districts and thirty-one rural districts, each with an elected council whose functions, composition and sources of revenue broadly resemble those of their English counterparts. Since 1921 there have been extensive changes in local government services.[1] A general tendency has been to transfer functions from districts to counties and to create statutory authorities for special purposes. This trend is similar to that in England, but in Ulster even more services are centralized. They include the police (Royal Ulster Constabulary), civil defence (Ministry of Home Affairs), the fire service (Northern Ireland Fire Authority), electricity (Electricity Board for Northern Ireland), youth employment (Northern Ireland Youth Employment Service Board), housing (Northern Ireland Housing Trust), general health services (Northern Ireland General Health Services Board), hospital and specialist services (Northern Ireland Hospitals Authority) and public transport(Ulster Transport Authority).[2]

[1] Many of these are described in Part III (Public Services).

[2] The Ministries of Education and Home Affairs are responsible to Parliament respectively for youth employment and the fire service but local authorities are represented on the two statutory bodies. County borough and district councils are also housing authorities, and Belfast Corporation has its own fire service and public transport system and (like Londonderry Corporation) generates electricity.

Other departures from the English local government system may be briefly summarized. In Northern Ireland there are no county aldermen; aldermen in county boroughs and boroughs are directly elected; all elections are triennial; and the franchise is restricted for the most part to ratepayers and weighted in favour of property.[1] In rural districts the county council is the rating authority. Government grants produce twice as much revenue as rates (£31 m. against £15 m. in 1964–65), mainly because agricultural land is exempt from ordinary rates, while industry still enjoys three-quarters exemption. Relations between councillors and constituents can be close because areas are small. Only seventeen of the boroughs and districts have more than 20,000 inhabitants and twenty-seven have fewer than 10,000. But Unionists or Nationalists control most councils, and antipathy between the two groups intensifies friendship within them.

The legal system also is broadly similar to that in England. Superior courts comprise the Supreme Court of Judicature (consisting of the Court of Appeal and the High Court of Justice) and the Court of Criminal Appeal. Appeals may be taken to the House of Lords. Inferior courts (which are within Stormont's jurisdiction) are county courts and courts of summary jurisdiction. The former have a limited jurisdiction in both criminal and civil cases. The latter are presided over, not by unpaid and legally unqualified justices, but by resident magistrates. A legal aid scheme comparable to that in England was introduced in 1965.

As already noted, any citizen with means can invoke the authority of the courts in order to determine whether laws made by the provincial Parliament conform to the constitution. There have been few cases.[2] When a Bill is submitted for the Royal assent the Attorney-General for Northern Ireland certifies that its

[1] The franchise is restricted to Northern Ireland parliamentary electors who either (*a*) reside as owner or tenant in a dwelling-house for three months ending on the qualifying date or (*b*) occupy other land or premises valued at not less than £10. The spouse of a resident qualifies under (*a*) but generally speaking an occupant of part of a house does not. In addition a company may nominate up to six electors, one for every £10 of the valuation of its premises, who must be British subjects. An elector may vote in the electoral area where he resides and also where he occupies other premises and where the company is situated, but in respect of qualifications (*a*) and (*b*) he can vote only once in one area. Electoral Law Act (N.I.), ss. 2, 29 (5), 31 (2). It is evident from the registers that more than a quarter of parliamentary electors have no local government vote.

[2] *Gallagher* v. *Lynn* [1937] A.C. 863 was of constitutional importance. See Quekett, op. cit., Part III.

provisions are within the powers of Parliament. Governments have kept scrupulously within the law, though on one occasion (in 1946) it was discovered that earlier legislation might be *ultra vires*.[1] Of the decided cases, many have turned on the interpretation of a prohibition in the constituent Act against taking 'any property without compensation', but that restriction was abolished in 1962.[2]

The question whether any Act, Order or Bill is beyond the powers of Parliament can be referred also to the Judicial Committee of the Privy Council. The reference is made by the Queen in Council on the representation of the Governor of Northern Ireland or a Secretary of State or on the petition of any person. The only case occurred in 1936, when Belfast Corporation unsuccessfully pleaded that a levy imposed on the poor rate and paid to the local Exchequer to help finance education was the same in character as income tax and so outside Stormont's powers.[3]

From this outline it is evident that Northern Ireland is in form a parliamentary democracy on the British model. Political power is concentrated in the Cabinet, but the Cabinet cannot do whatever it pleases. Ministers are responsible to a Parliament where the Opposition's right to criticize is secreted in procedure based on that of Westminster, at periodic elections political parties that oppose the government—and, equally, those that aim to abolish the constitution—can compete for votes, the Press is free, the rights of the citizen are secured by law and the judiciary is independent.

Ulster differs, however, from the rest of the United Kingdom in two important respects. The first arises from social relations which are discussed below. Whereas in Britain liberal democratic political forms have grown out of a homogeneous society, in Northern Ireland they have been imposed on a community that is deeply divided. The spirit of democracy—the willingness to tolerate opinions opposed to one's own and to discuss differences without resort to violence—is weak.

In the second place, the Parliament of Northern Ireland is by law subordinate. All Acts passed at Westminster extend to Ulster unless she is excluded expressly or by implication, for like every other part of the Kingdom she is subject to the rule of the British constitution that Parliament at Westminster is legally supreme. This subordinate status is specifically enshrined in the constituent

[1] See p. 120 below.

[2] Northern Ireland Act, 1962, s. 14.

[3] See p. 57 below.

Act by four rules: (*a*) the supreme authority in Northern Ireland of the United Kingdom Parliament remains undiminished;[1] (*b*) Stormont cannot repeal or alter the constituent Act or any United Kingdom statute passed after 3 May 1921 and extending to Northern Ireland;[2] (*c*) Northern Ireland statutes are void to the extent that they are repugnant to United Kingdom statutes passed after 3 May 1921 and extending to Northern Ireland;[3] (*d*) the Governor must comply with any instructions by the Crown in respect of any Bill and reserve the Royal assent if so directed.[4]

These restrictions, though potentially formidable, have in practice been of little significance. Westminster has never, as it appears, legislated on transferred matters without Stormont's consent,[5] and all United Kingdom Bills are scrutinized to ensure this does not happen.[6] Nevertheless, the power is there. It was invoked in 1930 when the British Government made it clear that they would revalue Northern Ireland for the purpose of income tax if Stormont refused to do so.[7] The Governor's power of reservation has been used only once. That was as long ago as 1922, and the Bill in question was given the Royal assent in the same year.[8] Finally, though Northern Ireland cannot alter the constitution, it has frequently been changed at her request, and the trend of amendment has been to clarify and enlarge her powers. To this generalization there is one notable exception. The Finance (No. 2) Act, 1940 added to the list of reserved taxes a purchase tax which

[1] Government of Ireland Act, 1920, s. 75.

[2] s. 6 (1). United Kingdom statutes and all other laws existing in Ireland at 3 May 1921 continued thereafter in force in Northern Ireland, but Stormont was given authority, subject to the restrictions in the constituent Act, to repeal or alter them.

[3] s. 6 (2).

[4] s. 12 (1), (2).

[5] The United Kingdom with Ulster's concurrence occasionally legislates on transferred matters when it is convenient to do so. The statute may then contain a provision to the effect that, so far as it relates to matters within the power of the Parliament of Northern Ireland, it shall be deemed to be an Act passed before the appointed day (3 May 1921). Stormont can then amend it whenever it wishes. Legislation of this sort is especially appropriate when effective action requires changes in the law relating to both transferred and reserved matters.

[6] Sir Frank Newsam, op. cit., p. 169.

[7] See p. 57 below.

[8] The Local Government Act (N.I.), 1922, which among other things abolished proportional representation for local government elections, passed through all its stages in the Senate and the House of Commons between 26 June and 5 July 1922. Although the Government intended the Bill to become law at once, it did not receive the Royal assent until 11 September 1922. In consequence, elections had to be postponed for a year. H.C. Deb. (N.I.), 2, cc. 1038–40.

would otherwise have been within Stormont's competence. This limitation, however, was to Ulster's advantage. It was certainly not against her will and may well have been imposed at her request.[1]

In general, therefore, harmony has marked the relations between Britain and Ulster. Common ideals and common interests bind them together. Most Ulstermen are happy to remain loyal subjects of the Crown, and political leaders in Britain are content to have it so. This is only to be expected in the case of the Conservative and Unionist Party, the ally of Ulster Unionists since the Home Rule agitation, but it was the British Labour Party that put on to the statute book the affirmation that 'in no event will Northern Ireland or any part thereof cease to be part of His Majesty's dominions and of the United Kingdom without the consent of the Parliament of Northern Ireland'.[2] Thus, over a period of more than forty years Ulster has been able to extend her legislative powers and entrench herself more firmly in the United Kingdom.

From constitutional rules we turn to social and economic conditions and political attitudes. Industrial civilization has left scars on few places in Ulster apart from the city of Belfast and its urban hinterland.[3] Here are shipyards, aircraft and engineering establishments and a myriad of factories, great and small, though since the war governments have pursued a policy of industrial dispersion. Here, too, live some 40 per cent. of the total population—in round figures 1,450,000.[4] The rest, about 850,000, are scattered

[1] See p. 83 below. The reservation of purchase tax illustrates one possible mode of constitutional amendment. The United Kingdom may in the same statute legislate for Great Britain and Northern Ireland and amend the Act of 1920. But to preserve Stormont's freedom, amendments normally take one of two other forms. (*a*) When legislating for England and Wales or for Great Britain on matters outside Stormont's competence, Westminster may provide that no restrictions imposed by the Government of Ireland Act shall preclude Stormont from passing similar legislation. This is very common. (*b*) An enabling Act may confer additional powers on Ulster or clarify her existing powers. In this category fall the Northern Ireland (Miscellaneous Provisions) Acts, 1928, 1932 and 1945 and the Northern Ireland Acts, 1947, 1955 and 1962.

[2] Northern Ireland Act, 1949, s. 1 (2).

[3] On Belfast see E. Jones, *A Social Geography of Belfast* (London, 1960). General surveys of social conditions include J. M. Mogey, *Rural Life in Northern Ireland* (London, 1947); *Belfast in its Regional Setting* (Belfast, 1952); C. F. Carter and D. Barritt, *The Northern Ireland Problem* (London, 1962); *Belfast Regional Survey and Plan 1962*, a Report prepared for the Government of Northern Ireland by Sir Robert H. Matthew (H.M.S.O., 1964).

[4] Statistics in this section of the text are taken, unless otherwise stated, from the *Ulster Year Book, 1963–65*. They can be brought up to date by reference to later editions.

in small towns and throughout the countryside. Of 30 towns with a population of 2,500 or more, only one (the city of Londonderry) has more than 50,000 inhabitants, and 27 have fewer than 20,000. Farms by English standards are diminutive, thanks to the Land Purchase Acts which enabled tenants to buy out their landlords. Almost half of all the 54,300 farms have fewer than 20 acres, and only 2,500 have 100 and more. A rough official estimate in December 1963 showed that 15,000 farmers had net farm incomes below £300 a year, 10,000 fell in the range £300–£500, and only 1,000 received more than £2,000.[1] Apart from agriculture, the principal industries fall into three groups—textiles and clothing, shipbuilding and engineering, and the preparation and processing of food, drink and tobacco. Small firms are numerous but relatively unimportant: concerns with 25 or more employees account for 90 per cent. of all factory workers.

Ulster's economic life is pegged to Britain's by rules of law, facts of geography and the wishes of her people. All decisions about trade, defence, external relations and monetary and credit policy, and virtually all decisions about taxation, are taken in London. Trade with or *via* Great Britain accounts for about 75 per cent. by value of imports and 90 per cent. by value of exports. Trade across the land boundary with the Irish Republic is insignificant. Of the 190,864 members of registered trade unions, 182,438 belong to unions with headquarters in Britain. Most of them, however, are represented in a Northern Ireland Committee of the Dublin-based Irish Congress of Trade Unions, and for many years the Government of Northern Ireland were unable officially to recognize the Committee. One reason for this was that it was not clear from the constitution of the Congress that the Committee enjoyed a measure of local autonomy. After Captain O'Neill became Prime Minister in 1963, this obstacle was soon removed. The Congress amended its constitution in 1964 and the provincial Government then established an Economic Council on which the trade unions are represented. Minimum wage rates in manufacturing industry more or less equal those in Britain, especially since many agreements between employers' associations and trade unions extend to the whole United Kingdom. Actual earnings are substantially lower, by between 10 and 20 per cent. *Per capita* incomes are

[1] H.C. Deb. (N.I.), 55, c. 1455. The income was that of the farmer himself after payment of wages to members of the family working at home.

lower still, the difference being of the order of 25 per cent.[1] Among the reasons for this is unemployment, which is and always has been more severe than on the mainland.

Despite this relative poverty, all the people of Ulster enjoy high standards of public services. This has not always been so. Between the wars public provision in general fell below British standards—not because the Ulsterman was conservative, but because his Government was chronically short of money. The manner in which penury was succeeded by affluence forms a principal theme of later chapters. Today, national insurance, family allowances, national assistance and health and welfare services are generally of the same nature and quality as in Britain. So, too, in its main features is the educational system. In all these services and in housing, hospitals, roads and public amenities the post-war years have seen massive improvement.

The Christian religion still dominates the Ulsterman's outer life. Well-attended churches and chapels are centres of a host of social activities, and the priest and minister command respect and dispose of authority which the fissiparous nature of nonconformity has done little to weaken. The 1961 census showed that 35 per cent. of the people were Roman Catholic. Of the rest, 29 per cent. were Presbyterian, some 24 per cent. Episcopalian (Church of Ireland), 10 per cent. adhered to other Protestant denominations, and 2 per cent. did not state their allegiance.

From this sketch it is evident that Ulster is poorer than Britain, she suffers more from unemployment, her population is less urban (though with a fair proportion of trade unionists), and she has relatively more small farmers. If we put these points against the fact that Stormont has adopted the British electoral system (which tends to produce two large political parties and discourages small ones), we would expect to find a conservative party based on farmers, small shopkeepers and the middle class, and a labour party supported mainly by industrial workers and lower income groups, with some stiffening from religious nonconformity. That a left-wing party could be a formidable force will be apparent from the following figures. The Northern Ireland electorate excluding the university constituency was 898,177 in 1964. In the

[1] *Report of the Joint Working Party on the Economy of Northern Ireland*, Cmd. 446 (1962), p. 11. On economic conditions see also K. S. Isles and N. Cuthbert, *An Economic Survey of Northern Ireland* (H.M.S.O., 1957); *Economic Development in Northern Ireland*, Cmd. 479 (1965).

same year there were 126,722 national insurance retirement pensioners and 452,000 men and women insured employees. Most of these were manual workers who were qualified to vote. With their spouses and other adult members of their families they obviously constituted a block of votes from which a left-wing party could expect to draw strong and continuous support in normal circumstances.

Circumstances are not normal though. For one thing, successive governments have copied social improvements introduced at Westminster by both the Conservative and Labour Parties. This has widened the appeal of the Ulster Unionist Party and narrowed the scope of a left-wing Opposition. For another, there is hardly any relation between the severity of taxation and the level of provincial expenditure. Ulstermen are in general obliged to pay taxes at United Kingdom rates, and they have a common interest in getting as much as they can out of the United Kingdom Exchequer.

These, however, are minor points. Class differences were obscured by the dust of the Home Rule struggle long before 1921, and political activity since that time has been moulded by the aspirations of two communities who live in the same territory but in every other respect are worlds apart. Roman Catholics who abhor the partition of Ireland bent all their efforts to end it. Protestants, whether employers or workmen, Presbyterians or Episcopalians, town or country dwellers, rich or poor on the whole identified themselves with the Unionist Party and, in large part, with the Orange Order. The latter, through its lodges and halls throughout the country, and by public demonstrations that were a feature of life in the nineteenth century, provided a ready-made organization for social activity and for resolute—and often bigoted —support of the constitution. The influence on local politics of this semi-secret society has been profound but, to an outsider, never obvious. A unionist without an Orangeman's sash has always stood little chance of election to the Commons and even less of an appointment in government. Occasionally, too, the Order has pressed Ministers to modify their policies, most noticeably in education. This said, it should be emphasized that the Orange Order remains a separate entity and that government is not its creature.[1] Although the division between Orange and

[1] In 1924, when unionists were struggling to establish the constitution, District Inspector Nixon was charged with making a political speech at an Orange Lodge in contravention of disciplinary regulations governing the

Green (a synonym for anti-partitionists) has lost much of its sharpness since the war, it still dominates the political scene. So today, as more than forty years ago, the Unionist Party is in power and its leaders enjoy inordinately long periods in office. Sir James Craig (later Lord Craigavon) was Prime Minister from 1921 to 1940, and Sir Basil Brooke (later Lord Brookeborough) held that post from 1943 to 1963.

We have already indicated that these pathological conditions are the outcome of the Home Rule convulsion. After 1886 the tension between Protestants who wished to maintain the Union and Catholics who wished to modify or destroy it became so acute as completely to polarize party politics. The Liberal Party, once strong in a province that has never lacked men of liberal views (Ulster returned nine Liberals to Parliament in 1880) was ground out of existence by friction between two extremes.

There is another and less obvious connexion between local politics and the events narrated in the last chapter. It was shown that Northern Ireland was saddled with a financial system which her own principal architect (Lord Carson) declared to be unworkable. Yet Ulster has not merely survived as a distinct political unit. Her public relations with Britain have never been anything but harmonious, for the spirit of co-operation between both governments has proved strong enough to enable them gradually to transform the financial provisions of the Government of Ireland Act. This transformation has not, however, been favourable at all times and in every respect to Ulster. Her leaders have occasionally been obliged to take very unpopular decisions as a result of pressure from London, and in order to secure improvement in public services they have had to yield to Whitehall a share in the control of matters that were transferred to them alone. By the law of the constitution Northern Ireland is still mistress in her own house, but the size and shape of that house are determined in large measure by the United Kingdom.

Whether this could have been avoided, and at what cost, are questions that we cannot attempt to answer until we have analysed the nature of the choices that have confronted local political leaders. What may be said at this point, in order to fix attention on the connexion between Ulster's internal politics and her

---

Constabulary. Despite strong opposition in the House of Commons and within the Orange Order, he was dismissed. *Belfast News-Letter*, 30 January, 29 February 1924; H.C. Deb. (N.I.), 4, cc. 66 et seq.

relations with the United Kingdom, is this: a local political party that was determined to retain sole control of transferred matters, or to improve social conditions faster than has been the case, could hardly have avoided conflict with Britain. But conflict, or even friction, has been wholly absent. Ulstermen did not want even the limited degree of independence that was thrust upon them; and separatist pressure has both deepened the majority's attachment to the United Kingdom and inclined them to repose such confidence in their leaders that they have generally ignored agreements that were of material benefit to them and acquiesced without much complaint in those that were not.

The same train of events therefore produced both a singularly inept scheme of self-government and also the conditions that could secure its frictionless operation. Ulster's leaders and the majority of her people never demanded a parliament. They were, indeed, resolved to make it work, but not at the expense of conflict with Britain. However difficult their financial and economic problems might become, Ministers could rely on the massive, if not uncritical, support of the Unionist Party and the Orange Order.

The movement of this dialectic can be discerned from the moment Northern Ireland came into existence. In 1921 Sir James Craig and his colleagues had to do two things if the new constitution was to survive. The first was to persuade Britain to revise the financial arrangements, for these proved to be quite unworkable. Cuts in taxation by the Chancellor of the Exchequer reduced Ulster's revenue, the unrealistic nature of the principles underlying the imperial contribution became manifest, and the amount of the contribution proved to be excessive.[1] The negotiations that followed were of transcendent importance for Ulster's future and would have stimulated lively discussion in an area where people were eager to govern themselves, but they attracted virtually no attention. They were overshadowed by a more exciting and, in the short run, an even more vital task—to establish the Government's authority in the face of fanatical opposition.

While Protestants were determined to uphold a constitution that enabled them to stay in the Union, most Catholics were equally determined to overthrow it, if necessary by violence or by the traditional Irish weapon of the boycott. Gunmen and gangsters

[1] These points are explained in Chapter Three.

tried to wreck the régime by murder and arson, Southern Ireland sought to strangle it by a trade embargo, Roman Catholic prelates refused to recognize it, the six Nationalist and six Sinn Féin members elected in 1921 to the House of Commons declined to take their seats, local authorities with Nationalist majorities refused to discharge their duties, and managers and teachers of some 300 Roman Catholic schools refused to recognize the new Ministry of Education or even to accept the salaries it paid.[1]

In this situation the Government had no choice but to impose their will on the recalcitrant minority. The Civil Authorities (Special Powers) Act (N.I.), 1922 empowered the Minister of Home Affairs to 'take all such steps and issue all such orders as may be necessary for preserving the peace and maintaining order', and the Royal Ulster Constabulary was reinforced by a Special Constabulary which, originally formed by the British Government in 1920, was transferred to Northern Ireland's control in 1921. Not that Ministers relied on organized force alone. The Ministry of Education (whose first Permanent Secretary, incidentally, was a distinguished Catholic) invited Catholic representatives to serve on a committee of inquiry into the educational system but was rebuffed.[2] The Ministry of Home Affairs went out of its way to try to establish cordial relations with all local authorities but was obliged to appoint commissioners in place of twenty-one defaulting councils. These bodies were reconstituted in time for elections that took place in urban areas in January 1923 and in rural areas in June 1924, though in the meantime (in September 1922) proportional representation for local government elections was abolished.[3]

By these means, and with the support of most citizens, Ministers rapidly asserted their authority. By 1925 order was restored, curfew restrictions were removed, the Special Constabulary as a whole-time force was practically disbanded, and the Governments of the United Kingdom, the Irish Free State and Northern Ireland concluded an agreement[4] by which, 'being united in amity' and

[1] *Report on the Administration of Local Government Services*, 1921–23, Cmd. 30 (1924), p. 9; *Report of the Ministry of Education*, 1922–23, Cmd. 16 (1923), pp. 2, 3, 16; P. Blanshard, *The Irish and Catholic Power* (London, 1954), pp. 216 et seq.

[2] *Interim Report of Departmental Committee on the Educational Services in Northern Ireland*, Cmd. 6 (1922), p. 9.

[3] For details see Cmd. 30, p. 9 and H.C. Deb. (N.I.), 1, cc. 400 et seq.

[4] Ireland (Confirmation of Agreement) Act, 1925, Schedule.

'resolved mutually to aid one another in a spirit of neighbourly comradeship', they dissolved at least some of the acrimony in the dispute about the boundary between the two parts of Ireland.

Yet few Catholic Irishmen were reconciled to partition. The gun and the bomb were still used at intervals to destroy life and property; and although Nationalist M.P.s finally took their seats in the Commons in 1928, they refused to form an Opposition critical of government but loyal to the constitution. The primary aim of their verbal attacks henceforth was less to improve conditions in Northern Ireland than to sap its standing before liberal opinion. The measures provoked by their own intransigence gave them ample ground for complaint. The use of special powers, including internment without trial; the abolition, in 1922 and 1929 respectively, of proportional representation for local government and parliamentary elections;[1] charges of gerrymandering and of discrimination against Catholics in every field of public life—debates on these matters have since consumed interminable hours of the provincial Parliament's time and given rise to a library of polemical literature.

This vituperation and violence ranged the majority of the population solidly behind the Unionist Party. Protestants in every walk of life and of every shade of opinion were acutely aware that nothing but their own solidarity stood between them and government from Dublin. Any attempt to form a new political party, any persistent criticism of government, and indeed any serious thought about 'politics' could alike jeopardize the constitution. So Nationalists gave to Unionist leaders the greatest gift that any politician can hope for—permanent immunity from competition.

[1] There can be little doubt that Nationalist resistance precipitated the abolition of P.R. in local government. It seems probable, however, that Northern Ireland would sooner or later have returned to the British (and traditional Irish) system of election in all territorial constituencies, as indeed Mr. de Valera proposed in the Republic of Ireland in 1959.

CHAPTER THREE

Between the Wars

THE Cabinet formed in 1921 consisted of Sir James Craig (Prime Minister), Mr. H. M. Pollock (Minister of Finance), Sir R. Dawson Bates (Minister of Home Affairs), Mr. J. M. Andrews (Minister of Labour), the seventh Marquis of Londonderry (Minister of Education) and Mr. E. M. Archdale (Minister of Agriculture and of Commerce). This team, as we have explained, lacked the spur of a constitutional Opposition. Indeed, for several years they had virtually no opponents in Parliament at all. Two Nationalists took their seats in the Commons in 1925 but the rest declined to do so until 1928,[1] and for more than forty years (until 1965) the Nationalist Party resolutely refused to become an official Opposition which co-operates with a government in order to criticize and supplant it.

This handicap to good administration was offset by special circumstances. Every informed person in Ireland, north and south, knew that public services were worse than in England. Later chapters will show that between 1906 and 1920 one official inquiry after another had advocated radical reforms to eliminate the dirt, disease, ill health, poverty, illiteracy and maladministration which for one reason and another were the heritage of British rule. The need for improvement was obvious and could not be ignored. That was not all. Craig and his colleagues were men of public spirit. They brought to their offices both the will to improve conditions of life for men, women and children of all creeds, and the knowledge that material progress would be Ulster's greatest asset in the long run; and, like any new broom, they were anxious to make a clean sweep.

It was natural, therefore, that immersed though they were in the tasks of restoring order and building an administrative machine, they should have aspired to do in Ulster what Britain had failed to do in Ireland. The Prime Minister himself sounded the

[1] The general election in 1921 returned 40 Unionists, 6 Nationalists and 6 Republicans. The second in 1925 gave Unionists 37 seats (including 4 Independent Unionists), Nationalists 10, Labour 3 and Republicans 2. Subsequent elections were dominated by Unionists and Nationalists.

keynote on 23 June 1921, the day after the formal opening of Parliament:

We have nothing in our view except the welfare of the people. Our duty and our privilege are from now onwards to have our Parliament well established, to look to the people as a whole, to set ourselves to probe to the bottom those problems that have retarded progress in the past, to do everything that lies in our power to help forward developments in the town and country, so that the Parliament established yesterday by His Gracious Majesty may at all events be a Parliament which has set out upon its task fully realizing the responsibility that rests upon it, and fully determined to maintain the highest traditions of any Parliament in the British Empire.[1]

To probe to the bottom—in this spirit other Ministers emphasized the contrast between things as they were and as they might be. Since Northern Ireland is often thought to be conservative or 'reactionary', it is worth quoting from their speeches. The Minister of Home Affairs stressed the need to improve local government services:

Poor law administration has been the subject matter of various commissions, but I think most of the reports of those commissions shared the fate of those of other commissions and little or nothing was done. I hope when this Ministry gets its feet under it we will be able to see to this very necessary reform of the poor law system.[2]

Health administration was archaic and the responsibility of a host of authorities:

There is no connecting link between any of these bodies, with the result that there is waste in every direction and inefficiency. I propose, as I said before in regard to poor law relief, that this matter should also receive the earliest consideration of the Department. . . . Then we have the various Housing Acts. . . . There are something like forty of these Acts, and no one seems to have thought of consolidating them and giving them some practical form.[3]

On highways, which he described as being 'for the most part a disgrace to any community', he said:

I found in taking over the various departments from Dublin that up to the present time they were all controlled by a series of boards, and these boards actually acted independently of each other, which I think very largely accounts for the fact that when legislation was introduced

[1] H.C. Deb. (N.I.), 1, c. 36. [2] ibid., c. 469. [3] ibid., c. 470.

the officials in connexion with these boards were more anxious to see that their vested interests were secure rather than that the legislation that was being enacted was suitable for the needs of the community.[1]

On public libraries, which all councils were empowered to provide, the Minister remarked, 'I regret to say that few of the local authorities have taken advantage of their powers.'[2]

Land drainage was of peculiar importance in Ulster, which is ringed by hills and mountains that direct water to the centre of the country where, however, there was no sufficient outlet to the sea. Ten drainage boards dating from 1842 and 1863 had done little to prevent periodic flooding on a vast scale. The Minister of Finance, a man given to under-statement, said, 'The extent to which they have justified their existence is open to serious doubt.'[3]

Education, a centralized and bureaucratic system, attracted the sharpest criticism. The Prime Minister, always keenly interested in the welfare of children, said:

I cannot help thinking, and it is admitted on all hands, that our educational system in the North is not one that can be even amended, but one that requires to be absolutely rooted out of the soil in order that we may begin to plant a new fabric.[4]

The Parliamentary Secretary to the Ministry of Education declared:

No one realizes more than I do, and no one realizes more than the Minister of Education, that secondary education was handed over to the Northern Parliament in a condition which is absolutely and undoubtedly deplorable. . . . Due steps are being taken by the Ministry in order to obtain . . . whatever evidence we require in order to take up this matter as speedily as we possibly can. . . . It is the wish and the desire of the Ministry of Education to see that every child throughout the Northern Province receives the same encouragement and has the same facilities for education as children have in other parts of the United Kingdom. And it will be our desire to forge and fashion a measure of reform which I believe will bring that about, and perhaps . . . we may be able to produce a measure of reform which will put this province somewhat ahead of any other kingdom or province in the world.[5]

These strictures were followed from 1923 to 1925 by legislation. A contributory pensions scheme was copied from Britain, local authorities got Exchequer help to build houses, and county

[1] ibid., c. 471.
[2] Senate Deb., 4, c. 32.
[3] H.C. Deb. (N.I.), 6, c. 1459.
[4] ibid., 1, c. 172.
[5] ibid., cc. 106–7.

councils were given wider powers in respect of libraries, land drainage, hospitals and roads. A Departmental Committee on Education proposed sweeping changes which were incorporated in the Education Act (N.I.), 1923. Local government reform raised complex problems, but the Government did not doubt that they, like other obstacles, could be overcome by intelligence and resolution. Sir James Craig told the Commons in November 1923 that they intended to get together 'the best brains of the country on local government' and that they hoped eventually to introduce 'the grandest measure of reform that this House will be asked to pass'.[1] There followed, in April 1924, the appointment of a Departmental Commission whose Report in 1927 recommended a host of notable reforms, among them abolition of workhouses and boards of guardians and improvement in health and sanitary services.

In the event none of these reforms or proposals fulfilled the ambitions of Ministers. They encountered crippling difficulties for the explanation of which we must turn to the basic features of Ulster's financial situation.

Under the constitution, revenue flowed from two main sources. Transferred taxes (principally motor vehicle and death duties) were controlled by Northern Ireland, but they produced only about one-tenth of total revenue. Most of the rest came from reserved taxes (mainly customs and reserved excise duties and taxes on incomes) which were imposed and collected at uniform rates throughout the United Kingdom. The proportion due to Ulster was calculated by the Joint Exchequer Board. From that proportion the United Kingdom deducted (*a*) the net cost of reserved services (e.g. the Supreme Court in Northern Ireland) and (*b*) Ulster's contribution to imperial services. The residue was made over to the provincial Exchequer, and it was mainly on this—the residuary share of reserved taxes—that the Minister of Finance relied to pay for transferred services. So although the provincial Parliament was constitutionally responsible for those services, the amount it could spend on them was determined for the most part by two factors that it did not control—the imperial contribution and the United Kingdom's fiscal policy.

This odd arrangement had provoked hard argument when the Act of 1920 was passing through Parliament. Ulstermen who

[1] H.C. Deb. (N.I.), 3, c. 1845.

aspired to improve transferred services pressed for a small imperial contribution.[1] The British Government, for their part, pledged themselves to treat both Northern and Southern Ireland not only with justice but generosity. The Minister in charge of the Bill (Sir Laming Worthington-Evans) declared on 22 October 1920:

The Government recognize that it is most desirable that the Irish Governments should not be hampered but should be allowed a substantial margin with which to meet any additional expense which may be incurred by the establishment of the new Parliaments or may be called for by various services which have hitherto not been developed perhaps in accordance with the requirements of the Irish people.[2]

Estimates published in May 1920[3] showed that reserved revenue would total £14·7 m. and transferred revenue £1·8 m. From this total of £16·5 m. the United Kingdom proposed to retain £10·1 m.—£2·2 m. for reserved services and £7·9 m. by way of imperial contribution for each of the two years 1923 and 1924. There would thus remain £6·4 m. for domestic services, but it was reckoned that they would cost only £4·1 m. when the new Government was set up and £4·5 m. in the foreseeable future. The Minister continued:

This gives Northern Ireland a total surplus of £2·25 m. I do not think, therefore, that it can be said that an imperial contribution has been fixed too high upon the information at present available. On the contrary, it has been fixed at an amount which leaves for expenditure in Ireland a sum very much in excess of the highest rate of expenditure that there has ever been in Ireland in times past. . . . These provisions were settled in no niggling spirit. They are generous, and sufficient to enable the two Parliaments to enter upon their duties without fear that their efforts will be stultified by want of money.[4]

Ulster Unionists accepted this forecast with reserve. Estimates framed in a period of post-war prosperity and high taxation might well prove baseless in later years. Nevertheless, as Sir Edward Carson emphasized during the debate on the Bill, no progress could be made in an atmosphere of suspicion. He and his followers,

[1] See especially the debate on the financial resolution in 133 H.C. Deb., 5 s. and the statements by the Minister of Finance in H.C. Deb. (N.I.), 1, c. 130 and 6, cc. 450–1.

[2] 133 H.C. Deb., 5 s., 1234.

[3] *Government of Ireland Bill: Further Memorandum on Financial Provisions*, U.K. Cmd. 707 (1920).

[4] 133 H.C. Deb., 5 s., 1234, 1238.

having accepted with reluctance a separate Parliament, implicitly trusted the British Government to see it was not hamstrung.

That Parliament had hardly been launched when Sir James Craig had to press for financial revision. Instead of being blessed with a substantial surplus, Northern Ireland would have sustained a heavy deficit had the imperial contribution remained at £7·9 m. Table 1 shows the estimates for 1921 and, in very round figures, the actual outcome from 1923 (the first full financial year) to 1925.[1]

TABLE 1. *Revenue and Expenditure, 1921–25*

£ million

	Revenue			*Expenditure*			*Residue*
	Trans-ferred	*Re-served*	*Total*	*Trans-ferred services*	*Re-served services*	*Total*	
1920–21	1·8	14·7	16·5	4·1	2·2	6·3	10·2
1922–23	1·9	11·8	13·8	5·0	1·9	6·9	6·9
1923–24	1·9	10·1	12·0	5·9	1·7	7·6	4·4
1924–25	2·2	8·8	11·1	5·9	1·7	7·6	3·5

For detail see Appendix Two

Reserved revenue fell by 1925 to little more than half the estimate, partly because industrial depression and unemployment struck Ulster with special severity and reduced the yield of taxation, and partly because of cuts in tax rates.[2] But expenditure rose. Part of the unforeseen cost of restoring order and relieving unemployment fell on Ulster's Exchequer. Her leaders also began to improve local services, for they believed that the assurance given on behalf of the British Government would be honoured. As the Minister of Finance said in September 1921:

We claim that there is something even more than a moral obligation on Great Britain to see that at least in the first year of the functioning of our Ulster Parliament there shall be, after all our expenses are paid, a surplus of £2·25 m. Otherwise the intentions of the Government will

[1] Tables 1, 2 and 3 are based on figures in Appendix Two, which are themselves rounded. Totals may be discrepant.

[2] Estimates of Ulster's revenue showed a loss of £802,000 in 1924 because of changes in the British Budget. *Financial Statement* (*N.I.*), *1924–25*, H.C. 51, p. 13.

not have been carried out, and the generous treatment on which they prided themselves so much will not be in evidence. I have not the slightest fear, however, but that the Joint Exchequer Board . . . will deal fairly with us.[1]

The United Kingdom, however, was unwilling to allow domestic expenditure to eat up the imperial contribution. There followed what the Minister of Finance described as 'long and irritating controversies with the Treasury'[2] until in 1923 an arbitration committee under the chairmanship of Lord Colwyn was appointed to consider whether 'any alteration is needed in the present scale of the contribution of Northern Ireland to the cost of imperial services'.

The Act of 1920[3] fixed the contribution for 1923 and 1924 at £7·9 m. a year.[4] Since, however, Ulster's difficulties were attributable more to the shortfall in revenue than to any extravagance on her part, £7·9 m. was clearly excessive, and in their first Report in September 1923[5] the Colwyn Committee recommended that after certain adjustments the contribution for 1923 and 1924 should be the surplus of revenue over expenditure.

The Committee's main problem—to devise a formula for subsequent years—raised issues of great interest and complexity. The Act of 1920[6] provided that the contribution after the first two years should be such sum as the Joint Exchequer Board, having regard to the relative taxable capacities of Northern Ireland and of Great Britain and Ireland, determined to be just. Now, experience since 1921 showed that to make the contribution a first charge on Ulster's revenue was quite impracticable, and the Colwyn Committee recognized that certain basic needs must be satisfied. There was no alternative but to make the contribution itself a residue instead of domestic expenditure. That expenditure would then need to be limited by principles binding on Northern Ireland, for otherwise the amount of residue would depend on her decision

[1] H.C. Deb. (N.I.), 1, c. 132.

[2] ibid., 6, c. 451.

[3] s. 23, as amended by the Irish Free State (Consequential Provisions) Act, 1922, Schedule I, para. 4 (1) (b).

[4] Or such less sum as the Joint Exchequer Board might substitute. The Board did reduce the contribution to £6 m.

[5] *First Report of the Northern Ireland Special Arbitration Committee*, U.K. Cmd. 2072 (1924).

[6] s. 23, as amended by the Irish Free State (Consequential Provisions) Act, 1922, Schedule I, para. 4 (1) (c).

alone. The basic issue, therefore, was to find an acceptable method of restricting domestic expenditure, taking account of relative taxable capacity.

'Taxable capacity', as the history of Ireland has well shown, means different things to different people.[1] It could plausibly be argued that Ulstermen would be taxed according to their relative capacity if they were subject to principles and rates of taxation which in all relevant respects were the same as in Britain. It is true that Ulster as a unit was poor—her *per capita* yield of income tax and surtax in 1924 was £3 6*s*., against £7 10*s*. in Britain—but the provincial Government held the burden to be as just as anywhere else in the United Kingdom because taxation falls on individuals. If that were admitted, there were two fair ways to limit domestic expenditure. The first was to allow Ulstermen to enjoy services of more or less the same kind and quality as in Britain—so far, at least, as they were financed by taxes as distinct from local rates. The second was to allocate to Northern Ireland each year a sum related in some determinate manner to aggregate expenditure in Britain on services comparable to those controlled by Northern Ireland. Each course would give Ulster one conspicuous advantage. The first would mean heavy expenditure at the expense of the imperial contribution (and therefore of the United Kingdom as a whole) to raise services to British levels. The second would give the provincial Parliament freedom to dispose of revenue as it pleased. Neither course alone could be counted on to give both advantages.

The Government of Northern Ireland, however, wanted the best of both worlds. They put to the Colwyn Committee a formula designed to ensure that Exchequer spending in Ulster would keep pace with comparable spending in Britain. They also took the view that in social services (unemployment insurance, old age pensions and apparently health services),[2] Ulstermen were entitled to exactly the same benefits as other citizens of the United

[1] The inquiry by the Royal Commission on Financial Relations in 1896 resulted in eight different reports and memoranda by the fifteen members. The Committee on Irish Finance in 1912 recorded their view that the problem of assessing relative taxable capacities was insoluble, not in the sense that no answer was possible, but because 'so many plausible answers are possible that the number of solutions threatens to equal the number of solvers'. U.K. Cd. 6153 (1912), p. 11. In 1920 Sir Edward Carson tried without success to get the Government to define 'taxable capacity' more closely. 133 H.C. Deb., 5 s., 1245.

[2] *Ulster Year Book, 1950*, p. xxx.

Kingdom. 'We have gone on the assumption', said the Minister of Finance in October 1924, 'that in all matters of social welfare we should be entitled to the same benefits as in Great Britain; that local autonomy did not necessarily imply any lower social status.'[1]

That assumption was not accepted by the Colwyn Committee. In their final Report in March 1925[2] the Committee recorded their view that common taxation was to some extent a measure of relative gross taxable capacity. That is to say, the severity of all taxation (whether reserved or transferred) in Ulster would henceforth be on a par with that in Great Britain.[3] They also adopted the formula submitted by Northern Ireland,[4] and they proposed that domestic expenditure[5] in Britain and Ulster in 1924 should be taken as a standard and that after that year *per capita* expenditure in Ulster should increase at the same rate as in Britain. The Committee did not, however, allow that Ulster should necessarily enjoy the same standard of services as Britain, or that she should create services that had no counterpart there. They said that the imperial contribution should be based on the difference between Ulster's revenue and her actual and necessary expenditure, and necessary expenditure was not to include spending on services that did not exist in Britain or that were superior to services there, taking into account not only average standards in the two countries but also 'any lower general level of prices, of wages, or of standards of comfort or social amenity which may exist in Northern Ireland as compared with Great Britain'. After 1924, therefore, Ulster's permissible expenditure would be limited in two ways: first by the *per capita* formula, and secondly by an estimate of her economic and social disparity. On the basis of these two principles the Joint Exchequer Board were to assess each year the exact amount of the contribution.

This settlement, which took effect at once, was welcomed by the provincial Government. Since their own services would henceforth rank as the first charge on revenue, they could contemplate

[1] Senate Deb., 4, c. 206. See also H.C. Deb. (N.I.), 6, c. 531.

[2] *Final Report of the Northern Ireland Special Arbitration Committee*, U.K. Cmd. 2389 (1925).

[3] Northern Ireland was permitted to vary the composition of transferred taxation, but a precisely worded formula ensured that the ratio between the yield of transferred revenue and the yield of comparable revenue in Britain in the standard year (1924) should remain constant, subject to some qualifications.

[4] The Minister of Finance said in 1925 that the formula was virtually identical to that which Northern Ireland submitted. H.C. Deb. (N.I.), 6, c. 452.

[5] With some exceptions, notably expenditure on unemployment.

with equanimity the prospect of a diminishing imperial contribution if revenue continued to fall. Indeed, the contribution might not merely diminish; it could wholly disappear and be replaced by a payment from the United Kingdom. That, at least, was Sir James Craig's view. During the Budget debate in 1925 local M.P.s complained (as they have many times since) that the imperial contribution was too high. The Prime Minister said:

The time may arise, and it may not be very far distant, when owing to the reduction of either direct or indirect taxation, this contribution without any refusal on our part to pay it to Great Britain may of itself melt away altogether. . . . It is conceivable that sixpence or a shilling more off the income tax or a reduction in the tea and other duties may produce the effect that the contribution, instead of being paid by Northern Ireland to Great Britain, may be paid by Great Britain to Northern Ireland in order to preserve the same standard of living amongst the population as prevails on the other side. . . . That is the long view, and that is the view which my right hon. Friend (Mr. Pollock) [the Minister of Finance] and his colleagues take.[1]

There can be no doubt that Craig was quite confident that Britain would eventually make a net payment to Ulster. He repeated the point in 1927.[2] His prophecy, to all intents and purposes, has come true today, as we shall see. Before the war, however, the British Government did not share his view, and the Colwyn Committee's remit—'to consider whether any alteration is needed in the present scale of the contribution'—clearly implied that Ulster's ordinary revenue would exceed her domestic expenditure: the contribution would invariably be positive.

In his reference to 'the same standard of living' the Prime Minister was also going further than the Colwyn Report, which contemplated disparities in Ulster justified by differences in prices, wages and conventional standards. It did not even follow from the *per capita* expenditure formula that provincial services would improve at the same rate as in Britain—equal increments in *per capita* spending in different areas may give unequal standards—but Ulster expected to gain on the swings what she lost on the roundabouts, and the formula she had advocated did at any rate seem to ensure that her spending would always increase *pari passu* with Britain's. As the Minister of Finance explained in 1925:

[1] H.C. Deb. (N.I.), 6, cc. 468–9.
[2] ibid., 8, c. 1386.

The principle is that Northern Ireland's total expenditure on local services should be admitted to keep pace with the total expenditure of Britain on an equivalent basis per head of the population; that is, if Great Britain increased her local expenditure by ten shillings per head of her population, we in Northern Ireland can do the same.[1]

This advantage had apparently been secured without too much sacrifice of legislative autonomy. The Northern Ireland Parliament was bound henceforth to keep transferred taxes in parity with Britain, but it was free to vary their composition (in any event they produced little revenue), and it could adjust the pattern of local spending to local needs, subject only to the restrictions against creating new services or raising the average standard of services to a relatively higher level than in Britain. The Minister continued:

This basis of calculation on our relative populations tends very greatly to simplicity and gives us much greater flexibility in our administration . . . and on the whole I am satisfied that it is to the benefit of Northern Ireland that its Parliament should get the freedom which is conferred by a general basis of calculation and which it would not secure if it were feasible, which I doubt, to make a separate equitable calculation in each particular case.[2]

In the event the expectations of Ministers were only partially fulfilled. The formula they had advocated was abandoned, the freedom they had sought for Parliament proved to be illusory, the financial security they had counted on turned out to be fragile, and their plans for reform were found to be premature. The reasons for all this will emerge as the narrative develops, but it may be helpful at this point to fix attention on the crux of the matter.

After 1924 expenditure and revenue continued to move in different directions. Supply expenditure (voted by Parliament) rose rapidly. The legislature had little latitude though. Most of the increase went on unemployment insurance, old age pensions and derating, for despite the Colwyn Report the Government were resolved to keep cash social services in step with those in Britain, and they had no real alternative but to adopt the British scheme of derating. Revenue, on the other hand, fell away. It was, of course, determined for the most part by the Chancellor of the Exchequer against the background of Britain's rather than Ulster's needs. Year by year, therefore, the surplus that constituted the imperial

[1] ibid., 6, c. 452. [2] ibid.

contribution narrowed until in the 1930's it virtually disappeared and the Minister of Finance could balance his Budget only by stop-gap methods.

This was the situation foreseen by Sir James Craig. But the United Kingdom did not then recognize any obligation to make good a deficit in the provincial Budget, and a claim by Ulster could easily be contested because she insisted on keeping unemployment insurance and old age pensions in absolute equality with Britain, though the Colwyn Committee had not agreed to this. It is true that Northern Ireland was not necessarily bound by the Colwyn principles in the 1930's; she could have asked for new arbitration.[1] By that time, however, there was little room for impartial review, for while Ulster was determined to maintain social benefits at British levels, the United Kingdom was equally determined to secure equity in finance.

We have said that rates of taxation throughout the United Kingdom were similar. Nevertheless, Ulstermen enjoyed privileges that were hardly defensible on any ground but prescription. Before 1920 Irish ratepayers had no control of and paid no rates for education or (except in Dublin) the police, whereas in Britain about half the cost of both services was a charge on local rates. This disparity continued in Northern Ireland.[2] Since, therefore, the provincial Exchequer defrayed expenditure that fell on the rates in Britain, it made an unduly low imperial contribution. Taxpayers in the province also enjoyed a special advantage, for their liability in respect of Schedule A income tax was based on valuations for rating made between 1857 and 1865 and never generally revised, whereas in England assessments were corrected every five years.[3] To eliminate these anomalies, it was reckoned in 1925, would impose on Ulster a burden of some £2 m. a year, about one-sixth of ordinary revenue.[4] That burden, as matters stood, fell on the United Kingdom as a whole. Since Ulster's

[1] The Committee considered that their principles should not necessarily be applied for more than five years without reconsideration unless they proved satisfactory to both sides.

[2] The Education Act (N.I.), 1923, shifted only a fractional part of the cost of education to the rates. Belfast Corporation was the only local authority required to contribute to the cost of the Royal Ulster Constabulary.

[3] The lack of general revision also meant gross unfairness in the distribution of the rate burden except in Belfast, which was revalued between 1900 and 1906. *Interim* and *Final Report of Departmental Committee on Valuation*, Cmd. 23 (1923), 26 (1924).

[4] H.C. Deb. (N.I.), 6, cc. 530–1.

domestic expenditure was tied to the British standard, any increase in the yield of taxes and of local rates for education and police would mean a larger imperial contribution and a commensurate reduction in United Kingdom taxation. The taxpayer on the mainland in effect was helping to pay for education and police in Ulster and subsidizing owners of property.[1] As Northern Ireland's expenditure cut more deeply into the imperial contribution, the United Kingdom (itself beset by financial difficulties) began to insist that she should bear a proper share of rates and taxes. So after 1925 the Joint Exchequer Board was gradually superseded by direct negotiations, with Ulster pressing for equality in cash social services and Britain pressing for less inequality in finance. The Colwyn Report proved to be, not the end, but only the beginning of the evolution of equitable financial relations.

We turn now to the actual course of events from 1924 to 1939. The major theme is the attempt to find a point of equilibrium acceptable to both Britain and Ulster. In this attempt three periods can be distinguished: 1924–31, 1932–35 and 1936–39. In each period, as throughout the province's whole history, financial questions of great public interest and importance were shrouded in secrecy. The Joint Exchequer Board has never published any reports, and it is apparently taken for granted that the public have no right to know, except in purely general terms, how Ulster's revenue and permissible expenditure are fixed. The available evidence nevertheless seems sufficient to enable us to reconstruct the main developments with little risk of serious error.

From 1924 to 1931, as reference to Appendix Two will show, ordinary revenue fell by £1·1 m., the imperial contribution dwindled from £4·5 m. to £0·5 m., but transferred expenditure rose by £3·6 m.—more than 50 per cent. Despite this remarkable expansion, there was little improvement in most services, nor did the Minister of Finance enjoy the freedom and flexibility he had anticipated. His Budgets were dominated by the need to follow Britain's lead in three directions–old age pensions, unemployment insurance and derating.

Non-contributory old age pensions in Ireland in 1920 were already payable at British rates, and these were maintained in

[1] The Colwyn Report did not mention these matters, but they were probably brought to light in the Committee by arguments put by the Treasury which, as the Minister said, was represented by its very ablest advocates. H.C. Deb. (N.I.), 6., c. 452.

Ulster in the inter-war years. When Mr. Neville Chamberlain inaugurated contributory widows', orphans' and old age pensions in 1925, Mr. J. M. Andrews (Minister of Labour) at once introduced an identical scheme. He again followed Britain's lead in extending the scope of pensions in 1929 and 1931. The local Exchequer had to find £1·7 m. for pensions in 1931, against £1·1 m. in 1924.

Among the reasons for this 'step-by-step' policy (which extended also to unemployment insurance), probably the most compelling was that Ulstermen had no choice but to pay taxes at British rates and make an imperial contribution.[1] Complaints about the size of the contribution were not infrequent after 1921. If Ministers had failed to keep in step with Britain, they would undoubtedly have strained their followers' loyalty and sharpened their resentment against Britain's financial supremacy. Therefore, on the question of cash social benefits the Government's attitude from the outset was uncompromising. At the beginning of 1922, when the Northern Ireland Cabinet decided to keep in step, Sir James Craig proclaimed that it would never be said 'that the workers in our midst worked under conditions worse than those across the water'.[2]

It was easier to make the prophecy than to fulfil it in respect of unemployment insurance. That scheme in Ulster was identical to Britain's, benefits in both countries being paid at the same rates from separate Unemployment Funds financed by employers, employees and the respective Exchequers; but Northern Ireland was able to keep up with her wealthier neighbour only by sinking into a morass of debt. By 1925, when 24 per cent. of her insured population were out of work compared with 11 per cent. in Britain, the deficit on her Fund was £3·6 m., an enormous sum for an area whose whole Budget came to little more than £5 m.[3] Worse still, her leaders could do practically nothing to stop the growth of debt. Neither remedies nor palliatives for unemployment lay within their power, even had they been within their knowledge. Currency devaluation, tariff protection, foreign trade agreements—these matters and the general fiscal and economic policy of the United Kingdom were determined in London. Nor was it feasible to re-

[1] The origins of the 'step-by-step' policy are discussed in Chapter Nine (Social Security).

[2] H.C. Deb. (N.I.), 2, cc. 19, 413.

[3] The deficit on the British Fund was £7·9 m. Ulster's proportionate deficit on the basis of insured population would have been about 2·3 per cent. of that sum, i.e. £183,000. *Unemployment Insvrance (Agreement): Memorandum explaining Financial Resolution*, Cmd. 57 (1926), p. 2.

arrange the finance of the Unemployment Fund. The Colwyn Report allowed them to make an Exchequer contribution at only the same rate as in Britain.[1] The one action they could take—drastically to reduce benefits or increase employers' and workers' contributions—was politically impracticable. The Cabinet were pledged publicly to maintain British standards, and to depart from them could mean the end of Home Rule. As the Prime Minister said on 9 March 1926, when the immediate crisis was past:

> It was a dreadful thought to carry always with one, that Ulster, having emerged from the other many difficulties which surrounded her, and having vindicated her determination to remain part and parcel of Great Britain and the Empire, might find herself so hampered financially that she could not carry on as a definite subordinate unit.[2]

Yet in the nature of this predicament lay its resolution. The United Kingdom had retained such extensive powers that she could hardly divest herself of commensurate responsibility. Such apparently was the case put up by Northern Ireland for special help.[3] The argument was successful. A Committee under the chairmanship of Lord Cave set up by the British Government in 1925 recommended in effect that unemployment insurance in Britain and Ulster should be partially integrated.[4] Special arrangements were then made to enable the province to keep benefits and contributions at British rates without being waterlogged by debt.

The essential points of the Unemployment Insurance Agreement of 1926 were two. First, the extent to which Northern Ireland could increase the deficit on her Unemployment Fund (the course hitherto adopted) was limited: as from 1 October 1925 she undertook

[1] The allowable contribution was 'the amount which would actually be contributable for the year if the contribution in Northern Ireland were calculated on the same basis of contribution as in Great Britain'.

[2] H.C. Deb. (N.I.), 7, c. 17.

[3] The Minister of Finance said in May 1949, 'The origin of reinsurance was the recognition by the Imperial Government that the provision of employment, although a transferred matter, was one which, being governed to a large extent by factors such as overseas trade, must carry divided responsibility, and that the cost of unemployment in any particular area of the United Kingdom should be met by the United Kingdom as a whole.' H.C. Deb. (N.I.), 33, cc. 870–1.

[4] The Committee also recommended that health and old age pensions should be 'reinsured' with corresponding services in Britain, but the proposal was dropped because it conflicted with the principles of the Colwyn Report. *Ulster Year Book, 1950*, p. xxx.

to provide each year from her Exchequer an 'equalization payment' sufficient to make the deficit per head of insured population equal to the corresponding deficit on the British Fund. But secondly, if in any year her Exchequer payment per head of population exceeded the corresponding British payment, then Britain was to meet three-fourths of the excess.[1] The amount of this subvention depended on the incidence of unemployment in Britain and Ulster, since rates of benefit and contribution were identical and changes in the size of populations in the short term were insignificant.[2]

This relieved Ulster's immediate anxiety, but it did not represent pure gain. Having accepted greater financial responsibility for the province's affairs, the United Kingdom gained even more influence over them. The provincial Government gave an assurance that they would welcome the fullest investigation by the Treasury or the British Ministry of Labour into the administration of their Unemployment Fund[3] and, what was more, that they would spend no money on any new items without first informing the Treasury.[4] Then, too, unemployment insurance henceforth absorbed a large slice of current revenue. They did continue to borrow for a few years (though only at the same rate as Britain), but when in 1931 the National Government stopped all borrowing for the British Unemployment Fund, they were obliged to do the same.[5] Unemployment insurance cost the local Exchequer £1·2 m. in 1931, against £0·4 m. in 1924.

[1] The proportionately greater debt on the Northern Ireland Fund (£3·4 m. in 1925) was transferred to a Suspense Account which Ulster undertook to extinguish by 1959. An attempt to do this from general revenue failed at first because the Joint Exchequer Board would not allow the redemption payments to rank against the imperial contribution. However, by arrangements made in 1936 and 1942, the province was permitted to divert substantial sums to the Suspense Account and to extinguish the debt by 1945. P.A.C. 1936–37, H.C. 442, p. 79; C.A.G. 1944–45, H.C. 685, p. xx.

[2] The British Government in 1926 declined to amalgamate the two Funds (as Ulster suggested on several occasions) because they wished to limit their financial liability and to encourage economical administration by the Belfast Government. 192 H.C. Deb., 5 s., 91, 148, 2393. Britain again rejected amalgamation in 1936 as being 'contrary to the whole spirit of the Act of 1920, which was that the social services should be administered by Northern Ireland and not by Whitehall'. 309 H.C. Deb., 5 s., 1682. It should be noted that though the 1926 Agreement was reciprocal, Northern Ireland never had to make any payment to Britain. The Agreement is scheduled to the Unemployment Insurance (Agreement) Acts (N.I.), 1926 and 1929.

[3] Cmd. 57, p. 6.

[4] P.A.C. 1947–48, H.C. 873, p. 66.

[5] P.A.C. 1932–33, H.C. 319, p. 55.

Meanwhile, an uglier word than unemployment had come into vogue. Derating, adopted by Britain in 1929, was a measure to subsidize agriculture and manufacturing industry by relieving them of local rates. The Exchequer made grants to local authorities to offset the loss of rate income. The Ulster Government had hardly set up a committee to consider a similar scheme when they announced their intention to follow Britain's lead.[1] They had no alternative if farms and factories were to continue to compete successfully in Britain, the principal market for Ulster produce.[2] Besides, in accordance with the Colwyn Report, rating relief could reduce the imperial contribution.[3] Derating (to coin an Irishism) was a gift horse that could kick if you looked him in the mouth. So after 1929, in Ulster as in Britain, the farmer paid virtually no rates and the industrialist's liability was reduced by three-quarters. In Ulster, too, local authorities were given bigger Exchequer grants, the money being found by drawing upon the imperial contribution. In consequence the contribution fell to £0·5 m. in 1931. In that year, however, Northern Ireland received from Britain a subvention of £0·5 m. under the Unemployment Insurance Agreement. The contribution had virtually disappeared.

TABLE 2. *Revenue and Expenditure, 1924 and 1931*

£ million

Revenue

	Ordinary	*From U.K. Exchequer*	*Total*
1923–24	12·0	—	12·0
1930–31	11·3*	0·5	11·8

* Includes £0·4 m. from a special account to finance derating.

Any discrepancies in totals are due to rounding up the figures.

[1] *Report of Committee on the Financial Relations between the State and Local Authorities*, Cmd. 131 (1931), p. 46.

[2] H.C. Deb. (N.I.), 17, c. 1842.

[3] 'In the case of any future shifting of expenditure from or to local rates in Great Britain, allowance shall be made so that Northern Ireland shall not suffer or benefit as the case may be merely on account of such change.' U.K. Cmd. 2389, p. 8.

Expenditure

	Imperial contribution	*Reserved services*	*Transferred services*			*Total*
			Consolidated Fund	*Supply*		
				Insurance, pensions, derating	*Other*	
1923–24	4·5	1·7	0·4	1·8	3·9	12·1
1930–31	0·5	1·8	0·8	4·7	3·9	11·8

In 1924 the surplus of ordinary revenue (represented by the imperial contribution) was £4·5 m. By 1931 increased expenditure, due almost entirely to pensions, unemployment and derating, had combined with diminished revenue to wipe out the surplus. The aspirations voiced by the Prime Minister in 1923 thus faded and died. There could no longer be any question of large-scale improvement, nor of trying to secure more freedom for the local Parliament. The problem henceforth was to keep in step with Britain in a limited range of services without an unbalanced Budget.

The second period, the four years 1932–35, began with the abandonment of the formula relating to *per capita* expenditure.

Until 1931 domestic expenditure was limited by the Colwyn Committee's two principles: (*a*) the imperial contribution should be the surplus of revenue over necessary expenditure; (*b*) *per capita* expenditure should increase *pari passu* with that in Britain. The calculations actually made each year have never been published,[1] but it is evident that the Treasury and the Ministry of Finance each prepared two sets of figures on the basis of (*a*) and (*b*) and after consultation made an agreed submission to the Joint Exchequer Board. When, however, they did their sums for 1932

[1] They cannot be worked out by an outsider. Among other things, we do not know which items of expenditure were included. For example, the Public Accounts Committee reported in 1949 that 'from the outset certain types of expenditure (e.g. on unemployment) had to be excluded from the calculations'. H.C. 873, p. 15. But in 1950 the then Second Secretary of the Ministry of Finance told the Committee that 'expenditure on unemployment is included, and always has been included, in the calculation'. P.A.C. 1948–49, H.C. 935, p. 28.

they found that formula (*b*) would entail a negative contribution of £640,000. That is to say, if *per capita* expenditure were to keep pace with that in Britain, the contribution would not merely disappear but would be replaced by a direct payment from the United Kingdom Exchequer in aid of general expenditure in the province. The British Government, however, made no such payment. The formula was simply abandoned, never to be revived.[1]

At this juncture also the Unemployment Insurance Agreement ceased to work as expected, for the rate of unemployment in Britain after 1929 increased so much faster than in Ulster that the latter's special receipts from the British Exchequer fell away and, after 1932, vanished entirely. Appendix Three shows how the Agreement worked. From 1932, therefore, Northern Ireland again had to bear the whole cost of unemployment, but she could no longer borrow (as before 1926) because Britain had stopped borrowing. The provincial Unemployment Fund had to be kept in parity with the British Fund from current revenue alone. Add to this the facts that the imperial contribution (hitherto in effect a reserve) was virtually extinct and that the security the Prime Minister had counted on had proved baseless, and it must be clear that Ulster's plight was desperate.

There were three courses open. The first—to cut expenditure—was urged in 1931 by a Committee on the Financial Relations between the State and Local Authorities:

> The limit of resources has been reached and the only effective remedy is for both government and local authorities to concentrate on the utmost measures of economy. . . . If such economies are not effected, we can foresee that the Government, in order to find an imperial contribution, may be forced to place part of the present state expenditure upon the already over-burdened ratepayers; and we cannot recommend any serious transference of the burden of expenditure from the Exchequer to the rates. We favour the alternative of drastic retrenchment, and we think that, so far as the state is concerned, that path should be pursued even if it leads to the adoption in respect of unemployment benefit and other social services of a level below that which is accepted as the standard for Great Britain.[2]

Sir James Craig (created Viscount Craigavon in 1927) and his colleagues rejected this advice. They were prepared to economize,

[1] C.A.G. 1947–48, H.C. 843, pp. 15–18; H.C. 873, pp. 14–16, 65–69; H.C. 935, pp. 26–29.

[2] Cmd. 131, pp. 51–52.

and they did economize in most fields, but they were determined to maintain absolute equality in unemployment insurance, pensions and derating, though these were the chief causes of their difficulties. If Ulster could not draw level with Britain, her leaders were at least resolved not to fall much further behind.

The second course was to increase local taxation. Transferred taxes (mainly death duties and motor vehicle and stamp duties) produced one-sixth of all tax revenue in 1931, and no rule in the constitution prohibited higher duties than in Britain or the imposition of a wholly new tax. To resort to such expedients would nevertheless have been folly. Extra taxation would handicap the economy without producing much, if any, extra revenue; for the British Government might conceivably have claimed the revenue,[1] and Ulstermen could avoid some of the taxation by removing to Britain dutiable assets (e.g. personal property) and dutiable activities (e.g. the transfer of stocks and shares). Moreover, by trying to raise more money to cover a Budget deficit, the Minister of Finance would accept responsibility for it; but the provincial Government considered their predicament to be mainly a by-product of British fiscal and economic policy. They had little control over their revenue and even less over economic decisions that intimately affected them.

The argument pointed to the third course. But they got no help from the United Kingdom during the years in question. On the contrary, as we have said, the Colwyn formula was abandoned; and from 1932 to 1935 the Minister of Finance had to balance his Budget by extraordinary measures. He pruned expenditure with the utmost rigour, restricted derating grants, raided the Road Fund and transferred to the Exchequer substantial sums from a Reserve Fund created primarily to reduce public debt.[2]

[1] The Minister of Finance said in 1943: 'Before the war, provided the Government deemed it expedient to make substantial increases within the limited field of Northern Ireland's transferred taxes, thereby raising such taxes above the levels ruling in Great Britain in the same field of taxation, it would have been possible to use such increased revenue to improve the standards of social and other services in Northern Ireland beyond the Great Britain standard, but only if the Joint Exchequer Board were satisfied that an adequate imperial contribution was being made, and subject to the effect which such departure might have on the understanding with the Treasury on unemployment reinsurance.' H.C. Deb. (N.I.), 26, c. 371.

[2] See C.A.G. 1931–32, H.C. 278, p. 12; 1932–33, H.C. 301, p. 12; 1933–34, H.C. 325, pp. 10–12; 1934–35, H.C. 361, p. 10; H.C. Deb. (N.I.), 25, c. 2205.

The imperial contribution, cut to £24,000 in 1935, became a token.

In these circumstances it might be expected that the problem would have been submitted to the Joint Exchequer Board or referred to arbitration, as in 1923. Why this was not done has never been disclosed, but it seems that the United Kingdom—herself in the middle of a financial crisis—had at length decided to require Ulster to diminish the financial privileges referred to above.[1] The Government at Stormont had for some years successfully resisted Britain's proposals to revalue Northern Ireland and impose an education rate.[2] Now they could resist no more. The United Kingdom would have revalued the province over Stormont's head;[3] and, as the Minister of Finance said, 'We have either to say that we are willing to accept partial responsibility for the education of our children or upset our whole relations with the Imperial Government.'[4] So in 1932 the Parliament passed a measure providing for quinquennial general revaluations,[5] and in 1934 local authorities were obliged to pay each year to the provincial Exchequer the produce of a shilling education rate.[6]

These impositions, which in a full year augmented revenue by some £0·6 m.[7] (about one-third of transferred taxation) provoked the sharpest protests. Belfast Corporation contested the legality of the education levy on the ground that it was substantially the same in character as income tax, and so beyond the powers of the legislature. The Judicial Committee of the Privy Council, to which the question was referred under s. 51 of the Government of

[1] In 1934 Lord Craigavon was challenged to justify his statement to the effect that in the long term he looked for a British contribution. He replied, in part, 'Naturally, we could not expect to get a contribution from Great Britain if we ourselves were not living on parallel lines to what they are on the other side.' H.C. Deb. (N.I.), 16, c. 2004.

[2] The Chancellor of the Exchequer first proposed revaluation in 1927. ibid., 17, c. 1589.

[3] The Minister of Finance disclosed in 1937 that the British Government intended to insert in the Finance Bill of 1930 a clause to revalue property in Ulster for income tax purposes and that 'as an alternative our government undertook to carry out a revaluation for rating purposes which the British Government would be prepared to adopt for income tax assessments'. ibid., 19, cc. 2141–2.

[4] ibid., 16, c. 1758.

[5] Valuation Acts Amendment Act (N.I.), 1932.

[6] Finance Act (N.I.), 1934, s. 3.

[7] In 1937 (the first year after revaluation) income tax yielded £482,799 more than in 1936, but some of this was due to a rise in the standard rate and improved trade. The education levy was £232,360 in 1938.

Ireland Act, decided that a rate was not a tax.[1] Opposition at Stormont came to nothing. The Government could rely on their majority in the Commons and on the cohesion of their party—a split could shatter the constitution. At the same time, the Minister of Finance emphasized that the two measures, though imposed at the United Kingdom's behest, were fair. On revaluation he made two points:

> The first is: we must pass this measure in this Parliament or have it forced upon us at Westminster. That is definite. The second is: we have always claimed equal rights and equal services with the rest of the Kingdom. Can we logically repudiate Britain's right to claim from Northern Ireland the same conditions in respect of revaluation as obtain in Britain?[2]

In the same vein he argued that the education levy was as inescapable as it was equitable:

> We have been reminded over and over again that we are not living up to our responsibilities and that if we were not prepared to take over the education of our own children some other arrangement would have to be made. After all, if we are getting and taking all the advantages of British citizenship in respect of all the social services, which claim such an enormous amount of money, and are helped by the British Government in that respect, I do not think it is unreasonable, when you bring the matter down to hard argument, that the British Government should expect that we would endeavour to live up to our responsibilities.[3]

These adjustments made, Britain was evidently satisfied that Ulster was bearing her fair share. There is no evidence that she applied further pressure. On the contrary, both governments were evidently in accord, for the Joint Exchequer Board (which met only when the Treasury and the Ministry of Finance differed) was not convened at all between 1935 and 1947. Members of the Board were notified of agreements made by the Treasury and the Ministry of Finance, and the chairman signed any necessary Orders.[4] Moreover, Ulster again received special help from Britain during the third of our periods (1936–39), to which we turn next.

On the completion of revaluation in 1936, the Unemployment

[1] *Re Reference under Government of Ireland Act, 1920, Re Sect. 3 of Finance Act (N.I.), 1934,* [1936] A.C. 352. See also Quekett, op. cit., Part III.

[2] H.C. Deb. (N.I.), 13, cc. 2428–9.

[3] ibid., 16, cc. 1757–8.

[4] ibid., 31, c. 950. P.A.C. 1946–47, H.C 817, p. 47.

Insurance Agreement, which had tumbled so quickly about Ulster's ears, was converted into a more solid shelter. The main change was simple and effective. *Per capita* equalization payments by the two Exchequers to their Unemployment Funds were henceforth calculated, not on total, but on insured populations. Reference to Appendix Three will show that the proportion of the population in insurable employment in Ulster was much smaller than in Great Britain. The former's *per capita* payments (to which help from Britain was related) were therefore inflated. The new Agreement also covered unemployment assistance (introduced in 1934) as well as insurance.[1] Thus, after 1935 the United Kingdom paid to the province larger sums than ever before.

Lord Craigavon and his colleagues were now, however, acutely conscious of their lack of security. The initiation by the United Kingdom of either reduced rates of taxation or new and expensive ventures which, as in the case of derating, they would have no option but to copy, could again plunge them into a predicament similar to that recently surmounted. Yet Ulster's survival as a self-governing unit was more clearly in Britain's interest than ever before. The creation in Ireland of separate Parliaments that had freely chosen not to unite was gradually demonstrating that partition was due to the wish of Irishmen themselves rather than to British bayonets, so that the storm centre of Irish politics was blowing away from Westminster. Furthermore, in 1938 the United Kingdom relinquished her rights over the Irish Free State treaty ports. In time of war Ulster alone could be relied on freely to provide facilities to protect the United Kingdom's Atlantic flank.

There is no evidence that Ulster pressed these considerations (though it would be surprising if Britain ever overlooked them), nor is there the slightest reason to suppose that Ulster's leaders would falter in loyalty to the Crown. Their case in seeking some measure of financial security was simply that they had always played the game. Beset by problems not primarily of their making, they had nevertheless fulfilled their obligation to make from rates as well as taxes as large a contribution to common services as equity required. It could be argued that they were both compelled and entitled to look to Britain for help in future budgetary difficulties.

[1] For details see Unemployment (Agreement) Act (N.I.), 1936, Schedule; C.A.G. 1935–36, H.C. 393, pp. 16–17; P.A.C. 1935–36, H.C. 412, pp. 31, 59.

Was it an unreasonable argument? The late Mr. J. M. Andrews, Minister of Finance from 1937 to 1941 (and to whom, incidentally, Ulster must owe a profound debt for his previous work until 1937 as Minister of Labour and for his subsequent services until 1943 as Prime Minister), recalled in 1945 how he had put that question to the Chancellor of the Exchequer. In reply Sir John Simon announced on 12 May 1938 that it would be equitable that means should be found to make good a deficit on the Northern Ireland Budget that was not the result of a standard of social expenditure higher than, or of a standard of taxation lower than, that of Britain.[1]

That [said Mr. Andrews] gives us a wonderful security. But remember, it was based on the assumption that we would play fair right along the line. We can always have parity as long as we pay our share of parity, but we can never expect the British Government to agree to bear our local authorities' share which is borne by the local authorities in Great Britain.[2]

In the event there was no need to call on Britain. Increased rates of taxation, the new Unemployment Agreement, revaluation and the education levy drove revenue to a higher level than ever before. But pensions, unemployment, and derating grants continued to absorb virtually all the money that was left after allowing for an imperial contribution and the cost of reserved services.

TABLE 3. *Expenditure on Supply Services, 1924 and 1939*

	£ million	
	1923–24	*1938–39*
Pensions, State insurance, unemployment assistance and derating grants	1·8	6·9
Other grants to local authorities, excluding education	0·2	0·4
Education	1·8	2·2
Justice and police	1·2	0·9
Administrative departments	0·4	0·5
Other expenditure	0·3	0·6
	£5·6	£11·5

'Other expenditure' was inflated in 1939 by public buildings (largely paid for by Britain in 1924) and civil defence.

[1] 335 H.C. Deb., 5 s., 1709.
[2] H.C. Deb. (N.I.), 28, cc. 78–79.

Among the wide range of local government services (in general markedly inferior to those in Britain), only education got appreciably more assistance. The heavy burden of poor relief and in progressive areas of better hospitals, health services and other amenities fell mainly on ratepayers. Rates per head of population rose from £1 5*s*. 8*d*. in 1931 (the first full year of derating) to £1 18*s*. 10*d*. in 1939, whereas derating grants actually fell.

TABLE 4. *Rates and Government Grants, 1931 and 1939*[1]

	£000	
	1930–31	*1938–39*
Rates	1,614	2,485
Government grants—		
Derating	1,116	999
Education	25	332
Other	252	260

By 1939 Lord Craigavon and a Unionist junta had directed the province's affairs for eighteen years. It was Craigavon's dominant aim, and his signal achievement, not only to keep Ulster within the United Kingdom, but to secure for Ulstermen of all creeds a measure of social security identical to that in Britain. His government had also confounded prophecies that devolution would not work and gained the financial security that was lacking until 1938. But he had not realized all his ambitions. For one thing, he had failed to get a wide measure of freedom for the provincial legislature. On the ramshackle foundations of the Act of 1920 he and his colleagues had built, not a half-way house, but a lean-to whose stability depended on the ties that bound it to Britain. For another, his desire radically to improve public services had only partially been fulfilled. So Ulstermen in 1939 still endured poverty, unemployment, ill health, poor housing, inadequate roads and indifferent education.

Yet neither this, nor the limitations imposed on the legislature, nor even the introduction at Britain's behest of higher rates and taxes, aroused much public resentment. There was certainly no organized campaign in any quarter. Careful study of newspapers and parliamentary debates fails to reveal any sustained movement of public opinion.

[1] Sources: *Local Taxation Returns*, 1930–31, 1938–39. Receipts from the Road Fund (a Consolidated Fund charge) and grants for capital purposes are omitted. The statistics are defective: grants to local education authorities in the Appropriation Accounts, 1930–31 were £164,300.

Before concluding this chapter it may be useful to summarize what appear to be the chief reasons for this profound apathy. In the first place, the Parliament of Northern Ireland never really struck root. Not that it was wholly ineffective, as later chapters will show. The point is that its impact on the intelligence and imagination of Ulstermen was never sharp. Neither Unionists nor Nationalists had ever demanded a legislature for Northern Ireland alone: the former looked to Westminster for salvation, the latter to Dublin. The one thing that might have stimulated all citizens to lift their eyes to Stormont—local taxation on the grand scale—was wanting.

The second point is related to the first. Nationalists throughout the inter-war years directed all their energies, not merely against the Government, but against the constitution. By their constant attacks on the legitimacy of Stormont and by their single-minded preoccupation with allegations of discrimination against Catholics, they both diverted attention from shortcomings in public services and also strengthened the Unionist Party and the Orange Order. They could hardly have chosen a more effective way to keep the same party in power for two decades and discourage public debate on matters of common interest.

Finally, external attacks also strengthened Unionist solidarity. The decline in the imperial contribution (which many took to be an important index of Ulster's value as part of the United Kingdom), subventions by Britain, and measures by Stormont to maintain its authority provoked criticism from responsible quarters in Britain.[1]

For these reasons Unionists and those who shared their outlook were content simply to trust their leaders. In that trust lay strength—and weakness. Single-party government and secrecy in public finance sapped the vitality of discussion to an extent that few democratic countries, and certainly no other part of the United Kingdom, would have tolerated.

[1] For example, A. Berriedale Keith, the celebrated authority on the British constitution, wrote that the people of Northern Ireland received large British subsidies, made no proper contribution to imperial charges, and their government had shown itself oppressive and unfair to the minority. *The Constitution of England from Queen Victoria to George VI* (London, 1940), vol. ii, p. 199. H. Harrison's *Ulster and the British Empire* (with statistics prepared by the intelligence branch of *The Economist*) (London, 1939) is a biting criticism of Ulster. In 1936 the National Council for Civil Liberties severely criticized measures to maintain order.

CHAPTER FOUR

The Impact of War

THE war marks a turning-point in Ulster's evolution. Automatically at war as part of the United Kingdom from 3 September 1939, the Government of Northern Ireland at once determined, in Lord Craigavon's words, 'to place the whole of our resources at the command of the Government in Britain'.[1] The manner in which this undertaking was fulfilled needs little recapitulation.[2] The deeds of Ulstermen (all volunteers)[3] who fought at sea, on land and in the air were matched at home by unremitting effort to expand the output of farms, factories and shipyards. The civilian population, subject to rationing and other controls, also did their utmost to help finance the war. Higher taxation and earnings drove revenue from £16·2 m. in 1939 to £54·3 m. in 1945, but the Government undertook to spend on domestic services no more than in peace-time[4] and willingly left the surplus with the United Kingdom. The imperial contribution soared from £1·3 m. in 1939 to £36·3 m. in 1945. The Government also agreed to administer in the province several national services (e.g. national registration, control of agricultural products and civil defence) and to bear their cost until the United Kingdom reimbursed them.

As a contributor to victory, however, Ulster sprang into prominence chiefly because of her geographical situation. Germany after the summer of 1940 controlled the coasts of Norway, Denmark, Holland, Belgium and France; her aircraft and U-boats could range far into the Atlantic and prey on shipping off Britain's east and south coasts; yet the south-western approach, of immense potential value in these conditions, was vulnerable to the point of uselessness by reason of Eire's neutrality. In a tribute to Mr. J. M. Andrews in 1943 Sir Winston Churchill wrote:

[1] H.C. Deb. (N.I.), 22, c. 1902.

[2] See J. W. Blake, *Northern Ireland in the Second World War* (H.M.S.O., 1956) and references to Northern Ireland in United Kingdom Histories of the Second World War, especially K. A. H. Murray, *Agriculture* (1955) and Captain S. W. Roskill, R.N., *The War at Sea, 1939–45*, vol. i (1954).

[3] Britain, to the chagrin of Ulster Unionists, deemed it unwise to cast the net of conscription over any part of Ireland.

[4] Except where additional expenditure was made essential by war conditions.

That was a dark and dangerous hour. We were alone, and had to face single-handed the full fury of the German attack, raining down death and destruction on our cities and, still more deadly, seeking to strangle our life by cutting off the entry to our ports of the ships which brought us our food and the weapons we so sorely needed. Only one great channel of entry remained open. That channel remained open because loyal Ulster gave us the full use of the Northern Irish ports and waters, and thus ensured the free working of the Clyde and the Mersey. But for the loyalty of Northern Ireland and its devotion to what has now become the cause of thirty governments or nations, we should have been confronted with slavery and death, and the light which now shines so strongly throughout the world would have been quenched. . . . During your Premiership the bonds of affection between Great Britain and the people of Northern Ireland have been tempered by fire and are now, I firmly believe, unbreakable.[1]

In the same year Mr. Herbert Morrison,[2] then Home Secretary, also paid tribute to Ulster's crucial contribution.[3] So war bound Great Britain and Northern Ireland together in indissoluble union. The possibility that any government in London might press Belfast to come to terms with Dublin (as after the First World War) had grown remote with the years. It was now non-existent.

In Ulster, as in Britain, war stimulated keen expectations of social improvement. It also provoked a volume of responsible criticism without precedent since 1921. There were two counts to the indictment. Unemployment, which averaged 19·4 per cent. in 1940, still stood at 5 per cent. two years later. This waste was not only an affront to the fierce patriotism of the loyal Ulsterman; it threw a shadow over his future. If his country was unable to attract more war factories at a time when Britain's economy was at full stretch, what prospect had she of finding work for her rapidly growing labour force after the war? A second issue, pressed with mounting persistence as the war reached its climax, was post-war policy in social security, housing, health and other social services. Was Ulster to be condemned for ever to unequal services but equal taxation? Ought she not to turn her thoughts to post-war reconstruction, as Britain did as early as 1941?

Already, by the middle of 1940, two members of the Govern-

[1] H.C. Deb. (N.I.), 26, cc. 645–6.
[2] Later Lord Morrison of Lambeth.
[3] *The Annual Register*, vol. 185 (1943), p. 106.

ment had become convinced that the Administration was too old and stale to acquit itself with distinction. Craigavon (then approaching his seventieth year) and most of his Cabinet had been continuously in office since 1921.[1] The Parliamentary Secretary of the Ministry of Finance (Lt.-Col. A. R. G. Gordon) left the Government in June because of its lack of drive.[2] His resignation was preceded by that of another Parliamentary Secretary (Mr. J. E. Warnock), who in September went to the length (unprecedented for a member of the Unionist Party) of moving a vote of censure. 'This Government', declared Mr. Warnock, 'has been too long in office and is in the main composed of tired and jaded men.'

No limpet clings to a rock with the tenacity with which the members of the Government of Northern Ireland have clung to their posts.... The Opposition in this Parliament has been numerically insignificant. The spur which is necessary to keep any government, the best government in the world, up to the mark, is lacking here.

And with prophetic insight:

The Prime Minister may save his Government, but his responsibility is to maintain Ulster, and by maintaining his present Cabinet until the hand of God removes him is not the way to serve this province.[3]

The Prime Minister had little difficulty in saving his government. Two months later (on 24 November 1940) Lord Craigavon died while still in office.

His successor, Mr. J. M. Andrews (previously Minister of Finance and before that Minister of Labour) made no radical

[1] The following table shows the Ministers in charge of departments on 1 June 1940 and the first office held by each of them.

	Department (1940)	*First Office*
Lord Craigavon	Prime Minister	Prime Minister (1921)
Mr. J. M. Andrews	Finance	Minister of Labour (1921)
Sir Dawson Bates	Home Affairs	Minister of Home Affairs (1921)
Mr J. F. Gordon	Labour	Parl. Sec., Min. of Labour (1921)
Mr. J. H. Robb	Education	Parl. Sec., Min. of Education (1925)
Sir Basil Brooke	Agriculture	Asst. Parl. Sec., Min. of Finance (1929)
Mr. J. M. Barbour	Commerce	Parl. and Financial Sec., Min. of Finance (1921)

[2] H.C. Deb. (N.I.), 23, cc. 2155–6.

[3] ibid., c. 2162.

changes in the Ministry[1] and encountered a swelling volume of criticism. For twenty years Ulstermen had in large part been treated as second-class citizens except for the purpose of taxation. In health, housing, education, poor relief and most other services apart from insurance schemes they were still far behind Britain. To take one example from many that will be given when we examine public services: between the wars maternal mortality diminished everywhere in the British Isles except in Ulster. There it increased until it was higher than in England and Wales or Scotland or Eire. Thousands of Ulsterwomen died in childbirth simply because they lacked proper attention. The constitutional responsibility for this was Ulster's—but hardly the blame. It was only with difficulty that she had been able to persuade the United Kingdom to pay for part of the cost of unemployment insurance; and it seems certain that she could have done no better before 1939, when Britain herself was in financial difficulties and the imperial contribution was negligible. Appreciation of this, and the weight of Lord Craigavon's personality, had kept criticism in check. His death, together with increases in taxation and the imperial contribution, and misgivings about the Government's ability to mobilize the country for war and prepare it for peace, made its supporters increasingly restive.

So Stormont fastened on shortcomings in social services with unwonted vigour and persistence. An unsuccessful demand in 1941 for a Select Committee on Housing[2] was followed by other debates on the same subject until the Commons finally resolved on the 'vital necessity' of providing, at the earliest possible moment and on a large scale, houses at a rent that working people could pay.[3] The need for a distinct Ministry of Health, heard in Ulster for the first time since the Irish Public Health Council of 1920, was pressed by a physician (Dr. W. Lyle, representing Queen's

[1] The Cabinet formed by Mr. Andrews in January 1941 was:

Prime Minister—Mr. J. M. Andrews
Minister of Finance—Mr. J. M. Barbour
Minister of Home Affairs—Sir Dawson Bates
Minister of Labour—Mr. J. F. Gordon
Minister of Education—Mr. J. H. Robb
Minister of Agriculture—Lord Glentoran
Minister of Commerce—Sir Basil Brooke
Minister of Public Security—Mr. J. C. MacDermott (appointed by Lord Craigavon, 25 June 1940)

[2] H.C. Deb. (N.I.), 24, cc. 1604 et seq.

[3] ibid., 27, c. 871.

University of Belfast) in precise and devastating argument based on comparative mortality rates in Ulster and England.[1] The problem of destitution, it was argued, should be tackled by sweeping away boards of guardians and poor relief and giving effect to the Beveridge Report.[2] The Minister of Home Affairs, who for twenty-one years had supervised local councils, castigated them for their failure to make the country sweeter and cleaner. 'I would ask the local authorities to show a little more public spirit in dealing with the problems of public health', he said. 'The neglect that has been shown in certain instances is shocking.'[3]

In the country the high tide of official Unionism ebbed. Between 1941 and 1943 government-supported candidates were defeated in three by-elections, two for Stormont and one for Westminster. An Independent Unionist (Mr. T. Bailie) captured Lord Craigavon's old seat of North Down. A Belfast constituency counted safely Unionist went to the Labour leader, Mr. H. Midgley. The loss of a seat at Westminster to a Labour candidate (Mr. J. Beattie) was attributed to the intervention of another Independent Unionist. These reverses, interpreted at the time as a public protest against the old, negative spirit of Ulster Unionism, left the government with an unsympathetic and even critical Unionist press.[4]

War blasted away complacency in other ways. In 1941, when Belfast slum-dwellers were driven out of their bomb-damaged houses to find refuge elsewhere, the Moderator of the General Assembly of the Presbyterian Church was moved to uncommon frankness. After describing how inexpressibly shocked he was by the sight of the people he saw walking the streets after the 'blitz', he said, 'I have been working nineteen years in Belfast and I never saw the like of them before. If something is not done now to remedy this rank inequality there will be a revolution after the war.'[5] At the same time Belfast City Council became gravely concerned about the people's health. Tuberculosis was rife and caused almost half of all deaths in the age-group 15–25. Infant mortality, excessive when compared with that in English industrial centres, was higher in 1940 than for twenty years past. In January 1941, when the Government grant for maternity and

[1] ibid., 25, c. 3121; 27, c. 660; 28, c. 91.
[2] ibid., 26, c. 203.
[3] ibid., 25, c. 2928.
[4] *The Round Table*, vol. xxxii (1942), p. 270.
[5] *Belfast News-Letter*, 3 June 1941.

child welfare was running at only 21 per cent. instead of a permissible 50 per cent., the Council began to press for more assistance.[1]

In September of the same year a special committee appointed to examine the city's health services invited a former deputy Chief Medical Officer of the English Ministry of Health (Dr. T. Carnwath) to make an independent investigation. He found that in its personal medical services Belfast fell far short of what might reasonably have been expected in a city of its size and importance. The existence of the poor law medical service[2] and conflict with the Government on finance meant that the Council were not quite certain what they were doing, whether it was worth doing, or whether they were the people to do it.[3] Even so, evacuation of children revealed to social workers a striking disparity between conditions in the city and the countryside. 'During the war', said a woman M.P., 'I discovered that maternity and child welfare services were practically non-existent throughout Northern Ireland.'[4] And the personal habits of evacuated slum-dwellers were such that (in the words of an official report)[5] 'the shock to householders who granted them sanctuary was second only to the shock they had received on learning of the disaster which had befallen Belfast'. Finally, in country areas, war made local people acutely aware that land drainage (of importance for food output) and fire services were primitive or non-existent.

These stirrings of public opinion were in vivid contrast to pre-war quiescence. True, Unionism in both the party and constitutional sense still held the field; men and women of public spirit were seeking neither a new party nor wholesale political reconstruction, but simply more vigorous leaders. Yet it must seem that they were fortunate at this time to be served by a Prime Minister in whose memory was embedded the whole of Ulster's complex experience. Mr. Andrews had taken part in financial negotiations with Britain before 1921,[6] and after that year he had observed from the vantage point of a Cabinet Minister his colleagues' reforming zeal and their disillusionment. As Minister of Labour he had been prominent in shaping the Unemployment Insurance

[1] *Belfast News-Letter*, 11 January 1941.

[2] This is described in Chapter Seven.

[3] *Belfast News-Letter*, 29 December 1941.

[4] H.C. Deb. (N.I.), 30, c. 938.

[5] *Report on Health and Local Government Administration, 1938–46*, Cmd. 258 (1948), p. 122.

[6] H.C. Deb. (N.I.), 26, c. 654.

Agreements of 1926 and 1936, and as Minister of Finance after 1937 he was intimately acquainted with the circumstances that led to the Chancellor of the Exchequer's assurance in 1938 about a Budget deficit. He, more than any living politician in Ulster, saw clearly the folly of public discussion about the future—and, still more, of public announcements by Ministers—before Britain's assent to proposed changes had been obtained. He, unlike many other members of the provincial Parliament, understood how narrow was the passage between the Scylla of dissension within the Unionist Party and the Charybdis of disagreement with Britain on finance. In his speeches he used his knowledge of the past to chart a safe course for the future. Thus, when urged in March 1943 to bring the Beveridge Report into operation, he said:

May I be excused if I make a short personal reference? In succession I have been Minister of Labour and Minister of Finance, and during the last two-and-a-quarter years I have been in the key position of Prime Minister. From all these different points of view I have had special opportunities of studying the problem, and therefore it may be thought that I speak with some knowledge of the subject.... In my opinion if we were to go on our own it would be folly. This is a small area, and it is not a safe insurance risk, as hon. Members know. It is one of the poorer parts of the United Kingdom. What keeps the matter right in Great Britain is the fact that there are great rich areas such as London which help to carry the burden of the areas not so favourably circumstanced. Our claim here is that as part of the United Kingdom we have the right to expect the same security.[1]

To gain Britain's recognition of that claim was Mr. Andrews' crowning achievement. By 1942 the pre-war Unemployment Insurance Agreement was no longer necessary. It was not, however, abolished but simply suspended with the Treasury's agreement until new arrangements had been made in the light of post-war social legislation.[2] This enabled the Prime Minister to say with confidence that the Beveridge plan would extend to Ulster as soon as Britain implemented it.[3] But Mr. Andrews was not content merely to keep in step in social security, as hitherto in unemployment insurance and pensions. He wished to establish all public services on a par with those in Britain, and he raised this issue with the Chancellor of the Exchequer in 1942. The time was

[1] ibid., cc. 291–3.
[2] P.A.C. 1941–42, H.C. 602, p. 47.
[3] H.C. Deb. (N.I.), 26, cc. 32, 314.

propitious. As we have seen, war raised Ulster's stature. To say it strengthened her bargaining power would also be true, but probably not very much to the point. The root of the matter lay deeper. In spirit as well as law Ulster was irrevocably bound to Britain and was prepared to stand by her, no matter what the consequences. There can be little doubt that it was this instinctive and massive sense of common citizenship, rather than any importunity by Mr. Andrews, that was decisive. The Chancellor replied on 14 September 1942:

With regard to the treatment of your local problems which was referred to in your letter, I recognize that in certain spheres Northern Ireland has considerable leeway to make up in order to attain equality of standard with the United Kingdom, and you can confidently rely on the Treasury always considering such a case sympathetically, as indeed the principle of parity requires us to do.[1]

Mr. Andrews himself did not make this assurance public until 1945,[2] and by that time he had been out of power for two years. For by 1943 he no longer enjoyed the confidence of the Unionist Parliamentary Party. Unemployment remained excessive, and there was a general feeling that men in office since 1921 lacked the vitality fully to mobilize the country's resources, impress on the United Kingdom the urgency of making complete use of them, and plan for the post-war world. The seeds planted by Mr. Warnock in 1940 had taken root; and Mr. Andrews, despite his continued control of the party machine and the support of the Ulster Unionist Council, was unable to eradicate them. At a private meeting in January 1943 back-benchers demanded the rejuvenation of the Cabinet. Thereafter the Prime Minister's authority evaporated. He resigned in May, to be succeeded by Sir Basil Brooke (later Lord Brookeborough).[3]

'The office of a Cabinet Minister is not, and should not be, a

[1] H. C. Deb. (N.I.), 28, c. 79.

[2] In November 1943 (after Mr. Andrews' government had fallen) the new Minister of Finance said, 'Last week, in pursuing our negotiations about the housing situation, we were authorized by His Majesty's Treasury to make the following statement: "It follows from the principle of parity of services that the Imperial authorities will give sympathetic consideration to the case for special measures as regards any service in which Northern Ireland has leeway to make up in order to attain equality of standard with the United Kingdom".' ibid., 26, c. 2090.

[3] *The Round Table*, vol. xxxiii (1943), pp. 166, 370; *Belfast News-Letter*, 20 January, 3 May 1943.

life appointment.'[1] Inspired by this principle, the new Premier discarded all members of the old Cabinet save one, brought in younger, untried and even virtually unknown men,[2] and secured a solid vote of confidence on his threefold policy: to maintain the constitution, vigorously assist the war effort, and prepare for post-war problems.[3]

Planning for the future, as Mr. Andrews had seen, could come to nothing without Britain's help. That, by mid-1943, had still to be secured, though the Chancellor of the Exchequer in effect had invited Ulster to put up a case for making good leeway in certain spheres. The first essential, then, was to convince the British Government of the need to improve backward services, notably health, housing and planning, education and highways. Pensions and insurance schemes were already in step with those in Britain; and poor law reform, though overdue, must await Britain's initiative because Northern Ireland could not unilaterally shift expenditure from rates to the local Exchequer. Ulster's leaders could not, however, expect to make a convincing case by submitting to Britain a purely general formula similar to that which they had proposed to the Colwyn Committee. What was needed was investigation of specific services, wherever possible in quantitative terms.[4]

Accordingly, the services mentioned above were subjected to searching examination. An inquiry into health services by a Select

[1] H.C. Deb. (N.I.), 26, c. 460.

[2] The Cabinet formed by Sir Basil Brooke in May 1943 was:
Prime Minister and Minister of Commerce and Production—Sir Basil Brooke
Minister of Finance—Major J. M. Sinclair
Minister of Home Affairs—Mr. W. Lowry
Minister of Labour—Mr. W. Grant
Minister of Education—Rev. R. Corkey
Minister of Agriculture—Rev. R. Moore
Minister of Public Security—Mr. H. C. Midgley

[3] H.C. Deb. (N.I.), 26, c. 466.

[4] In a report made in 1942 on the instructions of a Cabinet sub-committee the Ministry of Home Affairs said: 'Up to the present the problem of the financial assistance to be afforded for reconstruction has not been taken beyond agreement on certain broad principles which affect all parts of the United Kingdom equally, but when more detailed consideration is reached it is necessary that the particular requirements of the province should be known in order that a case for a fair share in the available resources may be properly presented.' W. R. Davidge, *Preliminary Report on Reconstruction and Planning* (H.M.S.O., 1944), p. 2. In 1943 the Government stressed the need for a housing survey to produce facts and figures on which to base their claim for money and materials. H.C. Deb. (N.I.), 26, cc. 2217–18.

Committee of the House of Commons[1] was supplemented by reports on maternity services[2] and mental deficiency.[3] In hospital administration Ulster was fortunate to get the help of the Nuffield Provincial Hospitals Trust (already established in Britain by the generosity of Lord Nuffield), with whose support was formed a Regional Hospitals Council of representatives of hospital authorities and other interested bodies. The Trust in 1943 appointed three surveyors who visited almost every hospital, and on the basis of their Report[4] the Council framed proposals for improving hospital services.[5] A planning consultant in 1942 advocated reconstruction of the City of Belfast to add to its efficiency, amenity and civic beauty; comprehensive planning of the whole Belfast region; and control of land use throughout the entire province. To this end he proposed that one Ministry should be the central planning authority, assisted by a Planning Advisory Board and by a Planning Commission of technical experts.[6] The Board and Commission were rapidly established. The former examined problems of water supply and sewerage,[7] housing[8] and location of industry,[9] while the Commission produced schemes for roads[10] and for the Belfast area.[11] The Ministry of Home Affairs conducted the first housing survey ever made in Ulster. A White Paper on Educational Reconstruction in 1944[12] followed the English Education Act of that year.

It should perhaps be emphasized that neither in education nor in other spheres did Ulster set out to copy Great Britain. She was inevitably influenced by her larger and wealthier neighbour because she sought parity, but local traditions and problems needed distinctive treatment. How best to achieve this was one

[1] *Special Interim and Final Reports of the Select Committee on Health Services in Northern Ireland*, H.C. 601 (1944).

[2] *Report of Maternity Services Committee*, Cmd. 219 (1943).

[3] *Mental Deficiency in Northern Ireland* (H.M.S.O., 1946).

[4] Nuffield Provincial Hospitals Trust, *Survey of the Hospital Services of Northern Ireland* (n.d.).

[5] *The Red Book: A Plan for the Hospital Services of Northern Ireland* (Belfast, 1946).

[6] W. R. Davidge, op. cit.

[7] *Report on the Problems of Water Supply and Sewerage in Northern Ireland*, Cmd. 223 (1944).

[8] *Housing in Northern Ireland*, Cmd. 224 (1944).

[9] *Location of Industry in Northern Ireland*, Cmd. 225 (1944).

[10] *Road Communications in Northern Ireland*, Cmd. 241 (1946).

[11] *Planning Proposals for the Belfast Area*, Cmd. 227 (1945). See also *Second Report*, Cmd. 302 (1952).

[12] *Educational Reconstruction in Northern Ireland*, Cmd. 226 (1944).

object of many inquiries. Another was to persuade public opinion to accept radical improvement and the increased local rates it would entail. Yet another was to give Ministers some idea of how best to allocate to different services the money they would eventually control. All these matters, however, were of the second order of importance. The main thing was to convince the United Kingdom of the strength of Ulster's case.

The facts evidently spoke for themselves. In May 1945 the Minister of Finance announced that the province would enjoy the full range of Britain's post-war social security schemes.[1] Special Exchequer assistance would lift under-developed services to Britain's level.[2] Finance in future would be, not a curb, but a spur.[3]

[1] H.C. Deb. (N.I.), 28, c. 866.
[2] ibid., 27, c. 1258.
[3] ibid., 30, c. 431.

CHAPTER FIVE

The Post-War Pattern

THE years after the Second World War stand in marked contrast to those after the First. Then, Ulster was struggling to stay inside the United Kingdom; she had no choice but to work the Act of 1920; and debate about whether her form of government suited her needs was academic. After 1945 intelligence could play over a wider field. The links with Britain were secure; the critical attitudes noted in the last chapter were reinforced by the emergence of a new generation; and the Irish question, of which the Act of 1920 was a by-product, was almost as dead as Captain Boycott. So people began seriously to consider whether devolution was worth the candle. One urgent problem alone—unemployment—seemed to show that while Ulster had more responsibility than power, Britain had more power than responsibility. For some years a desultory debate ranged round the alternatives of seeking either real self-government or complete unity with Britain.

Yet either course could mean the fire instead of the frying-pan. A sufficient argument against dominion status (the form of self-government most commonly canvassed) was that the province's industries were insufficiently diversified to support her in bad times as well as good. In 1945 that was obvious to anyone with a little knowledge of the past. What was less obvious, at a time when there was still a substantial surplus of revenue over local expenditure, was that Ulster's relative poverty was so great that she would be unable to finance from her own resources the vast expansion in social services planned for post-war Britain. Her leaders, however, were well aware of this. The Minister of Finance (then Mr. W. B. Maginess) said in 1951:

> If we fall on evil times and have jettisoned what has been described as our sheet anchor, we may find ourselves adrift on a stormy and turbulent sea as yet inadequately charted. . . . Any wholesale departure from the principles under which we have operated during the past thirty years would, I believe, be disastrous.[1]

[1] H.C. Deb. (N.I.), 35, c. 1024.

Captain T. M. O'Neill, who entered the House of Commons at Stormont in 1946, served as Minister of Finance from 1956 to 1963 and then became Prime Minister, was even more forthright. There was a time after the war (he said in 1960) when some people felt that dominion status was the answer to all problems.

I was not a little attracted to the idea myself during my first few months at Stormont, though I was wise enough, or fortunate enough—I do not know which—not to make a speech on the subject. I did, however, make a speech suggesting that Scotland should follow in our devolutionary footsteps. The following day I was taken aside by the father of my right hon. Friend the Minister of Health and Local Government [the late Mr. J. M. Andrews]. 'Young man,' he said, 'you must never again make a suggestion like that.' He paused. 'We do not want any more provincial calves pulling at the one cow.' . . . It is at first sight attractive to have greater powers, but we receive such great benefits from being part of the United Kingdom that our last state might be very much worse than our first.[1]

On the other hand, to return to Westminster would mean losing a Parliament that reflected most Ulstermen's determination to resist absorption by Catholic Eire. The Report of the Ulster Unionist Council for 1936 declared:

The cry 'back to Westminster' is a subtle move fraught with great danger. Had we refused to accept a Parliament for Northern Ireland and remained at Westminster, there can be but little doubt that now we would either be inside the Free State or fighting desperately against incorporation. Northern Ireland without a Parliament of her own would be a standing temptation to certain British politicians to make another bid for a final settlement with Irish republicans.[2]

These sentiments, it might be thought, were no longer relevant in a climate transformed by war; but in vital matters men do not willingly give the smallest hostage to fortune. Westminster recognized this in 1949. The Ireland Act of that year declared the Republic of Ireland to be no longer part of the British Commonwealth (though it is not a foreign country) and affirmed the constitutional position and territorial integrity of Northern Ireland. No United Kingdom Parliament can bind its successors. Subject only to this, the Parliament of Northern Ireland was in effect given power to veto any attempt to eject Ulster from the

[1] ibid., 46, c. 843.

[2] Quoted in N. Mansergh, *Ireland in the Age of Reform and Revolution* (London, 1940), p. 179.

Commonwealth and the United Kingdom. Constitutional security was rooted in the soil of devolution.

Fundamental change being ruled out, the old problems recurred. Taxes imposed and collected by the United Kingdom still provided the bulk of Ulster's revenue. Ordinary revenue still bore no necessary relation to expenditure. Expenditure on domestic services still had to be limited without depriving Stormont of all liberty of action. While, however, the problems were old, their setting was new. Ulster could count on Britain's help. Her leaders no longer needed to trim their policies to the principle that domestic expenditure should not normally exceed ordinary revenue. The imperial contribution could in effect be negative.

At the same time, executive action could hardly ignore the constitution. The Exchequer and Consolidated Fund of Northern Ireland had to be separate from those of the United Kingdom;[1] appropriations had to be made by the provincial Parliament;[2] revenue from reserved taxes had to be determined by the Joint Exchequer Board;[3] and an imperial contribution had to be made each year.[4] A formal merger of the two Exchequers, even if contemplated, was out of the question. So was any arrangement that would eliminate the imperial contribution from Ulster's accounts. More subtle measures were called for. But whatever measures were adopted, it was certain that the United Kingdom must acquire more influence. If she was to assume a contingent liability—indeed, if she was to be satisfied that the recorded imperial contribution was not wholly inadequate—she needed to be sure that Ulstermen would bear their proper share of financial burdens and that Stormont would not without good reason spend more than was absolutely necessary to lift public services to British levels.

These considerations, it appears, led to three agreements with the Labour Government after 1945. The first, which governs inter-Exchequer relations, arose naturally from past experience. During the war (as explained in the last chapter) Ulster agreed to spend no more money than was essential and also to finance several national services until the United Kingdom reimbursed her. In order to ensure that expenditure was really essential and charged to the proper account, the Ministry of Finance undertook to submit to the Treasury all Estimates before presentation

[1] Government of Ireland Act, 1920, s. 20 (1).
[2] s. 20 (2). [3] s. 22 (2). [4] s. 23 (1).

to Parliament, and also to submit in detail for prior sanction all proposals for new services estimated to cost more than £50,000 a year, and the Comptroller and Auditor General for Northern Ireland was to certify annually that this had been done.[1]

This was superseded in 1946 by the following agreement. (*a*) Parity of services and taxation between Great Britain and Northern Ireland will be the guiding principle. (*b*) The Northern Ireland Budget will be agreed each year between the Treasury and the Ministry of Finance for submission to the Joint Exchequer Board. In submitting Budget proposals for discussion, the Ministry will draw attention to major items of expenditure, and in particular will indicate any proposed divergence from parity standards which is deemed necessary from the aspect of special local conditions. (*c*) All Northern Ireland Supplementary Estimates arising in the course of a year will be furnished to the Treasury for their information and agreement. (*d*) The Ministry will consult with the Treasury in advance in respect of any new items of Northern Ireland expenditure, other than expenditure incurred on services in parity with Great Britain, estimated to exceed £50,000 in amount.[2]

The second agreement, which covers national insurance, was also in large part the outcome of past experience. We have seen that Lord Craigavon was determined to keep unemployment insurance. Rather than abandon it, he envisaged the collapse of Home Rule. His obduracy was not unreasonable. Unemployment dominated the Budget of a relatively poor area that could do little to stimulate industrial growth. Before the war, however, the British Government, intent on maintaining the spirit of the 1920 Act and safeguarding Ulster's independence, would go no further than to pay three-quarters of the excess cost.[3] In the post-war climate Britain was less anxious about constitutional niceties and more willing to advance Ulster's material welfare. So the vestige of autonomy was virtually swept away when national insurance began throughout the United Kingdom on 5 July 1948. Insured persons (and in some cases their dependents) became entitled to cash payments during unemployment, sickness, maternity, widowhood, orphanhood, after retirement and at death. The

[1] C.A.G. 1944–45, H.C. 685, pp. viii–ix.

[2] C.A.G. 1947–48, H.C. 843, p. 18. See also *Ulster Year Book, 1950*, pp. xxvii et seq.

[3] See above, p. 52, n. (2).

payments in Britain and Ulster are made from separate National Insurance Funds fed from contributions by employers, insured persons and the Exchequer. From the start, Ulster adopted Britain's rates of contribution and benefit, but this gave her no assurance that her Fund's income would exceed its outgo. Thus, when in 1951–52 the Exchequer contribution was cut and benefits were raised, the local Fund sustained a considerable loss though the British Fund was still in surplus. Therefore, by an arrangement made in 1951 but which took effect from 5 July 1948, the two Funds were virtually amalgamated.[1] Sufficient money is transferred annually from one Fund to the other to make the ratio between their balances equal to the ratio between the two contributing populations.[2] For a number of reasons—in particular, the higher incidence of unemployment and sickness—payments to Northern Ireland have been required every year, but these do not figure in the Budget to offset the imperial contribution.[3]

In the third place, a Social Services Agreement which was concluded in 1949 but which took effect from 5 July 1948 covers national assistance, family allowances, non-contributory pensions and the health service. If the cost of these four services in Ulster is proportionately higher than in the United Kingdom, the latter bears 80 per cent. of the excess.[4] The arrangement, like that for

[1] The National Insurance Act, 1946, s. 63 (1) authorized the Minister of National Insurance, with the Treasury's consent, to arrange with the appropriate Northern Irish authority for co-ordinating insurance so that it might operate as a single system in Britain and Ulster. A similar power, to be exercised with the consent of the Ministry of Finance, was conferred on the Ministry of Labour and National Insurance by the National Insurance Act (N.I.), 1946, s. 60 (1).

[2] The combined balances in the two Funds as at 31 March each year are divided in the ratio of the two contributing populations, weighted for each class and sex with the appropriate rate of contribution. See P.A.C. 1949–50, H.C. 969 p. 57.

[3] Under the National Insurance (Industrial Injuries) Act (N.I.), 1946, which replaced a scheme of workmen's compensation, cash payments are made to or on behalf of insured persons who are killed or incapacitated in the course of their employment. Reciprocal arrangements similar to those for national insurance were made with Britain. For several reasons (e.g. the absence from Ulster of coalmining and other hazardous occupations and the existence there of greater unemployment), small sums have been transferred from the Northern Ireland Industrial Injuries Fund to the British Fund.

[4] In calculating proportionate costs, relative taxable capacities as well as populations are to be taken into account. Social Services (Agreement) Act (N.I.), 1949, Schedule, para. 2 (iii). Ulster's proportion was provisionally fixed at 2·5 per cent. in 1949 and this was unchanged by 1963. Her population proportion, on mid-1963 estimates, was actually 2·7 per cent. Any questions arising under the Agreement are decided by the Treasury and the Ministry of Finance or, if they cannot agree, by the Joint Exchequer Board.

national insurance, is reciprocal: if Britain's expenditure were disproportionate, 80 per cent. of the excess would fall on Ulster. In fact, payments have been one way only—from London to Belfast—and, as in the case of national insurance, the effect is that more money can be spent on transferred services without drawing down the imperial contribution.

Since financial burdens are shared to such a large extent, special care is taken to ensure that Ulstermen are treated neither more nor less favourably than other citizens. In inter-Exchequer relations there is parity of services as well as taxation. National insurance contributions and benefits are uniform. In national assistance, pensions and family allowances, Ulster undertook to keep rates of payment in general parity with Britain. In the health service, which provides skilled attention, drugs and mechanical aids instead of money, the criterion is that the citizen should get exactly the same value as in Britain.[1] To this end, Northern Ireland agreed to keep the scale and standard of comprehensive health services in general conformity with Britain, and to ensure that rates of remuneration of persons employed correspond with British rates. Although Ulster has not committed herself to administrative uniformity, it is not to her financial advantage to diverge. Administrative differences in the services covered by the Social Services Agreement may mean smaller payments from Britain.[2]

We turn now to post-war trends in revenue and expenditure. These require no detailed examination. For history is a record of dilemmas; and whereas after 1921 Ministers were confronted by one predicament after another, since 1946 they have been able to expand domestic expenditure at a dramatic rate and still show in their accounts an imperial contribution. Fortune, hard work and the financial agreements described above made this possible. Fortune, by condemning the United Kingdom to outrageous taxation for defence, sustained Ulster's revenue. Unremitting effort by the provincial Government to reduce unemployment by attracting new industries and injecting money into public and private enterprise, helped to raise *per capita* incomes and tax yields. The financial agreements enabled the local Exchequer to spend more on domestic services at the expense of the imperial

[1] H.C. Deb. (N.I.), 31, c. 2228.
[2] Social Services (Agreement) Act (N.I.), 1949, Schedule, para. 1 (ii) (b), (c).

contribution, lightened the burden of national insurance, and augmented revenue by direct transfers from Britain under the Social Services Agreement. In addition, by the Agriculture Act, 1957 the United Kingdom granted to Ulster farmers a special subsidy to offset their remoteness from markets on the mainland. This is paid to the Northern Ireland Exchequer. Ulster farmers also receive other British subsidies.[1] These, with some other items, are enumerated below (page 87) because they are not included in Northern Ireland's Exchequer Accounts.

Even if we confine ourselves to those Accounts, the picture is very favourable. Between 1946 and 1963 revenue rather more than doubled, but spending on transferred services increased almost sevenfold without wholly swallowing the recorded imperial contribution.

TABLE 5. *Revenue and Expenditure, 1946 and 1963*[2] *(£ million)*

Revenue

	Transferred	*Reserved*	*From U.K. Exchequer*	*Total*
1945–46	5·2	50·0	0·8	56·0
1962–63	16·2	109·0	8·1*	133·3

* Social Services Agreement, £6·95 m. Agriculture Act, 1957, £1·1 m.

Expenditure

	Imperial contribution	*Reserved services, etc.*	*Transferred services*		*Total*
			Consolidated Fund	*Supply*	
1945–46	34·5	3·4	1·5	16·2	55·6
1962–63	7·5	2·3	9·5	109·5	128·8

If the cost of common services were shared by reference to the relative populations of Britain and Ulster, the imperial contribu-

[1] Britain's agreement to pay agricultural subsidies dates from 1938. 335 H.C. Deb., 5 s., 1708.

[2] Sources: *Ulster Year Book, 1950*; Finance Accounts for 1962–63, H.C. 1568 and 1963–64, H.C. 1626 (for final statement of reserved revenue and services and imperial contribution).

tion would be of the order of £60 m.[1] It seems improbable, however, that the contribution will increase in the foreseeable future. Budget Estimates for 1965–66 put expenditure on transferred services at £170·9 m. (against £119 m. in 1962–63), receipts from the United Kingdom at £10·8 m., and provision for imperial contribution at the token sum of £3·5 m.[2] But the continued growth of domestic expenditure is not likely to call for radical revision of the financial system. Tax revenue is also expanding, and in May 1965 the Minister of Finance announced that a review by his Ministry and the Treasury had shown there was no need to make fundamental changes in financial relations.[3]

The pattern as well as the magnitude of expenditure has been transformed since the war. Unemployment and pensions dominated the Budget before 1939, but nowadays the whole range of national insurance constitutes an insignificant burden. For Ulster is more prosperous; she is spending large sums to stimulate industrial development and improve health and other services that were starved of money after 1921; and every year there are substantial transfers from London to her National Insurance Fund. For example, in 1962–63 the provincial Exchequer paid £4·5 m. into the Northern Ireland National Insurance and Industrial Injuries Funds, against £8·4 m. received from the National Insurance Fund of Great Britain.[4] More money has therefore been available for other services. Table 6 shows, in round figures, expenditure in 1963 and comparable expenditure in the last pre-war year.

Capital expenditure after the war seemed to be a special problem. Since Ulster has so little control over her revenue, she could have found it impossible to raise the large sums required to make up leeway on capital account without incurring debts which she would have no certainty of extinguishing. In the event, revenue proved to be buoyant. However, from 1947 onwards, when construction was limited more by scarcity of materials than by money, the Treasury permitted the Ministry of Finance to divert current revenue to a Capital Purposes Fund earmarked for industrial development and a wide range of other projects. The Fund was augmented by large savings on the annual Estimates, money voted by Parliament for one purpose being diverted by statutory

[1] *Report of the Joint Working Party on the Economy of Northern Ireland*, Cmd. 446 (1962), App. VI.

[2] Financial Statement, 1965–66, H.C. 1656.

[3] H.C. Deb. (N.I.), 60, c. 1722.

[4] Northern Ireland National Insurance Fund Accounts, 1962–63, H.C. 1579.

TABLE 6. *Expenditure on Transferred Services, 1939 and 1963*[1]

	1938–39		*1962–63*	
	£ m.	*Per cent.*	*£ m.*	*Per cent.*
Consolidated Fund services	1·3	10·2	9·5	8·0
Supply services:				
National insurance	3·9	30·4	4·5	3·8
Family allowances	—	—	6·2	5·2
National assistance and employment services	2·0	15·6	7·8	6·6
Education	2·2	17·2	20·8	17·5
Health and Welfare	0·2	1·6	22·9	19·2
Housing, water and sewerage	—	—	3·3	2·8
Justice and police	0·9	7·0	6·3	5·3
Agriculture	0·2	1·6	4·7	3·9
Commercial, industrial and development services	0·1	0·8	18·3	15·4
Administrative departments	0·5	3·9	5·3	4·5
Public works and buildings	0·2	1·6	1·4	1·2
Exchequer contributions to local revenues	1·0	7·8	6·8	5·7
Other expenditure	0·2	1·6	1·3	1·1
Total	£12·8	100·0	£119·0	100·0

authority to another, though at the cost of making the already complicated public accounts still more confusing.[2] Housing was financed in a similar manner. In Ulster, as in Britain, the Government undertook to contribute for sixty years to the cost of subsidized houses; but in order to relieve the provincial Exchequer of this long-term burden, the subsidy was generally commuted to a lump sum payable from a Housing Commutation Fund built up in essentially the same way as the Capital Purposes Fund. By 31 March 1964 expenditure from the two Funds totalled £158·8 m.[3] A great deal of other capital expenditure was borne directly on the

[1] Compiled from Finance Accounts, 1938–39, H.C. 474; 1962–63, H.C. 1568; Appropriation and Consolidated Fund Services Accounts, 1938–39, H.C. 494. Specific grants to local authorities are included in appropriate services. Discrepancies in totals are due to rounding of figures.

[2] P.A.C. 1947–48, H.C. 873, p. 68; 1950–51, H.C. 1011, pp. 21–24; C.A.G. 1950–51, H.C. 997, pp. x–xii.

[3] H.C. 1626, pp. 28–29.

Estimates each year. In consequence, by 1964 Northern Ireland was in the fortunate position of being free from net debt. The whole capital programme had been financed from current revenue, that is (as it is sometimes put) at the expense of the imperial contribution.[1]

Revenue since the war has not only expanded; its composition has also changed. Table 7 shows the relative magnitude of transferred and reserved taxation in 1962–63 and the annual average for ten-year periods immediately before and after the war.

TABLE 7. *Transferred and Reserved Taxation*[2]

Years ended 31 Mar.	*Transferred taxes*		*Reserved taxes*		*Total*	
	£ m.	*Per cent.*	*£ m.*	*Per cent.*	*£ m.*	*Per cent.*
1929–38 (average)	1·7	17·9	7·8	82·1	9·5	100·0
1945–54 (average)	4·2	7·4	52·4	92·6	56·6	100·0
1963	6·8	5·9	108·8*	94·2	115·5	100·0

* Excludes Post Office and miscellaneous receipts.

It is evident that transferred taxes (estate, stamp, motor vehicle and various licence duties) are now comparatively trivial. The cause of this may seem to be simply that taxation reserved to Westminster in 1920 (customs duties, excise duties on articles manufactured and produced, and taxes on incomes and profits) has grown faster than the produce of duties transferred to Stormont. That has, indeed, been the case, but there is a more important though less obvious consideration. The Minister of Finance explained in 1940 that purchase tax, then introduced at Westminster for the first time, was a transferred matter. Taxes reserved by the Government of Ireland Act did not include a duty on purchases within Northern Ireland itself. However, if Ulster had chosen to impose purchase tax, she could not have claimed revenue collected from wholesalers in Britain in respect of goods sold in Northern Ireland, and so she would have lost a large

[1] P.A.C. 1958–59, H.C. 1404, p. 32.

[2] Sources: *Ulster Year Books*; H.C. 1568; H.C. 1626.

proportion (some 40 per cent.) of the sum due to her; for although in the case of transferred taxes she gets only the revenue actually collected within her territory, the Act prescribes in effect that reserved taxation (whether collected in Britain or Ulster) deemed to be borne by Ulster shall be attributed to her. The provincial Government therefore proposed that purchase tax should be subject to attribution like a reserved tax. Britain agreed to this, though only after some discussion. Since, however, it was impossible to get accurate statistics of the consumption of taxable articles in Northern Ireland, the Joint Exchequer Board approved a proposal by the Treasury and the Ministry of Finance to divide the total yield of purchase tax between Britain and Ulster in the same ratio as other reserved duties.[1] Northern Ireland's share, at first fixed at 1·7 per cent., was later raised to 2·5 per cent., which in 1962–63 gave her Exchequer £14·3 m., more than twice the £6·8 m. produced by all transferred taxes.

TABLE 8. *Revenue from Taxation, 1963*[2]

£ million

Transferred		*Reserved*	
Estate, &c., duties	1·6	Taxes on incomes and profits	49·4
Stamp duties	0·9	Customs and excise (excluding purchase tax)	45·1
Excise duties	0·5	Purchase tax	14·3
Motor vehicle, &c., duties	3·8		
	£6·8		£108·8

[1] In 1940 the Minister of Finance did not disclose these facts but simply said that Northern Ireland ought not to assert its legislative power because purchase tax would be limited to the war period and separate collection would be inconvenient. H.C. Deb. (N.I.), 23, c. 1163. In 1947 the Accounting Officer, Ministry of Finance, told the Public Accounts Committee that administrative convenience was not the only consideration. He said, 'If it were a transferred tax there is no provision in the Government of Ireland Act for attribution. . . . We would get no credit for the goods made and sold from Great Britain to Northern Ireland unless we made this a reserved tax. . . . That is the reason for it.' P.A.C. 1945–46, H.C. 759, p. 43. There is no public record of discussions between the Treasury and the Ministry of Finance, but the Public Accounts Committee were told in 1942 that Britain first proposed that Northern Ireland should receive only the revenue collected in the province and that the provincial Government put the counter proposal that some simple method of attribution should be found. P.A.C. 1940–41, H.C. 574, p. 31. See also C.A.G. 1940–41, H.C. 565, p. 8; 1945–46, H.C. 719, p. xi.

[2] Sources: H.C. 1568, H.C. 1626.

It must seem ironic that members of the provincial House of Commons should have protested so often after the war against the crippling effect on the linen industry of a purchase tax which their Government could have retained.[1]

The discussion about purchase tax touches two questions that aroused sharp controversy during the debate on Home Rule but which we have hitherto ignored. What is to count as the true revenue of an area with limited powers of self-government, and how can that revenue be measured? The first question has occasionally given rise to complaints in Ulster that the division of the taxing power works unfairly. Property in Britain owned by persons domiciled in Northern Ireland is of greater value than property in Northern Ireland owned by residents of Britain. Hence, Ulster's accounts would benefit if estate duty were imposed by the United Kingdom and made subject to attribution, as are reserved taxes. The same consideration applies to stamp duty, though the amount involved is small. Much larger sums are entailed in the case of the transferred pool betting duty, for residents of Northern Ireland 'invest' far more in football pools in Britain than in their homeland.[2] These examples, like that of purchase tax, illustrate the point that it does not generally pay a poor area to levy taxes at all. Ulster's revenue would be greater if Britain were to impose all taxes, except those whose incidence is wholly confined to Northern Ireland, and to share the revenue on the basis of the taxpayer's place of residence.

That, however, gives rise to the second question. It is impossible to measure the taxation that actually falls on Ulstermen. The Joint Exchequer Board has a statutory duty to determine what part of the proceeds of reserved taxes are properly attributable to the province,[3] but their calculations can hardly be exact. To record every taxable transaction between Britain and Ulster and count the incomes that accrue in each country to residents of the other, would require an army of clerks in Government and in profit-making concerns as well as customs examination at the ports. The Joint Exchequer Board use less precise methods. For the purpose of purchase tax they take the round figure of 2·5 per cent., and this has also been taken since 1963 for the attribution of customs and

[1] See e.g. H.C. Deb. (N.I.), 39, c. 1463; 48, c. 2229.

[2] The loss each year in death duties is about £0·25 m., and in pool betting duty about £0·5 m. See C.A.G. 1946–47, H.C. 774, p. xv; P.A.C. 1946–47, H.C. 817, p. 122; 1961–62, H.C. 1556, pp. 38, 40.

[3] Government of Ireland Act, 1920, s. 22 (2).

excise duties. The yield of taxation on incomes arising in Britain, which probably accounts for about one-quarter of all Ulster's income tax revenue,[1] is estimated. Since the Board's proceedings and the figures put before them are never published, no outsider can know how they do their sums. When questioned at Stormont, Ministers have given general assurances that all is well.[2] Odd things can happen though. The Finance Accounts of Northern Ireland contain each year a final statement of the amount due in respect of the residuary share of reserved taxes.[3] In 1934, when Ulster was in financial difficulties, she received £420,000 for the financial years 1925–31, though final statements for that period had already been published.[4] In 1962 estimates of the yield of tobacco duty were reviewed and £2 m. was added to revenue.[5] Nowadays, when the imperial contribution is finally assessed, it is rounded down to the nearest half a million pounds and the balance is paid to Northern Ireland to compensate for any lost revenue.[6] The whole business seems rather rough and ready.

Local comment on these matters has never generated heat. The Ulsterman is in general no more interested in them than in the other complexities of parliamentary devolution. His indifference in this case has a logical basis, for the counting of revenue has lost much of its point. Originally it was an integral part of the plan to make both parts of Ireland distinct and self-sufficient financial units. From her own revenue (mainly transferred taxation collected on her soil and reserved taxation imputed to her) Ulster was expected to finance her own services and make an imperial contribution. She is no longer required to do this because governments in London and Belfast have gradually bent the financial framework of the constitution. The post-war financial agreements enable Stormont to vote money at the expense of the United Kingdom taxpayer. Moreover, as already noted, Britain gives assistance that is not revealed in Northern Ireland's accounts. The Ulster farmer gets subsidies borne on the Vote of the United Kingdom Ministry of Agriculture (though agriculture is a trans-

[1] This estimate was made in 1953. H.C. Deb. (N.I.), 37, c. 1111.

[2] ibid., 40, c. 1425; 42, c. 1123. But see 52, c. 383.

[3] Final statements are published at least one year in arrear because it takes time to calculate reserved revenue and expenditure and the imperial contribution.

[4] Finance Accounts, 1933–34, H.C. 322, p. 16.

[5] H.C. Deb. (N.I.), 52, c. 383.

[6] P.A.C. 1957–58, H.C. 1351, p. 44; 1960–61, H.C. 1506, p. 17.

ferred service), and manufacturing industry in the province has had special treatment. Since, therefore, Northern Ireland is no longer compelled to be self-sufficient, it seems rather pointless to try to compute her revenue.

It can easily be argued that this transformation is no more than just. The Ulsterman has accepted parity of taxation and equality of insurance contributions; the farmer helps to feed the nation; the industrialist and the worker earn foreign exchange. In every field persons in Britain and Ulster contribute on more or less the same terms; and in many areas of Great Britain, as in Northern Ireland, it is certain that Exchequer spending exceeds revenue.

At the same time, the existence of a separate legislature and system of public accounts also makes it possible to argue that Ulster has been treated, not with justice, but generosity. Financial assistance from the United Kingdom during the three financial years 1961–63 averaged £45 m. a year.[1] In the last of those years total payments of all kinds (whether included in Ulster's accounts or not) were as follows:

TABLE 9. *Payments by United Kingdom to Northern Ireland, 1963*[2]

	£ million
Social Services Agreement	6·95
Agriculture Act, 1957	1·10
Transfers from National Insurance Fund, Great Britain	8·36
Farming grants and subsidies	28·55
White fish and herring subsidy	0·07
Contributions under National Health Service Acts	0·22
Agency services, &c.	1·52
	£46·77

In addition a memorandum produced by the Home Office in May 1963[3] showed that the province enjoyed special measures to encourage industrial development at a cost to the United Kingdom taxpayer of some £15 m. a year.[4] About half of this was a charge on the provincial Exchequer and represented, not a direct payment

[1] H.C. Deb. (N.I.), 56, c. 1845.

[2] ibid., 54, c. 2049.

[3] 'Exceptional Measures in Favour of Northern Ireland at the Expense of the United Kingdom.' *Belfast Telegraph*, 9 May 1963, *Belfast News-Letter*, 10 May 1963.

[4] This included special grants to industry, construction of new factories, grants for water, sewerage and other basic services, industrial derating, a coal and oil subsidy and special assistance to Short Bros. & Harland Ltd.

from the United Kingdom, but a larger reduction in the imperial contribution than equity might warrant. But all of it was special in the sense that comparable expenditure in Britain was on a smaller scale or non-existent. The imperial contribution was £7·5 m. in 1963. So, to put the matter roughly, if Ulster were independent and had to pay for her own defence and for diplomatic, consular and other 'imperial' services, she would either have to cut domestic spending by some £50 m. a year or raise that sum by taxation. Either course would be catastrophic. Expenditure in 1962–63 was £119 m. and tax revenue £116 m. Lord Craigavon's prophecy to the effect that in the long run a contribution would be paid to, and not by, Northern Ireland has been borne out in full measure.

It must now be evident that the financial provisions of the Government of Ireland Act have in large part become legal fictions. By the law of the constitution Northern Ireland is still a distinct entity. Her revenue is segregated, she is required to pay for reserved services and make an imperial contribution, and after these deductions have been made the residuary share of reserved taxes is remitted to her Exchequer. The terms and procedures are retained and embodied in the public accounts, but they no longer accord with reality. They have been transformed by agreements that have broken the bonds of constitutional law because they enable Britain and Ulster to co-operate. It is an exaggeration to say that Northern Ireland has reverted to the position of Ireland under the Union and is part of a common Exchequer, but it is not a great exaggeration. Taxation is indiscriminate and virtually uniform, and expenditure is governed by the needs of individual citizens.

It follows that regional self-government also has in some measure become a fiction. Again the law of the constitution remains unchanged in essentials. Ministers are still responsible to a Parliament which alone has power to authorize local taxes, prescribe the nature of public services and vote money for them. In fact, its powers to tax and spend have been eroded.

In taxation the most general limiting factor is the parity agreement. So far as reserved taxes are concerned, Northern Ireland has, of course, never had much choice. When general revaluation of England and Wales was provided for in 1953, Stormont was persuaded to pass similar legislation,[1] despite some resistance from

[1] Valuation Acts Amendment Act (N.I.), 1954.

both government and opposition benches.[1] The Minister of Finance, like his predecessor in 1932, stressed the 'overriding consideration of our obligations as citizens of a part of the United Kingdom' and pointed out that radical departure from the system in Britain would invite consideration of amending legislation for income tax purposes.[2] The Act of 1920 (s. 25) does give Stormont power to grant relief from income tax, but this would mean cuts in domestic services because tax relief cannot be given at the expense of the imperial contribution.[3] It could also evoke protests from firms in Britain that compete with firms in Northern Ireland.[4] This is not to say that Ulster never merits exceptional treatment; on the contrary, we have seen that she does enjoy special advantages. The point is that her claims must be established by argument. She cannot expect to enjoy the benefits of a common Exchequer and the advantages of unilateral action by a local one without antagonizing citizens who have the one but not the other.

Parity extends also to transferred taxation, but in this field Ulster has more latitude. Parity does not mean uniformity. 'The total amount of money raised per head from the taxpayers of this country', said the Minister of Finance in 1947, 'should correspond to the total amount raised per head from the taxpayers on the other side, and the exact form which that takes can be varied within the discretion of this Parliament.'[5] Stormont has occasionally diverged.[6] The scope for divergence is, however, very narrow. For one thing, transferred taxation is now relatively unimportant. For another, free trade with the rest of the United Kingdom, and the desire to avoid friction, impels Ulster towards uniformity. Higher rates of tax in Northern Ireland could be partly avoided by transferring movable assets and activities to Great Britain, while lower rates could have the opposite effect. Thus, in 1940 Stormont could have kept control of purchase tax and levied it at lower rates or declined to levy it at all. That would have encouraged a

[1] H.C. Deb. (N.I.), 38, cc. 2680 et seq.

[2] ibid., c. 2684.

[3] ibid., 31, c. 2237.

[4] See the points made by the Hall Committee in 1962 on the questions of a general employment subsidy and annual grants against tax liability. *Report of the Joint Working Party on the Economy of Northern Ireland,* Cmd. 446 (1962), pp. 33, 37.

[5] H.C. Deb. (N.I.), 31, c. 1235.

[6] For example, in 1958 duty on estates between the ranges of £10,000 and £125,000 was lower than in Britain, but motor vehicle duties were slightly higher.

substantial movement of industry from Britain and confronted Whitehall with the choice of either imposing trade barriers or amending the constitution. Similarly, in 1948 Westminster imposed a tax on stake money paid to football and other pools. Northern Ireland did not at once introduce a similar duty, possibly because she was hoping for some of the revenue collected in Britain.[1] If so, she was disappointed. She did, however, eventually levy the tax in 1951 at the British rate. Its immediate effect was to cut the number of pools in Ulster from eight to two.[2] Had the tax continued to be withheld, pool betting in Ulster could now be an important industry; but the removal of pool promoters from Britain, the leakage of revenue from the United Kingdom Exchequer, and the creation of a Monaco within the United Kingdom could seriously disturb harmonious relations. These examples tend to show that when the taxing power is divided in so small and compact an area as the United Kingdom, one must expect either a substantial degree of uniformity or a considerable amount of friction. The provincial Parliament has chosen (or at least acquiesced in) the former, and Westminster has never had to wield its legal supremacy.

In expenditure, Stormont's constitutional right to exercise sole control, already limited before 1939, has since been further whittled down by its leaders' will. It has no option but to follow Great Britain in national insurance, it is precluded from making radical changes in services covered by the Social Services Agreement, and it must maintain parity in every field unless Ministers can convince the Treasury or the Joint Exchequer Board (or possibly in the last resort the British Cabinet) that there are good reasons for divergence. This profoundly affects both legislative and administrative activity. The scope for forward planning within the Ministry of Finance is limited because the level of future expenditure is so greatly influenced by United Kingdom decisions.[3] Northern Ireland is subject to Treasury control.[4]

Treasury control in Britain is subtle and varied. Its methods,

[1] Northern Ireland has suggested that pool betting duty should be made a reserved tax, but the Treasury was not willing to do this. H.C. 1506, p. 17.

[2] C.A.G. 1951–52, H.C. 1019, p. xv.

[3] P.A.C. 1960–61, Third Report, p. 22. (This Report is not numbered.)

[4] In October 1964 economic planning was transferred from the Treasury to the Department of Economic Affairs. It is too soon to say whether this will have any effect in Northern Ireland, but there is no evidence at the time of writing of any change in general relations with the United Kingdom.

appropriate to different times, circumstances and types of expenditure, fall under four main heads. The Treasury influences policy; its sanction is required to annual Estimates and to programmes of expenditure in advance of Estimates; its approval must be sought for new items of expenditure, new services and policy changes that involve increased spending; and it maintains a close interest in expenditure that has already been authorized.[1] The first three of these points are similar to the terms of the agreement reproduced on page 77 above. In addition it was agreed that the Ministry of Finance would draw the Treasury's attention to any proposed divergence from parity standards.

These controls are more than formal. Ministers at Stormont have often made it clear that Treasury consent has been sought. The wide scope of that consent can be illustrated by a few examples from different fields. The Treasury in 1939 agreed to the making good from the local Exchequer of a deficit on the nationalized Northern Ireland Road Transport Board;[2] in 1944 to financial arrangements for the Northern Ireland Housing Trust[3] and to increased derating grants;[4] in 1946 to the shifting of some educational expenditure from the rates to the local Exchequer;[5] in 1958 to higher housing subsidies and grants to local authorities,[6] and to the charging against current revenue of certain capital expenditure.[7] In 1963, when the House of Commons at Stormont set up a Select Committee on Parliamentary Salaries, the Prime Minister declared that any recommendations would have to be put to London before they could be agreed;[8] and in 1964 the Minister of Finance said that a pensions scheme for M.P.s would need to be acceptable to the Treasury.[9]

It may be asked how the Treasury can match omnipotence with omniscience. An enormous range of knowledge is needed for informed decisions about the relative merits of different sorts of expenditure and to avoid prodigious waste. The Select Committee on Public Accounts at Stormont subjects financial administration to rigorous scrutiny, but the Committee is not (and is not

[1] Select Committee on Estimates, Sixth Report ('Treasury Control of Expenditure'), U.K. H.C. 254–I of 1957–58. See especially memoranda by the Treasury in Minutes of Evidence, pp. 1–12, 48–54.
[2] H.C. Deb. (N.I.), 22, c. 1525; P.A.C. 1941–42, H.C. 602, p. 32.
[3] H.C. Deb. (N.I.), 27, c. 2577.
[4] ibid., c. 1015.
[5] ibid., 30, c. 2662.
[6] ibid., 42, c. 1042; 43, c. 133.
[7] ibid., 42, c. 1050.
[8] ibid., 54, c. 2039.
[9] ibid., 57, c. 1446.

intended to be) a substitute for close and continuous administrative control, nor is it concerned with future spending or with policy that has determined the scale and character of past expenditure. The Treasury doubtless relies heavily on the experience, zeal and integrity of officials in the Ministry of Finance, who in turn look to their colleagues in other departments. Nobody who studies public administration in Northern Ireland can fail to realize that she has always been fortunate in attracting civil servants of high ability. At the same time, their loyalty is to their own political masters. The Ministry of Finance is not a Treasury outpost and there have evidently been plenty of arguments.[1] This situation is not dissimilar from that in Britain. Co-operation between the Treasury and other departments in London contains disagreement, and plans to spend public money must survive critical scrutiny and be justified by argument and discussion.

In other ways, however, Northern Ireland is a special case. The Treasury deals, not directly with the spending departments in Northern Ireland, but with the Ministry of Finance; and discussions must often turn on the problem of clothing with concreteness the general principle of parity. While local politicians and officials want to be sure that parity is fully achieved, the Treasury needs to be equally certain that it is not exceeded without good reason. Departments in Britain and Ulster work with each others' Estimates,[2] but close comparison must sometimes be difficult because local conditions and administrative forms differ. Moreover, it is at the stage when policy is being formulated, and before it is embodied in Estimates at all, that financial control is most effective. One possible device would be inspection of provincial services by or on behalf of the Treasury. That may be thought to be too crude. It does not seem to be used in Ulster, though something of the sort is not unknown in federal states.[3] A more

[1] The Accounting Officer of the Ministry of Finance said in 1949 that if Northern Ireland were to spend without Treasury agreement 'it would mean that before the Joint Exchequer Board the Treasury would say, "We do not agree that Northern Ireland should have spent that money", and therefore they would suggest to the Joint Exchequer Board, *as they have done over a considerable number of years*, that Northern Ireland should not have spent that money, and it must meet that expenditure out of its own funds and not out of the imperial contribution.' H.C. 873, p. 66. (Author's italics.)

[2] The form of Northern Ireland Estimates in 1921 was modelled directly on that used in Great Britain. See P.A.C. 1961–62 (Special Report on Proposed Changes in the Form of Estimates), H.C. 1492, p. 10 and *passim*.

[3] Federal officials inspect grant-aided services in the United States. M. J. C. Vile, *The Structure of American Federalism* (London, 1961), p. 9 and chap. ix.

subtle variant would be to invite independent persons who command the confidence of both Governments and who carry in their heads notions of standards in Britain, to examine and report on local services. This is certainly very common. Investigations in Ulster are often made by or with the assistance of distinguished people from Great Britain. We should emphasize, though, that we have no positive evidence to show why Northern Ireland finds it so useful to rely on outside advice.

Leaving this point aside, the question that calls for answer is whether local self-government is now worth very much. A final assessment must be deferred until we have made some study of public services. Before we leave financial questions, however, we shall do well to note that Northern Ireland by no means lacks influence over her own affairs. She has distinct Estimates; the initiative in compiling them rests with her; and this gives her the first word, if not the last, in determining the magnitude and pattern of expenditure. Then, too, the post-war financial agreements were obviously drafted so as to give her some latitude. Parity is no more than a guiding principle, and it is explicitly provided that the Ministry of Finance may propose to diverge from parity if local conditions make that necessary. Rates of national assistance, pensions and family allowances are to be maintained only in general parity, and the scale and standard of comprehensive health services need be maintained only in general conformity with the scale and standard of those services in Britain. Finally, the Joint Exchequer Board, on which Northern Ireland is represented and which is evidently more active than before the war,[1] is an independent arbiter. The Board receives the Estimates, fixes the imperial contribution, determines Ulster's revenue, and over the whole field of financial relations is the judge in any dispute that may arise between the Treasury and the Ministry of Finance.

The finance of local government, like that of central government in Northern Ireland, has been transformed in the post-war period. We have space only to glance at one topic likely to be of special interest to students of parliamentary devolution, namely, the

[1] The Board met once in 1962–63. H.C. Deb. (N.I.), 54, c. 963. In 1956 the then chairman of the Board, Sir J. M. Erskine (now Lord Erskine) said that the Board met as might be necessary to fulfil its statutory duties and agreed the imperial contribution 'not only in theory but in practice'. Letter to *The Economist*, 13 October 1956. Lord Erskine of Rerrick was appointed Governor of Northern Ireland in December 1964.

financial relations between local authorities and the provincial Exchequer.

It was shown in Chapter Three that the Minister of Finance was unable to give local councils much help to improve their services before the war. The expansion in Government grants that did occur was due mainly to derating, for after 1929 the Exchequer in effect paid the rates on agricultural land and 75 per cent. of the rates formerly borne by industry. This, however, did not increase local revenues, and the burden of improvement fell mainly on the ordinary ratepayer. By contrast, since 1946 Government grants have increased twice as much as rates. (Industrial derating still stands at 75 per cent., though it was abolished in England and Wales from 1 April 1963.)

TABLE 10. *Revenue Receipts of Local Authorities*[1]

	Rates		*Government grants*		*Miscellaneous receipts*		*Total*	
	£000	*Per cent.*	*£000*	*Per cent.*	*£000*	*Per cent.*	*£000*	*Per cent.*
1921–22	2,953	74·4	503	12·6	515	13·0	3,971	100·0
1945–46	2,967	41·0	2,838	39·2	1,436	19·8	7,240	100·0
1964–65	15,321	29·9	31,345	61·1	4,625	9·0	51,291	100·0

The nature of Government assistance has also greatly changed. In 1948 the derating grant was superseded by a new grant called the General Exchequer Contribution. In its present form, which dates from 1958, this is designed to give full compensation for derating as well as extra help to poor local authorities, calculations to achieve these aims being based on a formula that takes account of valuation, road mileage and population in each area. The contribution is not tied to any specific service but is in aid of expenditure in general, and this is not subject to the same degree of ministerial scrutiny as expenditure on services that rank for

[1] Sources: *Report of the Committee on the Finances of Local Authorities*, Cmd. 369 (1957), p. 20; *Local Authority Rate Statistics*, 1964–65 (these are estimates). Miscellaneous receipts in the table consist mainly of rents, fees and other charges for public services. Net revenue from trading undertakings is very small.

specific grants. A local council thus enjoys some freedom. However, the Ministry can reduce the contribution if it is satisfied that a local authority is not maintaining a reasonable standard of efficiency or that its expenditure has been excessive and unreasonable. The Ministry must report to Parliament the amount of and the reasons for any reduction.[1] This power has rarely if ever been used.

The greatest expansion in grants since the war is not, however, attributable to the General Exchequer Contribution, but to grants in aid of education, health, welfare, roads and other specific services.

TABLE 11. *Government Grants to Local Authorities*[2]

	General Exchequer Contribution		*Grants for specific services*		*Total*	
	£000	*Per cent.*	*£000*	*Per cent.*	*£000*	*Per cent.*
1945–46	1,314*	46·3	1,524	53·7	2,838	100·0
1964–65	8,019	25·6	23,326	74·4	31,345	100·0

* Derating deficiency contribution.

From these statistics it is clear that the financial independence of local authorities is narrower than at any previous time. They have less discretion in spending grant money because a larger part of it is earmarked for particular services, and the proportion of total revenue which they themselves raise by way of rates has greatly diminished. In some areas, indeed, the connexion between local spending and local rates has been virtually destroyed. In an extreme case (Enniskillen Rural District, co. Fermanagh) in 1964–65, gross payments were estimated at £210,903, of which only £26,822 fell on ratepayers.

Local autonomy in finance is circumscribed in other ways. The local government audit, the power to surcharge unlawful expenditure, and ministerial sanction to borrowing resemble similar controls in Britain. Two other arrangements are for the most part

[1] Local Government (Finance) (No. 2) Act (N.I.), 1958, s. 10. This statute prescribes the manner in which the General Exchequer Contribution is to be calculated.

[2] Sources: *Local Taxation Returns*, 1945–46; *Local Authority Rate Statistics*, 1964–65.

peculiar to Northern Ireland. We have seen that several services which local authorities administer in England are centralized in Northern Ireland. The Ministry of Education is responsible to Parliament for the youth employment service, as is the Ministry of Home Affairs for the fire service and civil defence,[1] but ratepayers are required to contribute to these and also to the cost of drainage, a function of the Ministry of Agriculture. It is true that the charges levied upon them are relatively small,[2] and the local authorities are strongly represented on the statutory bodies that actually administer all but one of the services mentioned.[3] Nevertheless, there is resentment about some of these arrangements, and it hardly seems conducive to good government to compel elected bodies to pay towards services for which they are not accountable to their own ratepayers.

A more serious restriction arises from arrangements for financing education. The charge on local rates has gradually risen since local education authorities were created in 1923. In 1947 further reforms were introduced in the educational system and in its financial basis. Part of the cost of teachers' salaries and other items specified by statute is pooled among all local education authorities, the relative share of each area being determined, broadly speaking, by the ratio of its net annual value to the net annual value of Northern Ireland. The pooling arrangements, in which the Ministry of Education also participates, are complicated beyond belief, but their significance for local government can easily be grasped by looking at the round figures. Public expenditure on education in 1962–63 was £25 m., and three-quarters of this was borne by the Ministry. The rest (about £6 m.) fell on the rates as augmented by the General Exchequer Contribution. Of the £6 m., £4·7 m. was shared.[4] The local rate for education is thus determined, not only by the policy and spending of the Ministry and the local authority in question, but by that of all authorities put together. This device was designed to stimulate rapid development

[1] See above, p. 25.

[2] In a medium-sized borough (Ballymena, co. Antrim) in 1964–65 charges for fire service, drainage, youth employment and civil defence accounted for £5,515 out of total estimated payments, including county services, of £542,840.

[3] Local authority representatives are in the majority on the Northern Ireland Youth Employment Service Board, the Northern Ireland Fire Authority and the Drainage Council, which advises the Ministry of Agriculture, the drainage authority.

[4] See *Educational Development in Northern Ireland*, Cmd. 470 (1964), p. 26 and App.; Appropriation Accounts, 1962–63, H.C. 1569, p. 120.

in all areas, spread the expense among them, and gradually shift to the rates a larger part of the whole cost of education.[1] These aims, or at least the first two, are no doubt highly desirable, but there is a strong case for trying to achieve them by altering the system of Government grants. Pooling on the scale indicated must greatly weaken local self-government and blur still further the lines of responsibility between councils and electors.

The whole field of local government finance was last surveyed from 1955–57 by a Committee under the chairmanship of Sir Roland Nugent.[2] While advocating no radical change in the finance of education, the Committee were concerned about the ever-increasing dependence on State grants. Yet they could find no real solution. A local income tax was beyond the legislative competence of Parliament, and the taxes it did control were hardly suitable for transfer to local authorities. The Committee did recommend uniform valuation of all rateable hereditaments, including agricultural land, which has not been re-assessed in Ulster for a century. It is often argued that this would mean even larger Government grants because land (on which the Exchequer pays the rates) would then account for a larger proportion of the net annual value of Northern Ireland. However, the Minister of Finance said in 1958 that an increased grant for derating would have to be offset by reductions in other grants.[3] The Committee also advocated a measure of re-rating, but the Government with Britain's agreement kept industrial derating at 75 per cent. to promote economic growth.[4] This is unfortunate, not only because of the loss of local revenue, but also (as the Nugent Committee observed) because people who are largely insulated against rate increases have less incentive to interest themselves in local affairs. Complete re-rating could strengthen local independence and responsibility more than any other measure, though it is questionable whether Whitehall would sanction alternative methods of subsidizing industry and agriculture.

The issue of local autonomy has, however, tended to fall into the background since the Committee reported. Nowadays the sharpest grievance is that too much expenditure falls on the rates and that more of it should be shifted to the Exchequer. Ministers have resisted this for three good reasons. First, it is undesirable: the balance between rates and taxes should not be tipped so as to

[1] Cmd. 470, p. 25.
[2] Cmd. 369.
[3] H.C. Deb. (N.I.), 43, c. 139.
[4] ibid., 52, c. 698.

diminish local interest or dissuade able citizens from entering local government.[1] Second, it is not possible: Ulster's general financial relations with Britain mean that grants should be on the broad basis of parity except where special circumstances exist.[2] Third, it is not equitable: grants are already higher than elsewhere in the United Kingdom. Thus, the responsible Minister emphasized in 1963 that the rate of Exchequer assistance towards education, housing, playing fields and swimming pools was far higher than in Britain, and that ratepayers in Ulster made no contribution whatever towards the cost of the police force.[3]

Despite this assistance, it is often complained that local rates are excessive because Northern Ireland is one of the poorer parts of the United Kingdom. We have seen that *per capita* incomes are about 25 per cent. lower than in Britain.[4] Whether the rate burden is really unfair is a question that admits of no simple or exact answer. Valuations are not on the same basis as in England and Wales, nor are official statistics of rates collected.[5] We can do no more than make a guess and give reasons for it. In 1962–63 the amount of rates collected per head of population was estimated at £17 11*s.* for England and Wales[6] and £9 for Northern Ireland.[7] As they stand, these figures are misleading. The proportion of rateable value attributable to industrial hereditaments was smaller in Northern Ireland, both because in 1962–63 she had derating at 75 per cent. (against 50 per cent. in England and Wales), and also because she was less industrialized. Her rate per head ought therefore to be lower, for it would be unfair to expect ordinary householders to pay the share which industry bears in England. We can allow for this and other differences by scaling up the Northern Ireland figure to £11, which seems to be an over-estimate.[8] If, further, we take account of lower average incomes in Ulster, which may be held to justify a rate call at least 25 per cent.

[1] H. C. Deb. (N.I.), 54, cc. 700 et seq.
[2] ibid., 43, c. 134
[3] ibid., 54, cc. 700 et seq.
[4] Above, p. 30.
[5] In particular, many hereditaments which are rated in England and Wales are exempt in Northern Ireland.
[6] *Rates and Rateable Values in England and Wales*, 1962–63, Table C.
[7] *Local Authority Rate Statistics*, 1962–63, p. 13.
[8] In April 1962 about one-ninth of the *rateable* value of England and Wales was due to hereditaments used for industrial and freight transport purposes. The fraction in Northern Ireland was roughly about one-twentieth (industrial, &c., £0·5 m., and other non-agricultural hereditaments £10 m.). Increase this fraction to one-eighth by scaling up the £0·5 m. to £1·5 m., and rate revenue per head would rise by about £1. (The population in 1962–63 was 1·4 m., and

below that in England and Wales (say £13), there is a strong presumption, to put it no higher, that Ulster ratepayers suffer no great injustice. It is, of course, another question—and one that arouses lively controversy—whether the rate burden is fairly distributed within Northern Ireland. There are extremely wide variations in *per capita* rates collected in urban and rural areas. If the urban figures were adjusted to take account of all relevant differences, it might well be found that the real burden approximated closely to that in urban areas of England and Wales.[1]

It will be apparent from this sketch of a complex subject that parliamentary devolution has tended to restrict rather than enlarge local autonomy. To impute this to some Machiavellian design seems wrong-headed. Ministers at Stormont often stress the need for a strong and vigorous local government system, and in recent years they have brought in a number of reforms, though of a relatively minor character.[2] In finance, however, the tide still runs strongly against local freedom.

There appear to be two main currents. The more general is, of course, that rate revenue has not kept pace with local expenditure. To have increased the one as much as the other would mean that rates today would be greater by about one-third. An impost of that size, or anything like it, would undoubtedly arouse the most strenuous opposition in Ulster. It is not merely that the rate is not a particularly equitable tax or that it is not deducted at source, or even that it is demanded in lump sums, for the first and second of these defects are present in other taxes on outlay (e.g. the tobacco

---

the average poundage rate was £1 3*s*.) It is also probable that the proportion of rateable value due to large shop and office property was lower in Northern Ireland, though 40 per cent. of total net annual value was within the City of Belfast. However, to compensate for this and for revenue lost by rating exemptions, we have allowed another £1 per head (i.e. £1·4 m.), which is certainly too much. I am indebted to Mr. R. J. Lynn, Superintendent of Rate of the City of Belfast, for advice on these technical matters.

[1] Amount of rates estimated to be collected per head of population, 1962–63:

	Northern Ireland £ *s*.	*England and Wales* £ *s*.
London . . .	—	32 14
Leeds . . .	—	17 1
Belfast . . .	12 6	—
Non-county boroughs .	12 2	17 10 (combined)
Urban districts . .	11 19	
Rural districts . .	4 7	12 1

[2] See e.g. H.C. Deb. (N.I.), 54, c. 701.

duty), and the third is not insuperable. It is the combination of these points with the fact that the rate is inescapable that seems to make it so unpopular. Even this was tolerated as long as there was some relation between the rate struck in an area and the benefits derived from it, but this connexion in Northern Ireland has become so tenuous as to blur the distinction between local rates and central taxes.

In the second place, the combination of Ulster's unfavourable economic situation (which has meant retention of derating) and of constitutional rules and practices leaves little room for manœuvre. The scope for local taxation apart from rates is virtually non-existent; and the finance of local government is caught up in the general financial relations with the United Kingdom. For example, the provincial Government cannot of their own volition assume the whole financial responsibility for education (which takes about half of local authority expenditure) and leave local councils wider freedom to cultivate a smaller field. To substitute a general grant for most specific grants (as in England and Wales since 1959–60) might make it harder to be certain of eliminating any leeway that still exists in particular services. It is difficult to resist the conclusion that in local as in central government the tendency is to sacrifice liberty to improvement.

No review of the post-war years would be complete without reference to recent social and political changes. During the past decade the violence and fierce intolerance that marred life before the war have perceptibly diminished. Organized attacks on life and property by the Irish Republican Army have stopped; spontaneous disorder is infrequent; and Protestants and Catholics of good will are more disposed to co-operate.

This has had some impact on party politics. A revived Liberal Party holds one of the four University seats at Stormont. The Northern Ireland Labour Party has made headway in some urban areas and captured four Belfast constituencies at the general election in 1958. When Nationalists in the provincial House of Commons still declined to form an official Opposition, the Speaker recognized one of the Labour members as Leader of the Opposition. Stormont came nearer than at any time since 1921 to being a microcosm of Westminster. At the same time, traditional attitudes remain dominant. At the general election in May 1962 Labour increased its poll but only retained four seats. Unionists won thirty-four, Nationalists nine and other parties five. Twenty Unionists, including six of the nine members of the Cabinet, were returned unopposed. Over the greater part of the country there is still no effective challenge to Ulster Unionism.

Yet that party's outlook, and the emphasis in its policy, are shifting. Moderate views are often to be heard within its ranks; and its success in attaining pre-war aims—to establish the constitution and improve public services—together with the rise of Labour, combined to rivet attention on the one problem that has defied solution—unemployment.

Intensive effort by the Northern Ireland Government, reinforced by lavish financial inducements to industry, were by no means without fruit. By 1961 more people were at work than ever before. But unemployment was still five times greater than in Britain, for contraction of older industries offset expansion of newer ones, and the rate of natural increase of the working population (Ulster's birth-rate is the highest in the United Kingdom) exceeded the rate of migration. Requests to London for more help culminated in October 1962 in a Report by a Joint Working Party under the chairmanship of Sir Robert Hall of senior officials of United Kingdom and Northern Ireland departments.[1] The approach of the two sides was evidently rather different. Ulster's object was to eliminate unemployment, and she proposed subsidizing industry to the extent of ten shillings a week for all employees, at a cost of some £5·6 m. a year. Other members of the Working Party set the provincial problem more firmly in a national context. To them the primary aim was to encourage new growth industries able to compete in overseas markets: expensive general subsidies might not only become permanent and whet the appetite for more, but would reduce mobility of labour. The Working Party did agree on many points but were unable to propound any measure that would have a sharp and immediate impact.

In Ulster, where people had expected a panacea, the Report was at once a shock and a stimulus. Captain T. M. O'Neill, then Minister of Finance, said in November 1962:

> The Hall Report is a great watershed in our affairs. It has given us a cold, impersonal look at ourselves. It has tested the Imperial Government to help us in certain areas and met a negative response. Now we

[1] Cmd. 446.

as a government and those to whom we are responsible know where we stand. Very well, then. We must now proceed with a three-pronged attack upon our problems, relying largely on our own skill, determination and enterprise.[1]

Emphasis on self-help drove Unionists to seek more initiative at the centre of affairs. Lord Brookeborough, then aged seventy-four, had been Prime Minister since 1943. Under his leadership Ulster had marshalled her resources for war, entrenched her constitutional status and enhanced her material well-being. But the tide that had swept him to power turned against him. In March 1963, after a minor operation, he resigned.

His successor, Captain O'Neill, returning to the theme of self-help, proclaimed his Government's intention to transform the face of Ulster by further improving public services, driving forward economic expansion, and planning urban and rural development.[2] It is evident that no effort is to be spared to achieve these aims. In 1963 the Government accepted a plan prepared by Sir Robert Matthew for developing the Belfast region. In 1964 the Prime Minister reconstructed the Administration and created a Ministry of Development, and the long-standing problem of relations between Government and trade unions was resolved.[3] In 1965 relations between the north and south of Ireland, for so long marked by bitter hostility, entered a happier phase. On 14 January the Prime Minister of the Republic of Ireland (Mr. Sean Lemass) met Captain O'Neill at Stormont to discuss common problems. This initiative by the two statesmen at once impelled anti-partitionists in Ulster to re-examine their position. In February the Nationalist Party, while still cherishing the ideal of a United Ireland, applied for and received the status of official Opposition at Stormont, a role that had fallen to the numerically smaller Labour Party for nearly seven years. In the same month new plans for the economic development of the province were published.[4] Nineteen sixty-five may well mark a new turning-point in the affairs of Northern Ireland.

[1] *Belfast Telegraph*, 30 November 1962.
[2] H.C. Deb. (N.I.), 55, cc. 28 et seq.
[3] These matters are further discussed in Chapters Two and Eight.
[4] *Economic Development in Northern Ireland*, Cmd. 479 (1965).

PART THREE

Public Services

Introduction

PUBLIC finance and public services are aspects of a single activity, and our account of the one has necessarily entailed some examination of the other. The object of the following chapters is to widen and deepen that examination so as to expose more clearly certain themes that are implicit in the narrative up to this point.

The dominant theme is evidently the desire of Ulster's leaders to improve public services. Without detailed study we cannot appreciate the strength of that desire or the extent to which it has been satisfied. Nor can we understand why Ulstermen have been willing to pay the price of its satisfaction. The pressure for improvement has been instrumental in transforming the financial relations between Britain and Ulster, and hence the content (as distinct from the form) of parliamentary devolution. In order to finance social betterment, Stormont has had no alternative but to acquiesce in agreements that have diminished its autonomy.

What then is the value of devolution? A provisional answer is that it allows local people to exert a powerful if not decisive influence on local affairs. But in Northern Ireland the strength of public opinion and of other factors that mould public policy is secreted in detail to a far greater extent than in countries where political parties with different policies alternate in power. The principal role of Unionism has always been to form and support governments pledged to maintain the British connexion, and the influence on those governments of the Joint Exchequer Board and the Treasury is not negligible because it is largely concealed. By tracing the evolution of particular services we should be able to judge how they have been shaped by the wishes of local people and by the initiative of their own Government.

To review every aspect of public policy would, however, require a book in itself. We have selected four services—education, health, housing and planning, and social security. Even within this restricted field much has been omitted that is not relevant to our purpose. The structure of each chapter is deliberately designed to illustrate the need for improvement, the extent to which it has been attained, and the degree to which Government and people have determined its pace and direction.

CHAPTER SIX

Education

EDUCATION in Northern Ireland still bears the stamp of the remote past. We must therefore outline its evolution, though nothing short of a volume could unravel its tangled history.

The period before the Union of 1800 is disfigured by England's efforts to anglicize Ireland and propagate the doctrines of the established Church. These ventures, though pursued intermittently from 1536 to 1695 and thereafter pressed forward with fanatical zeal until the partial relaxation of the penal code in 1782, were a failure. Roman Catholics shunned the State-supported schools and, evading the penal laws with some success, built up their own inchoate forms of instruction.[1]

So after the Union, and more particularly after Roman Catholic emancipation in 1829, educational policy was of paramount importance. To wise men in Ireland and England alike, it was evident that common schooling offered the best if not the only chance of healing wounds and gradually creating a united country. On the Irish side Sir Thomas Wyse (a Catholic of luminous intellect) had profound influence. His ideas were given material form by Edward Stanley, Chief Secretary for Ireland,[2] whose plan for national elementary education in 1831 was designed to enlighten and unite the Irish people without subjecting them to proselytism.[3]

Success turned on securing the co-operation of all religious denominations. Eminent men of all persuasions, constituted a Board of Commissioners of National Education, were to see that children of different faiths were given combined literary and moral education and, at specified times, separate religious instruction. The Board controlled the secular curriculum, sanctioned publication of a book of extracts from the Bible and employed inspectors. Management of schools was entrusted to local 'patrons' and managers, many of them clergymen, who provided and

[1] T. Corcoran, *State Policy in Irish Education, 1536 to 1816* (Dublin, 1916), pp. 41–117; P. J. Dowling, *The Hedge Schools of Ireland* (Dublin, 1935).

[2] Afterwards fourteenth Earl of Derby and Conservative Prime Minister.

[3] J. J. Auchmuty, *Irish Education* (Dublin, 1937), chap. iv; *Sir Thomas Wyse, 1791–1862* (London, 1939), chap. x.

maintained school-houses, paid teachers and (subject to the Commissioners' regulations) engaged and dismissed them.[1] The Board, however, gradually assumed greater financial responsibility until by the end of the century almost the entire cost of primary education, except maintenance of certain school buildings, was borne on parliamentary votes.[2]

These so-called 'national' schools, instead of dispersing religious conflict, provided new foci for it. The established Church never liked the scheme. Presbyterians and Orangemen in Ulster (where nine schools were wrecked or closed between 1832 and 1835), raising the cry of 'the Bible unabridged and unmutilated', assailed restrictions on religious instruction until by 1840 the Board conceded their demands. Roman Catholics then began to insist on schools under their exclusive control. The upshot was educational partition. Although the Board itself always adhered to the principle of combined secular and separate religious teaching, by the end of the century the great majority of Catholic children went to schools with Catholic teachers, while Protestant denominations tended to segregate themselves from each other.[3]

So a rash of tiny clerical schools erupted across the face of Ireland. That country by 1917 had 8,118 State-aided primary schools; Scotland, with a bigger school population, had 3,167. Of the 13,357 Irish national school-teachers, 5,743 were assistants and 7,614 principals. The cost to the Exchequer of educating a child in an Irish national school was £4 17*s.* 1*d.*, against £3 0*s.* 1*d.* in England and Wales. These differences, no doubt, were partly due to the fact that the population of Ireland was more scattered. Yet State assistance, thinly spread, lost much of its value, as a Vice-Regal Committee showed in 1918.[4] Schools were cold, insanitary, overcrowded and poorly equipped; books were rarely provided;

[1] G. Balfour, *The Educational Systems of Great Britain and Ireland* (Oxford, 1898), pp. 80–118.

[2] *Final Report of Royal Commission on Local Taxation* (*Ireland*), 1902, U.K. Cd. 1068 (1902), p. 44. Different classes of national schools were financed on different principles. Schools vested in the Commissioners or in trustees received more State aid than non-vested schools and in consequence were more closely regulated. On 31 December 1919 there were 7,947 schools and less than half of them (3,620) were vested. *Report of Commissioners of National Education in Ireland*, 1919–20, U.K. Cmd. 1476 (1921), p. 12.

[3] Balfour, loc. cit. On early controversies see also R. B. McDowell, *Public Opinion and Government Policy in Ireland, 1801–46* (London, 1952).

[4] *Report of Vice-Regal Committee of Enquiry into Primary Education* (*Ireland*), 1918, U.K. Cmd. 60 (1919). The statistics cited are at pp. 31, 41.

and since education was not universally compulsory,[1] many boys and girls never went to school or left at a tender age or simply stayed away at will. Of 700,000 pupils, some 200,000 were on average absent every day during the three years 1917–19. Teachers' salaries were too low and their conditions were too depressing to attract sufficient good candidates.[2] And public opinion was indifferent. As the Vice-Regal Committee observed:

> The energies of the Irish people have been so constantly engrossed by large constitutional and agrarian issues that education, like other important matters, has been often pushed aside or ignored.[3]

Yet men of good will were not condemned to impotence. The original scheme had been shattered by local resistance; and local managers, responsible to no representative body, still exercised enormous influence. This excessive reliance on irresponsible, even if conscientious, effort meant that the Commissioners, 'forced to wait in helpless inaction for the appearance of voluntary effort', had no real power to insist on improvement. A partial remedy had often been suggested. A local rate for education would both produce more money and also call for local education authorities who at worst could be compelled to do their duty and at best might arouse enthusiasm. So the Vice-Regal Committee (which included the Roman Catholic Bishops of Raphoe and Tuam) recommended not only larger Exchequer grants, improvement and amalgamation of schools, compulsory attendance and better attention to pupils' needs, but also the creation of local committees appointed by county and county borough councils and the imposition of a local rate 'to arouse and foster in the public mind throughout Ireland a keener appreciation of the importance of the question of national education'.[4] Little came of this, apart from some increase in salaries in 1920. Northern Ireland therefore inherited a system which (as Sir James Craig said in 1921) needed to be rooted out of the soil to make room for a new fabric.

Secondary schools, neither aided nor closely regulated by the State for the first three-quarters of the nineteenth century, were

[1] Irish Education Act, 1892, s. 15 (2); U.K. Cmd. 1476, p. 30.

[2] This dismal picture was lightened by the model schools, built and maintained by the State, managed by the Commissioners, and intended as exemplars to adjacent national schools. By securing suitable buildings, adequate equipment and efficient teachers on special rates of salary, the Commissioners provided a first-class elementary education. But there were only thirty model schools, twelve of them being in Northern Ireland.

[3] op. cit., p. 5.

[4] op. cit., p. 6.

a medley. A few, like the grammar schools established by Erasmus Smith and other private benefactors, and the Royal Free schools founded in Ulster by royal charter, were fairly old foundations (generally Protestant) with endowments; many had been created by Roman Catholics after 1793; others were private ventures run for profit. Their standards were as diverse as their origins.[1]

Government at length intervened in 1878. A Board of Commissioners of Intermediate Education were empowered to award prizes and exhibitions and make grants to approved schools. Given no powers of inspection, they nevertheless needed to assess a school's efficiency before giving away public money. The expedient adopted (already inaugurated in England by Robert Lowe in 1862) was to make a grant to schools in respect of each pupil who passed the Board's examination. So the Commissioners were able to influence curricula and ensure that instruction—as gauged by examination results—was, in Lowe's words, either efficient or cheap.[2]

Payment by results cannot be ranked with the great administrative inventions. Concentrated cramming, especially of young children, was pernicious; and schools' grants, on which teachers' salaries partly depended, fluctuated with the prevalence of epidemics during examinations and the chance distribution of clever pupils, though touting for them was not unknown. Inspectors were not appointed until 1909, and in 1914 grants were made solely on their reports, but only for children from twelve to fourteen. Examinations were still the chief factor by 1919.

In that year another Vice-Regal Committee[3] disclosed the pitiful plight of intermediate education. Grants were small in total but complicated in composition; teachers were overworked, underpaid, without title to pension and liable to capricious dismissal; pupils were forced in an examination hothouse; and poor boys and girls were effectively barred from this utilitarian garden because public scholarships were unknown. The Committee urged that teachers' salaries and status should be raised; that grants should be simplified, increased and augmented by a local rate; that payment by results should be abolished; and that financial

[1] The Irish Parliament made some attempt to prevent improper use of endowments, and after the Union the endowed schools came under closer State control.

[2] Balfour, op. cit., pp. 203–18. S. J. Curtis, *History of Education in Great Britain* (London, 1948), p. 150.

[3] *Report of Vice-Regal Committee on Intermediate Education (Ireland)*, U.K. Cmd. 66 (1919).

help should be given to poor children of ability but withheld from schools conducted purely for private gain.

These proposals were still-born. At a time when Ireland was beginning to disintegrate, intermediate education was crumbling too. In 1920 the Intermediate Education Board, forsaking the dreary language of official reports, declared:

> It is difficult for us at this juncture—when the whole edifice of secondary education in Ireland is toppling to destruction—to refer to these matters in language of moderation and restraint. Of one thing, however, we feel quite certain, and that is that if something is not done immediately to place Irish secondary education in the position of financial equality with that of Great Britain, it is impossible to see how the complete disruption of the system can be avoided.[1]

This cursory survey has omitted much. We have not even mentioned technical instruction which, partly because of its banausic nature, was highly successful. (It was in the Catholic University in Ireland that J. H. Newman, afterwards Cardinal, in his lectures on the Idea of a University, insisted on the philosophic nature of true education.) We have, however, said enough to show that in its leading features, whether the outcome of Irish history like clerical control, or the product of English experience like payment by results, Irish education by 1921 was antiquated by the standards of the English Acts of 1902 and 1918.[2] It was out-moded, too, because it lacked co-ordination and direct public responsibility. The English Board of Education under a President accountable to Parliament dated from 1899. The Boards in Ireland, being directly responsible to no elected body, were practically immune from popular criticism, and as long as they remained distinct it was impossible even to begin to give children the sort of education they were best fitted for.

In Northern Ireland one Ministry of Education superseded the two Boards.[3] Lord Londonderry, the first Minister, in

[1] Quoted in *Interim Report of Departmental Committee on the Educational Services in Northern Ireland*, Cmd. 6 (1922), p. 48.

[2] 'We much regret', wrote the Commissioners in 1920, 'that at a time when far-reaching reforms and developments have been secured in the educational systems of Great Britain, there is little progress to chronicle in the conditions in Ireland.' *Report of the Commissioners of National Education in Ireland*, 1918–19, U.K. Cmd. 1048 (1920), p. 7.

[3] The functions of the Department of Agriculture and Technical Instruction relating to technical instruction were also transferred to the Ministry.

September 1921 appointed a Departmental Committee under the chairmanship of Mr. R. J. Lynn[1] on which were represented almost all interested bodies except the Roman Catholic Church, whose adherents refused to serve or give evidence. The Committee showed that Ulster was a microcosm of Ireland as portrayed by the Vice-Regal Committees. For example, of elementary school-teachers in the province, 2,036 were principals and only 2,170 vice-principals and assistants. In Belfast the citizens had endured the Churches' failure to provide schools for the rapidly growing population until it was reckoned there was no room at all for some 12,000 children. The Committee argued that radical reforms, including the creation of local education authorities, were imperative.[2]

The Education Act (N.I.), 1923 was a courageous attempt at wholesale reconstruction. Courageous, because education was then peculiarly explosive. As already noted, several schools were damaged; Roman Catholics boycotted the Ministry; Roman Catholic bishops in a manifesto expressed hostility to publicly provided schools;[3] and many Protestants were apprehensive about religious education. Nevertheless, county and county borough councils, acting through education committees, were made local education authorities with the duty to provide public elementary schools (as national schools were henceforth called) and the power to accept from voluntary managers the transfer of existing schools.

The Act had hardly been launched when it was swept on the rocks of religion. The storm had three centres: management of schools, religious instruction, and appointment of teachers. On these matters Catholics and Protestants, though otherwise fiercely opposed, joined in condemning the Government.

Their accusation that elementary education would be secular was not wholly without truth. The Act provided that every public elementary school, whether provided, transferred or voluntary, should be open to children of all religious denominations for combined literary and moral instruction, and that religious teaching should not be given within the hours of compulsory attendance.[4] In provided and transferred schools, which were wholly financed by public money, the local education authority was

[1] Afterwards Sir Robert Lynn.

[2] See Cmd. 6 and *Final Report of the Departmental Committee on the Educational Services in Northern Ireland*, Cmd. 15 (1923).

[3] *Belfast News-Letter*, 28 March 1923.

[4] Education Act (N.I.), 1923, s. 28.

forbidden to require teachers to belong to any particular church or denomination, or to provide religious instruction, though it was to afford opportunities outside the hours of compulsory attendance for any religious teaching to which parents did not object.[1] The authority was permitted to set up school management committees of parents, former managers of transferred schools and other interested persons, but their functions were purely secular, and appointment of teachers was expressly withheld from them.[2] A voluntary manager who declined to transfer on these terms and kept control of his school and of religious instruction was entitled to receive from the education authority half the cost of lighting, heating and cleaning. The Ministry itself paid the salaries of teachers in all public elementary schools. The voluntary manager would also get half the cost of repairs and general upkeep, and he could apply to the education authority for a contribution towards reconstruction and new building, but only if he agreed to a school management committee of four members appointed by himself and two by the authority[3] and this 'four and two' committee would control religious instruction and teachers' appointments.[4]

The nature of these choices aroused vehement protests. In 1925, when it was evident that fear of secularism was retarding transfers, the Government made minor changes.[5] They failed to mollify the Protestant churches and the Orange Order,[6] and these powerful groups wrung more substantial concessions in 1930. Former managers of transferred schools secured representation on the education committees through which local education authorities discharged their duties, a preponderant influence on school management committees (which were made mandatory), and an initiative in selecting teachers.[7] (A school management committee, of whose members half represented managers of transferred and superseded voluntary schools and a quarter parents, was to select three applicants for a teaching post and the education authority

[1] ss. 26, 66 (3).
[2] ss. 3, 66 (3).
[3] ss. 15 (2), 16 (1).
[4] ss. 27, 66 (4).
[5] In June 1925 the Ministry concluded what it described as 'a concordat which had the approval of all parties to the dispute'. This permitted local education authorities to require teachers in provided and transferred schools to give undenominational Bible instruction as part of the ordinary course of instruction, though not within the hours of compulsory attendance. *Report of the Ministry of Education*, 1925–26, H.C. 107, p. 9. See also Education Act (N.I.), 1925.
[6] H.C. Deb. (N.I.), 12, c. 777; Senate Deb., 27, c. 57.
[7] Education Act (N.I.), 1930, ss. 1, 2, 3.

was to appoint one of them.) In addition, in provided and transferred schools, it was the duty of the education authority to provide non-denominational Bible instruction if the parents of not fewer than ten children applied for it, and the duty of teachers to give such instruction.[1] So began an era in which prospective teachers found it wise to canvass members of both local education authorities and school management committees and in which, as the Prime Minister said, provided and transferred schools were 'safe for Protestant children'.[2]

Were they not safe for Roman Catholics? It was Ulster's plain duty to ensure they were, for her constitution prohibited religious discrimination. In a heated debate in the Commons, Lord Craigavon firmly proclaimed his Government's impartiality. Bible instruction, he insisted, need have no 'odour or taint' of Protestant teaching. Authorities of the Roman Church could draw up a programme to include 'the great and simple truths of our common Christianity', and school management committees could ensure that none but Catholic teachers were appointed. He continued:

> In this way I maintain with confidence that if Roman Catholics transferred their schools, those schools would be as secure of being conducted on Roman Catholic lines by the authority as Protestant schools will be of being conducted in harmony with the views of Protestant parents. And if this can be said with truth, how does the system we are setting up give a preference to Protestants?[3]

Roman Catholics found the argument unconvincing. Gerrymandering (they complained), by depriving them of any chance of gaining a majority on a local education authority, had destroyed their faith in public control.[4] They were now invited to agree to Bible teaching (which was subversive of their faith) and to legislation that could compel a Catholic teacher either to give such teaching if ten Protestant children joined his school or to suffer the consequences of refusal.

[1] Education Act (N.I.), 1930, s. 4.

[2] H.C. Deb. (N.I.), 12, c. 725.

[3] ibid., c. 727.

[4] ibid., cc. 783, 1163. In their manifesto in March 1923 (noted at p. 110 above) the Catholic bishops declared: 'If Catholic children are compelled to attend school, the religious education there should be in accord with Catholic convictions. . . . It is necessary to add that, under the arrangement to be made as regards training and certificates, which remain with the Ministry, it would be quite an easy matter to cut off the supply of young teachers for convent or even ordinary elementary schools. Certainly, if recent legislation abolishing proportional representation and rearranging the local government board areas, thereby ousting Catholics from the representation, is to be taken as an indication of what we may expect, the outlook is of the gravest character for our people.'

This point was more substantial than Lord Craigavon himself apparently realized, for we shall presently explain that the Government of Northern Ireland later came to the conclusion that it would be unconstitutional to expose any teacher to threat of dismissal on a religious issue. Yet it is doubtful whether the most scrupulous fairness would have induced Roman Catholics to transfer. They demanded Catholic teaching of Catholic children in Catholic schools under voluntary managers but paid for entirely by public money.[1] The fact remained that they—in general the poorer section of the population—were compelled as citizens to pay rates and taxes for a system they detested, and expected as churchmen to find all the money to improve their own schools unless the managers accepted a 'four and two' committee, which they generally declined to do. The outcome could easily be foreseen: their children would suffer. This evidently impressed Lord Craigavon, and on the committee stage of the Bill of 1930 the Government took powers to pay half the cost of building or reconstructing voluntary schools and to lend the other half, whether the schools had 'four and two' committees or not.[2]

So after 1930 in provided and transferred schools the way was open for Bible instruction by teachers appointed on the recommendation of school management committees, while in voluntary schools distinctive religious education was secure and improvement was less remote. This settlement lasted until 1947.

Against this turbulent background the Ministry and the local authorities drove forward plans to make former national schools fit for the rising generation. Three needs were dominant—to raise teaching standards, improve pupils' attendance and provide larger and better but fewer buildings.

The first was perhaps the least difficult, for since the Ministry paid the salaries of all teachers, it was singly responsible for their proficiency. Improvements in training, and the opening in 1922 of a new interdenominational college at Stranmillis, Belfast,[3] gradually made untrained teachers rare. Whereas in 1922 about

[1] ibid., cc. 716 et seq. Nationalists would not accept the arrangement that had prevailed in Scotland since 1918 by which Catholic bishops compiled lists of teachers but local authorities appointed teachers from the lists and managed and financed former Catholic schools. ibid., c. 743.

[2] ibid., cc. 1153, 1226. Education Act (N.I.), 1930, s. 10.

[3] In 1921 the only training college in Ulster for elementary teachers was St. Mary's Training College, Belfast, for Roman Catholic women. Stranmillis Training College, at first housed in temporary quarters, was formally opened in May 1930.

82 per cent. were trained, by 1938 the comparable figure was 93 per cent.[1]

Efficient teachers are wasted if children stay away. Throughout 1922 nearly a quarter of all pupils were absent. The compulsory attendance provisions of the Act of 1923, the efforts of education committees and livelier public interest, combined to raise average attendance to 86 per cent. in 1938.[2]

This sharpened the accommodation problem. In the five years 1922–26 the effective school population rose by some 17,000, mainly because children attended more regularly. Since, however, the province had so many tiny schools, the clamant need was for fewer but larger ones in which pupils could be more exactly classified by ability and teachers could be employed more economically. From its inception the Ministry wherever possible amalgamated small schools. But only the education committees could undertake new building. Their achievement justified faith in local initiative. By 1939 they provided 188 new schools and substantially reconstructed many of the 479 transferred to them. At the same time, closing of small buildings reduced the total number by 315. In 1923 schools with an average attendance of 240 or more numbered 96; by 1938 there were 169. At the other end of the scale, schools with an average attendance of less than 50 fell from 998 to 791.

Here in hard if dreary figures is evidence of solid progress. Yet in many ways the record was disappointing. The volume of new building, though impressive at a time when money was scarce, fell far short of what was needed. None of the education committees provided nursery schools; their school medical services were inadequate; their scholarship awards were niggardly; they bought books and stationery for only one child in ten; and they did little to help feed or clothe needy children, who in rural areas often ate nothing but dry bread throughout the day.[3] Even the two county boroughs failed to establish special schools or classes for mental defectives. In these respects Northern Ireland was still a generation or more behind most of England and Wales.

[1] These and subsequent statistics are taken from the *Reports of the Ministry of Education* and from *Educational Reconstruction in Northern Ireland*, Cmd. 226 (1944).

[2] These figures relate to children of all ages. Average attendance by pupils of compulsory school age rose from 84 per cent. in 1925 (the first year for which there are statistics) to 88 per cent. in 1938.

[3] *Report of the Ministry of Education*, 1938–39, H.C. 483, p. 17.

There remained a more intractable problem. Most managers refused to transfer their schools or to accept 'four and two' committees. By the end of 1938 more than half of all elementary schools, with almost half the total number of pupils, were voluntary. Denominational control, and all it implied in Ulster, was still strongly entrenched. And voluntary schools seemed worse than ever when contrasted with new buildings under public control. True, grants under the Act of 1930 helped to build thirty-four voluntary schools and reconstruct another twenty-four, but hundreds in 1939 were no better, if not worse, than in 1919. In many cases, too, voluntary managers were unable to provide fuel or pay even half the wage of a caretaker.[1] So old, dirty and insanitary structures remained, monuments to the past and a challenge to the future.

Secondary education after 1921 was free from religious difficulties. Protestant and Roman Catholic governing bodies continued to manage their own grammar and other secondary schools (which were largely financed by fees), and there was no pressure to bring them directly under public control.[2] Other changes, however, were imperative. Only a few schools, like Belfast Royal Academical Institution and Ballymena Academy, could count their pupils in hundreds. Many were Lilliputian, with thirty or even fewer pupils, run for private profit by the head master or mistress or farmed out to the principal by boards of governors. Most girls' schools (with the notable exception of convents) were modified private houses, overcrowded, badly lit and with poor ventilation and sanitary accommodation[3]. Government grants were still largely based on examination results. Teachers had neither superannuation rights nor security of tenure; their salaries, which depended on private bargains struck with employers, were on average lower than in elementary schools; more than half of them lacked even a pass degree, and many had no satisfactory qualification at all. The Lynn Committee reported in 1922:

> We have been confronted with the fact, ascertained beyond all question, that unless the secondary schools are placed without delay in a position to obtain qualified teachers for the work which they are

[1] H.C. Deb. (N.I.), 30, c. 3468; Cmd. 226, pp. 9, 11.

[2] Local education authorities had power to provide new secondary schools and to accept the transfer of existing schools, but they were able to do little in this sphere.

[3] *Report of the Ministry of Education*, 1923–24, H.C. 54, p. 16.

expected to perform, they cannot escape decay, if not extinction. A few may, by greatly increasing their fees, manage to survive on a reduced scale, but they will be placed beyond the reach of any but the children of the wealthy, and higher education will cease to be a real part of a national and popular system. We cannot but look with dismay upon a condition of things which makes it almost impossible to obtain teachers for the schools and closes them to all but the rich, or renders it necessary for parents to send their children to England and Scotland for the education which cannot be obtained in the native atmosphere and among their own people.[1]

Three notable reforms followed. The jungle of grants was cleared: a capitation grant for each pupil ended payment by results, and salary increments paid by the State removed from governing bodies the temptation to replace experienced teachers by younger and cheaper ones. Grants expanded from £51,529 in 1921 to £194,608 in 1938. Secondly, as a condition of State aid, the Ministry insisted that all schools should be managed by governing bodies under approved schemes, that none should be run for private profit, and that the whole income of a school from every source should be devoted to it. Finally, governing bodies were to conform to approved salary scales and teachers were given superannuation rights and required to possess appropriate qualifications. These changes stimulated striking improvements in quantity and quality. The number of pupils aged 12–19 rose from 6,253 in 1921 to 11,540 in 1938, buildings were improved, teaching standards were raised, and the failure rate in public examinations instituted by the Ministry in 1925 was sharply reduced.

This progress made more conspicuous the need for further reforms, of which two were of special urgency. Most children entering secondary schools were too old; and the road to higher education remained effectively barred to offspring of poor parents. In England and Wales it was generally recognized after the Hadow Report of 1926 that there should be a definite break in a child's career at about eleven and that pupils above that age should be taught in separate schools, or at least in senior classes, with a curriculum suited to them. Many English authorities conformed to this principle. In Ulster, however, all-age schools giving elementary instruction were still the rule. It was therefore the more necessary that children destined for an academic curriculum should enter secondary schools as soon after eleven as possible. In fact,

[1] Cmd. 6, pp. 47–48.

most of them were far older. This, as the Ministry noted in 1936, imposed on teachers and pupils a well-nigh impossible task.[1] The root cause, no doubt, was parents' reluctance to transfer children from free elementary to fee-paying secondary schools. So large numbers of boys and girls were handicapped and frustrated.

Even larger numbers had no chance whatever of reaching full intellectual stature. The Lynn Committee had proposed a liberal scheme of scholarships. Higher education, they said, was no preserve for the well-to-do, but an absolute necessity if the State was to gather to its service the ability of citizens and secure to them their just claim for equal rights. The education authorities probably did their best with limited financial resources,[2] but in 1938 only 5 per cent. of pupils in secondary schools held scholarships. In England and Wales, 47 per cent. paid no fees, 5 per cent. had fees reduced, and about 18 per cent. got maintenance allowances,[3] which had no counterpart in Ulster at all. Poor children aspiring to enter university fared even worse. In 1938, when 1,036 pupils passed the Ministry's senior certificate examination, local authorities awarded 28 university scholarships. The average for the five years 1934–38 was 24. Indeed, over the whole field of secondary education, local authorities did relatively little, though they had ample powers. By 1938 they managed only 8 of the 76 recognized schools.

Progress after the war was stimulated by Britain. When, in July 1943, the Coalition Government published plans for education, they inspired a debate at Stormont during which the Government announced their intention to provide for a commensurate advance.[4] Ulster's White Paper of December 1944[5] prepared the ground for the Education Act (N.I.), 1947. Public education comprises, not three distinct streams—elementary, grammar and technical—but three progressive stages—primary, secondary and further education. It is the duty of local education authorities to contribute to the spiritual, moral, mental and physical development of the community by making available efficient education at

[1] Of children who went from elementary to secondary schools in 1936, less than 3 per cent. were younger than twelve. *Report of the Ministry of Education*, 1935–36, H.C. 383, p. 18.

[2] See *Report of Committee on the Scholarship System in Northern Ireland*, Cmd. 192 (1938).

[3] Political and Economic Planning, *Report on the British Social Services* (London, 1937), pp. 64–65.

[4] H.C. Deb. (N.I.), 26, c. 1761.

[5] Cmd. 226.

each stage. Primary education normally ends at eleven plus, after which age all pupils are to receive secondary education, either in a grammar school or in a secondary intermediate or technical intermediate school. Selection was by examination conducted by the Ministry until 1965, when the examination was replaced by a different method that gives more weight to teachers' assessments.[1]

Ulster's plans thus followed Britain's in broad content as well as timing, but the provincial Government did not intend merely to copy England. The new system had to be 'acceptable to all the different interests which have given service to the cause of education in the past and which must be allowed to play their part in the future'.[2] The ideal was to be married with the practicable.

The terms of such a union aroused acrimonious dispute about primary schools. It began in January 1945 when the White Paper was debated, simmered for nearly two years, came to boiling point when the Bill was considered from October 1946 to January 1947, and boiled over in December 1949, when the Minister of Education (Lt.-Col. S. H. Hall-Thompson), sacrificing himself in the interests of party unity, resigned.[3]

The argument turned principally on the three points that had caused the storm between 1923 and 1930: appointment of teachers, religious instruction and grants to voluntary schools.

The question of appointments was bound up with that of management. We have seen that in 1930 the Government entrenched former voluntary managers on school management committees and gave the latter a voice in selecting teachers. Neither Ministers nor some M.P.s were happy about this. Management committees were assailed as being undemocratic; and parochialism, in the intimate conditions of Ulster society, had consequences that seemed undesirable. There was scope for jobbery and conflict; prospective teachers had to canvass members of management

[1] For details see *Education in Northern Ireland*, 1963–64, Cmd. 476, p. 10.

[2] Cmd. 226, p. 14.

[3] Others besides Lt.-Col. Hall-Thompson found the Ministry of Education an uncomfortable place. His predecessor, Rev. Professor R. Corkey, and the Parliamentary Secretary of the Ministry, Mrs. D. Parker (later Dame Dehra Parker) resigned in 1944. Professor Corkey declared that difficulties had arisen over religious instruction in schools. See H.C. Deb. (N.I.), 27, cc. 259 ff.; Senate Deb., 27, cc. 53 ff.; statement by the Moderator of the General Assembly of the Presbyterian Church, *Belfast News-Letter*, 17 March 1944. Mrs. Parker said she had been vindictively attacked and her religious views had been questioned at a time when it was most important for the Ministry to secure the goodwill of education authorities, teachers and parents. *Belfast News-Letter*, 18 March 1944.

committees and education authorities; and serving teachers displaced from one school had no assurance of appointment in another. But the pre-war settlement could not be materially altered. The Minister declared that the Churches would regard any weakening of their representation on management committees as a breach of faith.[1] It was equally impracticable to confer power to appoint teachers on education authorities alone or (as many teachers wished) on an independent appointments board. The Government did propose in effect to make management committees solely responsible for appointments, but although that would have confined canvassing to members of one body, it was unacceptable to the Commons.[2] The old system thus remained virtually unimpaired[3] and teachers still found it advisable to tout for posts, even in areas like Belfast and Londonderry where the education authority forbade canvassing.[4] This has been widely and sharply criticized in recent years. On 18 March 1964 the Minister of Education (Mr. Ivan Neill) pointed out that canvassing could not be eliminated merely by making rules, but that he was making progress in persuading education authorities to abolish it.[5]

Plans for religious education were similar to those in the English Act of 1944. In every school there was to be collective worship and religious instruction, both undenominational except in voluntary schools, where managers held full sway. In addition, ministers of religion were permitted to inspect and examine religious instruction and also to give denominational teaching, subject to safeguards for parents and pupils.[6] All this, which went far beyond simple Bible teaching, aroused little opposition except among Roman Catholics, from whose viewpoint collective worship in a State school was denominational.

One further change, however, provoked fierce resistance from Protestants. By the Act of 1930 teachers in provided and transferred schools could be compelled to give Bible instruction.

[1] H.C. Deb. (N.I.), 30, c. 2782.

[2] ibid., cc. 2912–33.

[3] In order to give teachers security of tenure, local education authorities were enabled to transfer redundant teachers from one county school to another, and this power was extended by the Education (Amendment) Act (N.I.), 1963. The system of appointment described above applied to county primary and intermediate schools (formerly, provided and transferred schools), not to technical intermediate or grammar schools.

[4] *Belfast Telegraph*, 26 March 1957, 18 April 1963; H.C. Deb. (N.I.), 54, cc. 1528 et seq.

[5] ibid., 56, c. 1866.

[6] Education Act (N.I.), 1947, s. 21.

Compulsion, maintained the Attorney-General, was both *ultra vires* and illiberal. It was *ultra vires* because the Government of Ireland Act prohibited Parliament from restricting the free exercise of religion or from imposing any disability or disadvantage on account of religious belief. It was illiberal because coercion of a man's free spirit and conscience was contrary to that right of private judgment on which Protestantism itself stood.[1] The latter point alone might have been expected to command immediate assent in a community whose chief watchword is religious and civil liberty; but the Government's belated discovery that their legislation for some fifteen years had been unconstitutional, and their determination to protect tender consciences, provoked an almost fanatical campaign whose organizers threatened to wreck the Bill.[2] It was only after protracted conferences with representatives of the Churches and other interested bodies that the Government succeeded in carrying their point, though opposition continued up to the committee stage in December 1946.

These disputes were dwarfed by the controversy about voluntary schools, most of which were under Roman Catholic management. As we have seen, they received substantial help from public funds, including the whole cost of teachers' salaries and half the cost of running expenses and of new building and reconstruction. Yet the burden of raising the other half, already heavy before the war, would become crushing in the post-war world of inflated prices and larger and better schools. In the White Paper the Government therefore proposed to increase grants if managers would accept 'four and two' committees.[3] The condition, declared the Minister of Education, was fundamental; if it were rejected no extra help would be given.[4] The managers were unmoved. By the end of 1946, when only 52 out of the 959 voluntary schools were under statutory committees (provided and transferred schools then numbered 690), the Minister was obliged to admit that the attempt to build a bridge between the local authority and the voluntary manager had failed.[5] So, as in 1930, the Government were in a dilemma. If they withheld extra assistance many children would suffer; if they gave it, they would strengthen a system that could ultimately destroy Northern Ireland as a distinct political unit.

[1] H.C. Deb. (N.I.), 27, c. 2854.
[2] ibid., 30, c. 3102.
[3] Cmd. 226, pp. 26–27.
[4] H.C. Deb. (N.I.), 27, c. 2751.
[5] ibid., 30, c. 2011.

Their decision did credit to their hearts—and probably to their heads. Determined that 'an Ulster child should not go wet or cold or be educated in a hovel merely because his manager is standing gloriously on principle', the Minister proposed that voluntary primary and intermediate schools should get 65 per cent. grants both for new building and reconstruction and for maintenance, lighting, heating and cleaning. The Ministry, as always, would continue to pay teachers' salaries. The Bill also gave education authorities extensive obligations to provide, for schools of every sort, medical inspection and treatment, transport, milk and meals, books and other requisites—all free. In addition the education authority would be responsible for all running costs of a voluntary school if the managers consented to a statutory committee (on which, as before, they would be in the majority) to control and manage the school. The Minister was bitterly and indeed vindictively attacked: by Nationalists who, continuing to play Oliver Twist, demanded 100 per cent.,[1] and by Unionists who insisted that 'appeasement' of the Roman Catholic Church should stop.[2] But he carried his case, though without the goodwill, or even the support, of many of his party.[3] He had probably gone as far as he could within the limits of party unity.

By 1947 the Government therefore managed to put on the statute book provisions which, though wholly acceptable to few, were nevertheless reasonably equitable. Both Protestants and Catholics had the assurance of statutory worship and religious instruction and power to select teachers; teachers' consciences were protected; and voluntary schools would receive more public money—and more, incidentally, than in England[4]—without accepting any element of public representation in their management. But victory for Lt.-Col. Hall-Thompson's policy meant his personal defeat. On 14 December 1949 the Grand Orange Lodge of Ireland discussed education and it became known that the Minister was to resign.[5] Announcing this the following day, the

[1] ibid., c. 3328. [2] ibid., c. 3306.

[3] The critical division on 10 December 1946 was carried by a majority of nineteen to eight—twenty-seven votes in a House, excluding the Speaker, of fifty-one. Among those who voted against were Mr. J. M. Andrews, then Grand Master of the Orange Order and a former Prime Minister, and Mr. H. C. Midgley, who became Minister of Education in 1950. ibid., c. 3473.

[4] Grants to church schools in England and Wales stood at 50 per cent. until the Education Act, 1959 raised them to 75 per cent. In Northern Ireland the whole cost of teachers' salaries has always been borne on public funds.

[5] *Belfast News-Letter*, 15 December 1949.

Prime Minister promised to review the whole system.[1] Two years later the new Minister (Mr. H. C. Midgley) declared that consultations with all interests had convinced him that no fundamental changes were possible,[2] news that was received with calmness if not indifference. 'You never get to the bottom of this most perplexing and damnable country' said Mr. Asquith when he visited Ireland in 1917.

In the meantime the Ministry was immersed in the task of reconstruction. Weight of numbers alone constituted a formidable problem. Between 1947–48 (when the Education Act came into operation) and 1964, pupils in grant-aided schools increased from 213,211 to 295,855, mainly owing to the high birth-rate, the tendency of pupils to stay longer in secondary (and especially grammar) schools, and the raising of the school leaving age to fifteen, which had to be put off until 1957.[3] But the task was not merely quantitative. To fulfil the promise of the Act of 1947, new types of teachers and schools were needed, not only in the right areas, but in proportions that would allow both local authorities and boards of governors and managers of various voluntary schools to make their proper contribution.

Success in teacher-training was remarkable. Expansion of existing colleges and provision of new ones[4] made it possible from 1947 to 1964 to increase the teaching force in primary and intermediate schools by two-thirds, to a total of 8,890. At the same time, training was remodelled to provide specialists for the new intermediate schools. In 1948 the course for primary teachers was lengthened from two to three years. A similar change in England, recommended by the McNair Committee in 1944, was deferred until 1960.

Building of county schools (the new name for all local authority schools except nursery and special schools) and of voluntary schools began slowly. The Act of 1947 required each local education authority to draw up a comprehensive development scheme for its area, and this task was complicated by the extensive duplication of county and voluntary schools and the need to consult

[1] H.C. Deb. (N.I.), 33, c. 2276.

[2] ibid., 35, c. 345.

[3] The Government have announced that the school leaving age will be raised to sixteen not later than 1970.

[4] The Ministry provided the Ulster College of Physical Education at Jordanstown, co. Antrim, in 1953. St. Joseph's Training College, a voluntary college under Roman Catholic management for men students, was opened in 1961.

different interests. Nevertheless, between 1947 and 1964, 250 new primary schools and 210 major extensions were built, giving places for more than 60,000 pupils at a cost of some £10 m. Here, in place of squalid hovels, were palaces of light sweetened in rural areas by water-borne sewerage. The policy of closing small and antiquated buildings also continued. Primary schools fell in number from 1,635 in 1948 to 1,463 in 1964, but in the latter year there were still 742 with only one or two teachers. The original development schemes showed that about 190 secondary intermediate schools (100 county and 90 voluntary) would be wanted. By 1964 there were 76 county schools and 53 under voluntary management, almost every one of them specially designed and built since the Act of 1947.

Political wisdom was of greater immediate importance than new building so far as grammar and cognate secondary schools were concerned. In 1947 only 10 were managed by local authorities and 67 were voluntary. Full use of the latter was obviously essential if pupils were to receive an academic education. While, however, the voluntary schools (like 'direct grant' English schools) got some State financial aid, their income from fees and in some cases endowments enabled them to keep a valued tradition of independence; and the Government were in no doubt that any attempt to transfer them to public control and abolish fees altogether would encounter strenuous resistance, if not withdrawal from the State system. The problem of finding places for qualified children would then be intensified, class distinction among grammar schools (hitherto virtually absent) would appear, and deeply-rooted traditions would perish. Moreover, to reserve every school place for qualified pupils would encourage wealthy parents to send unqualified children to English public schools, which have no exact counterparts in Ulster, instead of educating them in their native land.[1]

These misfortunes were avoided by compromise. It was agreed that governors of voluntary schools would reserve up to 80 per cent. of their places for qualified pupils (whose fees were covered by local authority scholarships) and that they would be allowed to fill the other 20 per cent. with fee-paying pupils.[2] The continued

[1] H.C. Deb. (N.I.), 30, cc. 2359, 3210.

[2] This had subsequently to be modified. In 1950 voluntary grammar schools were divided into two groups. Group A schools must keep for qualified pupils at least 80 per cent. of their places, they charge tuition fees (defrayed by scholarships in the case of qualified pupils) and claim capitation and salary grants from

co-operation of existing schools (52 of which underwent major extensions) and the building of 20 new ones made it possible to double the number of pupils, from 17,178 to 36,178, between 1948 and 1964. There were then 22 county and 59 voluntary schools, about half of the latter being under Protestant and half under Roman Catholic management. There were also 5,290 boys and girls in grammar school preparatory departments, which are another distinctive feature of Ulster's educational system. Preparatory departments receive grants from the Ministry, charge fees, and offer an alternative to the primary schools. The Government have resisted demands to deprive parents of the opportunity to spend money on education, and the general arguments for freedom in this sphere have special force in Northern Ireland, as we have already indicated. Whether such parents should be subsidized by the State is, however, a question that has aroused lively argument in recent years.

An examination of other aspects of education and ancillary services would reveal prodigious progress by pre-war standards. Free books and materials, meals and milk, medical and dental inspection and treatment, special provision for handicapped children, nursery schools, transport, scholarships and further education—all these, so conspicuously neglected in the past, are now provided.

Imperfections still remain, and new problems are replacing old ones. Both these themes were developed in a White Paper in 1964.[1] The worst blemish was the continued existence of small and outworn primary schools in rural areas and of large classes elsewhere. Defects of this sort will without doubt be made good within a measurable period of time if ratepayers are prepared to play their part.

The most serious problem concerned the future organization of secondary education. Should a single comprehensive school

---

the Ministry, but cannot use the tuition account for capital expenditure. This is met from a capital fee payable by parents and from a 65 per cent. grant. Group B schools need not reserve places for qualified pupils, their fees generally exceed the value of scholarships (the difference being payable by parents), and they get capitation and salary grants but no capital grant. At the outset 29 schools opted for Group A and 35 for B. By 1964 there were 49 Group A schools, 10 Group B schools and 22 county schools under the management of local education authorities.

[1] *Educational Development in Northern Ireland*, 1964, Cmd. 470 (1964).

replace the separate grammar and intermediate schools within a specified area? In discussing this, the Ministry pointed to two special considerations. First, virtually all intermediate and many grammar schools were new, but hardly any would accommodate the very large enrolment required for a comprehensive school. Second, the imposition of a comprehensive system could mean secession by some voluntary grammar schools, which might rely on greatly increased fees to maintain their independence. The Government would then have created the sort of social cleavage in education which they were at pains to avoid in 1947. For these and other reasons, the Ministry concluded that instead of trying to impose a rigid comprehensive system, it would be better to evolve non-selective secondary education gradually and by common consent. To this end, it proposed to narrow the differences between grammar and intermediate schools (e.g. by restyling the latter 'secondary schools' and removing disparities in staffing) and to encourage local variety and experiment with the aim of dispensing with the need to select pupils for different types of school. This pragmatic approach will no doubt amplify the features that already distinguish secondary education in Northern Ireland.

From the present writer's standpoint it seems that the Government's long-term policy has in general been resplendently successful. In only one respect must it be admitted to have failed. Lord Londonderry in 1923 set out, not only to improve the standard of education, but to make it a cohesive force under public control. The authorities of the Roman Catholic Church, however, have steadfastly declined to transfer their schools or even for the most part to accept statutory committees of management. Almost half of all primary school pupils are educated in Catholic voluntary schools.[1] It is less the nature of this problem (which is common to

[1] Pupils on rolls of primary schools, January 1964:

	Roman Catholic	*Other denominations*	*Total*
County schools	837	96,673	97,510
Voluntary schools under 'four and two' committees	905	3,424	4,329
Voluntary schools not under 'four and two' committees	87,439	987	88,426
	89,181	101,084	190,265

many countries) than its scale in the peculiar conditions of Ireland that has given rise among many Protestants to nagging doubts. Both before and after the war the voluntary schools were treated better than in England. Ruthless measures might conceivably have weakened them. The Government of Northern Ireland have acted in the faith that generosity does not evoke intransigence.

CHAPTER SEVEN

Health Services

HEALTH services inherited by Northern Ireland in 1921 consisted for the most part of four layers deposited over a period of some seventy years. The first, an offshoot of the poor law, dated from 1851, when poor law unions were divided into dispensary districts in which guardians of the poor were required to employ dispensary medical officers and midwives to minister to the destitute and indigent.[1] To the poor law, also, Ireland owed most of her hospitals: 159 of the 200 public general hospitals at the beginning of the twentieth century were workhouse infirmaries. Enterprise and charity had given the province of Ulster a number of private hospitals, but in each of the counties of Armagh, Cavan, Fermanagh, Monaghan and Tyrone the only hospital apart from workhouses was a county infirmary.[2]

The second layer, comprising public health (or environmental) services, began with the Irish Public Health Act of 1878, which used the poor law machinery to try to secure a minimum standard of sanitation in town and country. Cities and towns became urban sanitary districts under urban sanitary authorities, and poor law unions (except any part within an urban district) were made rural sanitary districts under the guardians as rural sanitary authorities. Both urban and rural authorities employed the poor law dispensary doctors as part-time medical officers of health,[3] and the guardians appointed their clerks of unions as executive sanitary officers and their relieving officers as sanitary sub-officers. Twenty years later, in 1898, these sanitary districts became urban and rural districts with elected councils,[4] but in rural districts the council and the board of guardians consisted of the same persons,[5]

[1] T. A. Mooney, *Compendium of the Irish Poor Law* (Dublin, 1887).

[2] *Appendix to Report of the Vice-Regal Commission on Poor Law Reform in Ireland*, U.K. Cd. 3203 (1906), Table 25.

[3] Dublin, Belfast and other large cities were required to appoint medical superintendent officers of health.

[4] G. T. B. Vanston, *The Law Relating to Local Government in Ireland* (Dublin, 1899), vol. i.

[5] Councillors and guardians in urban districts were separately elected, the urban guardians being added to the rural district councillors to form the board of guardians for the union.

and the system of part-time and unqualified officers remained intact.

The third layer was national health insurance. The National Insurance Act, 1911 began a scheme by which insured persons could receive, through approved insurance societies, sickness benefit (money payments during illness) and medical attention from a panel doctor. The Act extended to Ireland except in respect of medical benefit. So although Irishmen could claim money whenever they were certified as being too ill to work, they got no medical treatment (except through the poor law dispensary service) unless they paid for it themselves.

The last layer comprised special services created after 1898, in which year Ireland was given elective county, county borough, urban and rural district councils. The host of functions conferred on these authorities included prevention and treatment of tuberculosis, maternity and child welfare, medical inspection and treatment and feeding of schoolchildren, and supervision of midwives.[1]

So much for the bare bones of a system which, though complex, was conspicuously defective in at least two respects. First, none of the special services was properly developed. When Northern Ireland was established, 25 of the 64 county borough and district councils had taken no measures to prevent tuberculosis, 38 did nothing about maternity and child welfare, only one authority had begun to feed needy schoolchildren, and only one had arrangements (which were not fully operative) for their medical inspection.[2] Secondly, the administrative structure lacked coherence. Since the part-time medical officers of health depended mainly on fees from private patients, their private interest could easily conflict with the public interest. Neither they nor sanitary sub-officers were required to possess special qualifications in public health. The very ubiquity of the poor law dispensaries did not encourage local councils to develop their own services—why duplicate the work of dispensary doctors and midwives?—and, there being no single health authority in the counties nor any ministry of health for Ireland as a whole, responsibility was diffused and weak.

As in other directions, governments did not lack advice from distinguished citizens. In 1906 the Vice-Regal Commission on

[1] For details and a general historical summary see *Report of Departmental Commission on Local Government Administration in Northern Ireland*, Cmd. 73 (1927).

[2] *Report on the Administration of Local Government Services*, 1921–23, Cmd. 30 (1924), pp. 36–43.

Poor Law Reform, supported by the Irish Committee of the British Medical Association, advocated a State medical service and the remodelling of the hospital system.[1] In 1909 the Royal Commission on the Poor Laws proposed the appointment of whole-time county medical officers of health.[2] In 1913 the Irish Milk Commission showed how tubercular milk and infected meat could easily be offered for sale, and how the efforts of such progressive towns as Belfast and Bangor (co. Down) were nullified by rural inertia and the administrative structure. Summarizing evidence given before them, the Commission said:

> It is complained both in the case of the medical officer and the veterinary inspector that local influence and dependence on persons who may at the same time be clients and district councillors, make the efficient discharge of public duty by the professional officer extremely difficult.[3]

In 1920 (the year after the creation of the English Ministry of Health) the Irish Public Health Council tersely declared that 'reforms are urgently needed'.[4] They recommended an Irish ministry of health, the unification in each county and county borough of hospital, medical and public health services, and the creation of a system, dissociated from the poor law, to give both insured and needy persons medical, hospital and specialist treatment. This Report had even less chance of acceptance than the others. In the circumstances of 1920 there was never the slightest possibility that its ideas would come to life in undivided Ireland.

In 1921 the people of Northern Ireland were therefore poorly provided for. Indeed, judging by mortality rates, their health was worse than anywhere else in the British Isles.[5] Yet their average

[1] *Report of the Vice-Regal Commission on Poor Law Reform in Ireland*, U.K. Cd. 3202 (1906), pp. 18–34.

[2] *Royal Commission on the Poor Laws: Report on Ireland*, U.K. Cd. 4630 (1909), p. 65.

[3] *Final Report of the Irish Milk Commission*, U.K. Cd. 7129 (1913), p. 59.

[4] *Report of the Irish Public Health Council on the Public Health and Medical Services in Ireland*, U.K. Cmd. 761 (1920), p. 3.

[5] Death-rates per 1,000 population (three-year averages):

	1922–24	*1936–38*
England and Wales	12·2	12·0
Scotland	14·1	13·3
Eire	14·6	14·4
Northern Ireland	15·5	14·4

Statistics of mortality in this chapter are taken from the *Reports on Health and Local Government Administration in Northern Ireland* and the Northern Ireland *Registrar General's Annual Reports*. All death-rates are crude rates.

age was little more than thirty and half of them (49·2 per cent. at the first census in 1926) lived in rural areas.

Ministers had no illusions about this. As we have seen, the Prime Minister began his career with glittering ambitions; and the first Minister of Home Affairs, Sir Dawson Bates (who was responsible for all local government services as well as lunatic asylums, reformatories, prisons, police and the administration of justice) showed in his early speeches how anxious he was to inaugurate reform. In April 1924 he appointed a Departmental Commission[1] whose thirty-six members explored the labyrinth of local government for three years, until September 1927. Their proposals would have transformed Ulster's health. All personal health services in each county were to be administered by one committee employing a medical officer and other qualified staff; there were to be new and improved hospitals and better treatment for mothers and children; boards of guardians were to be abolished, workhouses were to be closed, and their inmates (who fell mainly into the categories of sick and infirm, old and young, and lunatics, idiots and epileptics) were to go to more suitable institutions. There would, however, be little point in trying to summarize fully the Commission's 153 recommendations, for in the financial climate after 1925 there was little prospect of their being realized. When, in May 1928, the Minister first referred to the Report, he made it clear that reform was no longer to be expected.[2] It became quite impossible in 1930 when derating transferred to the Exchequer the greater part of the burden of rates in rural areas.[3] The Government finally announced in 1932 that they intended to make no comprehensive changes.[4]

The basic structure was therefore unaltered. The only medical officers of health outside Belfast and Londonderry were doctors in private practice whom guardians appointed as poor law dispensary medical officers and who also acted in other capacities—as registrars of births, marriages and deaths, public vaccinators and school and police medical officers. Sanitary sub-officers in urban areas were often unqualified persons who filled such posts as those of water inspector, town inspector and clerk of markets, while in rural districts they collected the rents of council cottages and were employed as poor law relieving officers. It was a cheap system. A dispensary doctor's salary before the war averaged about £220 a year,

[1] Cmd. 73.
[2] H.C. Deb. (N.I.), 9, c. 1763.
[3] ibid., 13, c. 28.
[4] ibid., 15, c. 7.

to which was added £15 to £20 for his work as medical officer of health. But his remuneration was so low that to look for efficient service was to expect a good deal of human nature; he was required to possess no special qualification; his recommendations could be ignored because administrative areas were so small, local relations were so intimate and local influence was so strong; and (as already noted) his duty and interest could conflict whenever the question arose of condemning property owned by private patients.[1]

General sanitary conditions were therefore reminiscent more of medieval than modern times. Throughout the countryside there was no public service for collecting and disposing of refuse, which was dumped indiscriminately on waste ground and along river banks.[2] Rivers and tidal waters were polluted with industrial waste and sewage: Belfast Lough received crude sewage from Carrickfergus, Holywood and other places,[3] and in Omagh, the principal town of co. Tyrone, sewage went straight into a river that was liable to overflow its banks through flooding.[4]

Effective sewage disposal was impossible without piped water. Here, Belfast at least was fortunate. The enterprise and foresight of Belfast City and District Water Commissioners (established in 1840) gave the city and many adjacent areas abundant pure water from the Mourne Mountains. Londonderry, the second largest city, avoided water shortage only at ruinous cost. The city's heavy capital expenditure but low rateable valuation, together with scant Exchequer assistance, drove the rates to such heights that the drive for economy made it the dirtiest place of any size in Ulster.[5] Most other urban centres were too small to be independent water authorities. Twenty-five of the thirty-three boroughs and urban districts in 1937 had fewer than 10,000 inhabitants, but only four

[1] On the whole system see *Report of the Select Committee on Health Services in Northern Ireland*, H.C. 601 (1944).

[2] *Report on Health and Local Government Administration*, 1947–49, Cmd. 288 (1951), p. 118.

[3] H.C. 601, Minutes of Evidence, pp. 182, 708 and 56th day; *Report on the Administration of Local Government Services*, 1930–31, Cmd. 137 (1932), p. 73.

[4] *Belfast News-Letter*, 7 January 1936.

[5] In Londonderry (population 47,804 in 1937) capital expenditure for water supply from 1923 to 1934 totalled £421,241, against £211,090 for all boroughs and urban districts (combined population 191,647). The service of the debt was mainly responsible for driving rates in Londonderry from 13*s*. in 1923 to 19*s*. 6*d*. in 1934. In the latter year the Belfast rate (including water) stood at 13*s*. 5*d*., and in all boroughs and urban districts it averaged 12*s*. 5*d*. On sanitary conditions in Londonderry, see H.C. 601, p. 73, and Minutes of Evidence, 3rd day.

pooled resources to form joint water boards.[1] In some cases pipes supplying one town were laid through another whose own water came from a different source. Four towns with a population of over 1,000 had no piped water and many more lacked adequate sewerage. Rural districts were far worse off. Of the 109 communities with 250 to 1,000 inhabitants, the great majority had neither piped water nor sewers, and almost all country dwellers tolerated constant drudgery and occasional danger to health by using well water.[2]

Among other aspects of public health, the prevalence of impure food was probably most serious. District councils had ample powers to regulate the production and sale of food, both to safeguard health in general and to prevent tuberculosis in particular, but some of them neglected even the compulsory duty of milk supervision. Notified cases of typhoid fever, many of them traced to farms, rose from 70 in 1922 to 378 in 1930,[3] and in 1923 a leading citizen of Belfast (Sir Crawford McCullagh) said that 20 per cent. of cows slaughtered in the Corporation's abattoir were infected with tuberculosis.[4] The Ministry's own Reports after 1921 dwelt constantly on this problem; Belfast Corporation sought authority by private Bill to inspect sources of meat and milk outside the city;[5] and other progressive councils pressed for powers to supervise dairies outside their boundaries.

None of these expedients was ideal (for to dam the flow of dirty milk to one town would merely divert more to others) and none was successful. Instead the Ministry pursued a protracted campaign of inspection (by its own itinerant medical inspectors), admonition and occasional compulsion, and in 1929 it insisted that sanitary sub-officers in towns should be qualified.[6] Systematic

[1] Portadown and Banbridge in 1902 and Coleraine and Portstewart in 1933.

[2] *Report on the Problems of Water Supply and Sewerage in Northern Ireland*, Cmd. 223 (1944); *Report on the Administration of Local Government Services*, 1932–33, Cmd. 157 (1933), p. 48.

[3] These and subsequent figures relating to public health between the wars are taken, unless otherwise stated, from the *Reports on the Administration of Local Government Services*.

[4] H.C. Deb. (N.I.), 3, c. 222.

[5] ibid., c. 218.

[6] Sanitary sub-officers in urban districts with more than 4,000 inhabitants were required to possess the sanitary inspector's certificate of the Royal Sanitary Institute or an equivalent qualification. S.R. & O. (N.I.), 1929, No. 19. In rural districts the practice of employing relieving officers as sanitary sub-officers, inspectors of dairies and collectors of rents was made compulsory in 1933 after one council had tried to break away from it. S.R. & O. (N.I.), 1933, No. 121.

inspection of meat and milk outside a few large towns was still rare in 1931.[1] In the thirties, however, improvement in agricultural produce followed vigorous efforts by the Ministry of Agriculture to ensure that exports to Britain, the principal market, should conform to high standards. A variety of measures, including employment of whole-time veterinary officers, established the reputation of Ulster produce and incidentally afforded more protection to local consumers. But inspection of meat for sale remained patchy in urban districts and virtually non-existent in rural areas.[2]

In the personal health services one notable development was the restriction of the scope of the poor law. Boards of guardians, exercising powers they had possessed since 1898, converted several union infirmaries into district hospitals to which fee-paying patients could be admitted. The number of district hospitals rose from one in 1921 to eleven in 1933.[3] After 1930 the Government could not afford to welcome this, for derating shifted a large part of local rates to the provincial Exchequer. The Minister of Home Affairs, referring to proposals to create more district hospitals, said in 1934:

> An increase in local expenditure involves an increase in the Government derating grant, and it is therefore apparent that from the Government as well as from the local point of view it is essential that extravagant expenditure on any service should be avoided.[4]

Only one more district hospital was opened before the war.[5] There then remained twelve unconverted union infirmaries which, with the twelve district hospitals, six county infirmaries and a few voluntary institutions, comprised all the general hospitals. Their quality and geographical distribution were alike uneven. Fourteen of the thirty public hospitals and all the voluntary hospitals save one were in Belfast and the counties of Antrim and Down. The whole of co. Fermanagh had no provision for general hospital treatment outside the poor law, apart from one county infirmary; Armagh and Tyrone were better off to the extent of a

[1] Cmd. 137, p. 73.

[2] *Report on the Administration of Local Government Services*, 1936–37, Cmd. 190 (1938), p. 52.

[3] Six of these were in co. Antrim, three in co. Down, one in co. Londonderry and one in co. Tyrone.

[4] H.C. Deb. (N.I.), 16, c. 1577.

[5] In Lurgan (co. Armagh) in 1938.

district hospital each; and the citizens of Londonderry who wished to avoid the workhouse had to rely on a small county infirmary that served Londonderry county also.[1] Even so, people were reluctant to use union infirmaries. Mortality in them was high,[2] their structure and equipment were antiquated (some being lit by oil lamps or gas), and as the Minister himself said in 1937 many were 'managed by indifferent nurses and had the services of one part-time medical attendant who in no sense could be called a surgeon'.[3]

The poor law's scope was further restricted by the introduction in 1930 of national health insurance medical benefit which, as we have explained, was originally withheld from Ireland. Britain herself pressed Northern Ireland to come into line because she wished to ratify international health conventions for the whole United Kingdom.[4] Of greater practical importance was the fact that health insurance in Ulster was administered through United Kingdom societies.[5] Whereas, however, in Britain insured persons were entitled to cash payments during sickness and to attention from a panel doctor, in Ulster they could get the cash by producing a certificate, but not the treatment. The consequent untreated illness and opportunity for fraud[6] drove the cost of sickness and disablement benefit from £308,200 in 1923 to £624,000 in 1927, and the approved societies gave notice that they could not continue to operate unless conditions were changed. So in 1930 Stormont

[1] *Report on Health and Local Government Administration*, 1938–46, Cmd. 258 (1948), p. 17.

[2] Deaths in poor law institutions in 1938 totalled 2,317, equal to 13 per cent. of all deaths in Northern Ireland and nearly three times greater than the 832 deaths in the twelve district hospitals.

[3] H.C. Deb. (N.I.), 19, c. 988. See also L. Kidd, 'Public Health Administration in Northern Ireland', *British Medical Journal*, 1938, vol. ii, Supplement, p. 245.

[4] H.C. Deb. (N.I.), 12, c. 1355.

[5] Two-thirds of the insured population were members of United Kingdom societies. *Report of Inter-Departmental Committee on Medical Benefit in Northern Ireland*, Cmd. 113 (1930), p. 4.

[6] An applicant for sickness benefit required a doctor's certificate to support his claim. If he found it hard to convince one doctor that he needed a certificate, he could visit as many more as he chose in the hope of eventually getting the coveted bit of paper from an 'easy certifier', while a doctor could earn substantial sums merely for issuing certificates. The separation of medical attention from certification thus provided both stimulus and opportunity for fraud. When in 1927 the Ministry of Labour inaugurated a medical referee service, it found that abuses were not uncommon. Of 25,210 cases referred to the referees in 1928, only 42 per cent. were judged unfit for work; the rest were considered fit or abandoned their claim. See H.C. 601, Minutes of Evidence, 33rd day.

brought in medical benefit.[1] The measure affected more than half of all patients treated by poor law medical officers.[2] Yet so great was the demand for treatment that the number of poor law cases in the thirties exceeded that in the twenties.[3]

The special services, whose progress must now be summarized, were prevention and treatment of tuberculosis, maternity and child welfare and school medical and mental health services. Tuberculosis had long been such a scourge in Ireland that the first measure in the United Kingdom to provide specially for its treatment was the Tuberculosis (Ireland) Act, 1908. Yet in Ulster efforts to stamp out the disease still offered the greatest scope for reducing mortality during the early adult period of life. In 1938 tuberculous diseases caused 46 per cent. of all deaths between the ages of 15 and 25 and 38 per cent. of those between 25 and 35. The figures afford a striking example of incoherence in public administration. The death of a young parent could impoverish the family, making it not only a prey to further infection but a charge on public funds; and it made no sense to spend large sums on education if the citizen were to die while memories of schooldays were green.

Local authorities did make some progress,[4] but the Ministry damned their efforts with faint praise by reporting in 1937 that their schemes were 'well administered as far as they go'.[5] They did not go far enough because preventive measures were inadequate and facilities for treatment were meagre. We cannot review in a few words the myriad aspects of prevention, but one point can be put into figures. Notification of cases of infectious tuberculosis, though made compulsory in 1934,[6] was virtually ignored outside Belfast and Londonderry.[7] 'So many people had

[1] National Health Insurance Act (N.I.), 1930.

[2] Cmd. 113, p. 9.

[3] New cases attended and registered rose from 115,542 in 1922 to 182,917 in 1929, fell slightly from 1930 to 1932, and thereafter rose to 183,977 in 1938.

[4] Death-rates from tuberculosis per 100,000 population (three year averages):

	1922–24	*1936–38*
England and Wales	108	66
Scotland	118	72
Eire	151	116
Northern Ireland	164	98

[5] Cmd. 190, p. 53.

[6] Local Government Act (N.I.), 1934, s. 33 (1).

[7] In the three years 1936–38 the annual average of deaths from tuberculosis was 1,248 and of notified cases 597, of which 535 were in Belfast and Londonderry.

to be notified', testified a dispensary medical officer in 1943, 'that it became a dead letter.'[1] As for treatment, not until 1930 were schemes in operation in every county and county borough, and even then premises were often unsuitable. Three of the eight counties and county boroughs provided sanatoria with a total of 375 beds in 1923. No more public sanatoria were brought into use between the wars, and the number of beds, though slightly augmented, remained pitifully small.

In the maternity service neglect was far more conspicuous. Ulsterwomen in 1938 ran a greater risk of dying in childbirth than 15 years before,[2] though an expert committee reported in 1939 that at least half of all deaths were preventable.[3] This record is attributable in the main to want of money and bad administration. Boards of guardians provided rudimentary facilities for the poor, and employed before the war 168 medical officers and 139 midwives. District councils had more extensive (though permissive) powers, but the existence of the poor law discouraged them from doing very much. Moreover, the Government failed to make 50 per cent. grants. The Treasury was already restricting grants in 1920, the Ministry of Finance continued to do so, despite a battle with Home Affairs in 1930,[4] and the latter reported in 1937 that for financial reasons schemes had never been properly developed.[5] So both in Belfast (where the infant mortality rate in the five years 1934–38 averaged 97, against 77 for Northern Ireland) and in the country as a whole the poor law remained the core of a maternity service.[6] Not that paupers, or those who ministered to them, were fortunate. A high proportion of infants who died—perhaps one in

[1] H.C. 601, p. 220.

[2] Maternal and infant mortality rates per 1,000 live births (three-year averages):

	Maternal mortality		*Infant mortality*	
	1922–24	*1936–38*	*1922–24*	*1936–38*
England and Wales .	3·8	3·6	77	57
Scotland . .	6·3	5·1	93	77
Eire . . .	5·1	4·1	69	71
Northern Ireland .	4·7	5·5	79	76

[3] *Report of Maternity Services Committee*, Cmd. 219 (1943). This Committee, appointed in 1936, reported in 1939.

[4] P.A.C. 1930–31, H.C. 267, pp. 8, 51 et seq.

[5] Cmd. 190, p. 56.

[6] 'Generally speaking,' reported the Maternity Services Committee, 'for the whole of the population above the status of pauper, midwifery provision in its broader sense is a private matter.'

every four—perished in the workhouse.[1] And dispensary midwives were so overworked and underpaid (their total income, including fees from private patients, ranged from £52 to £92 a year) that the chairman of the Maternity Services Committee cited them as the greatest example of sweated labour he had ever known.[2]

The school medical service began in 1923, when the Education Act and subsequent regulations[3] made it the duty of education authorities to employ school medical officers, dentists and nurses. County councils were permitted to delegate their functions to regional committees. Three did so, and the service became the responsibility of sixteen different bodies. Progress outside Belfast, where a scheme was started in June 1923, was slow and uneven. Several bodies failed for years to discharge their statutory duty despite reminders by the Ministry, while others engaged as school nurses the dispensary midwives and as medical officers the dispensary doctors. In 1931 (seven years after the regulations were made), four regional committees relied on dispensary doctors, in three other areas the medical officers were part-time, in two others there was no medical officer at all, and eight committees employed no dentist, either whole-time or part-time. During the next seven years more progress was made, but the Ministry noted in 1938 that schemes had not been developed in any area and that many children did not get the attention they needed or had to wait too long for it because of limited facilities.[4]

[1] The *Registrar General's Annual Reports* give deaths of children by calendar years but not the number in institutions. The *Reports on Local Government Services* give deaths in workhouses for years ending 31 March. Putting both sources together, we get the following table:

Age	*Total deaths, 1937 and 1938 (average)*	*Deaths in workhouses, year ended 31 March 1938*
Under 1 year . .	1,951	516
1 to 5 years . .	693	196
5 to 15 years . .	404	83
	3,048	795

Some pauper deaths may have occurred in district hospitals, but the number cannot have been large. There were 54 paupers in extern hospitals on the last Saturday in March 1938, and throughout that year the average daily number in all extern institutions was 135.

[2] H.C. 601, p. 615.

[3] S.R. & O. (N.I.), 1924, No. 71.

[4] *Report on the Administration of Local Government Services*, 1937–38, Cmd. 200 (1938), p. 51.

School medical inspections in 1937 showed that 752 children (almost 1 per cent. of those examined) were mentally backward or defective. There are no statistics to indicate the incidence of arrested or incomplete mental development among the whole population, but in 1943 a medical inspector of the Ministry put the number of mental defectives at up to 10,000, of whom perhaps 3,000 needed institutional care.[1] Yet Northern Ireland had neither an institution for these afflicted persons nor any legal provision for their welfare.[2] Local education authorities were, indeed, required by statute to ascertain which schoolchildren were mentally defective and to provide suitable instruction for those who were educable.[3] Even in Belfast the duty was virtually ignored.[4] A few children were sent to special institutions in Eire, but most attended ordinary schools or stayed at home. Those above school age were left to relatives or to join the rag-bag of humanity in workhouses or to find their way into industrial schools, prisons and mental hospitals.[5] The proper function of the latter was to treat mental illness. Here some advance was made. Lunatic asylums were renamed public mental hospitals in 1932, and a more enlightened code enabled voluntary and temporary patients to enter them.[6] But lack of money checked material reforms. Government grants between the wars were fixed at the 1918–20 level, though the number of patients rose substantially. Only one hospital (at Purdysburn, Belfast) had adequate facilities for the proper grading of patients, and some were so antiquated (the oldest, in Londonderry, was built in 1824) that the Select Committee on Health Services reported in 1944 that the health and possible cure of patients had been adversely affected.[7]

To sum up: by and large, Ulster's health services were mediocre by British standards. Mortality was high and no doubt would have been higher had not almost half the population been scattered in rural areas. British administration before 1920 and financial stringency thereafter were mainly to blame. There can be no doubt that the Minister of Home Affairs was speaking from bitter experience when in 1942 he said, 'On every conceivable oppor-

[1] H.C. 601, pp. 416–17.
[2] Cmd. 258, p. 64.
[3] Education Act (N.I.), 1923, Part IX.
[4] The Ministry of Education opened a special school for educable mental defectives in Belfast in 1936, but enrolment was small.
[5] H.C. 601, p. 50; Minutes of Evidence, 21st day.
[6] Mental Treatment Act (N.I.), 1932.
[7] H.C. 601, p. 52.

tunity [*sic*] I have had friendly fights with the Ministry of Finance. I received any amount of sympathy but the whole difficulty was finance.'[1] Health was a Cinderella. And public opinion—such as it was—was indifferent to her plight because the Administration was designed neither to focus attention on the health services as a whole nor to stimulate debate about piecemeal change. For one thing, responsibility was divided among the Ministries of Home Affairs, Labour (national health insurance and health in factories), Education (the school medical service) and Agriculture (the milk scheme and the Diseases of Animals Acts). For another, the functions of the Ministry of Home Affairs were ill assorted. Political debate rarely rose far above the level at which the foundations of the State were assailed and defended, yet the Minister was responsible both for health and for public order and justice. Nationalists too often ignored the first subject and seized on the others when Estimates were debated. Common needs and interests were submerged in the most bitter party warfare.

As indicated in Chapter Four, public interest in health services came alive during the war. In this period Mr. J. M. Andrews (then Prime Minister) secured Britain's agreement that past neglect could be remedied. Thereafter local inquiries, notably by the Select Committee on Health Services, threw so bright a light into dark corners that (as a member of the Committee said), 'Some of the evidence was so bad that we had to stop it and ask the Minister of Home Affairs to take action.'[2] The Committee found the chief administrative defect to be the want of a single authority responsible to Parliament, and they proposed the immediate creation of a Ministry of Health. Their other conclusions were in many respects similar to those of the Departmental Commission of 1927—and, indeed, to those of inquiries in Ireland before 1921. Thus, one medical officer was to be charged with oversight of all health services in each county, the post of medical officer of health was to be dissociated from that of dispensary doctor, the maternity service was to be separated from the poor law, adequate standards of sanitary inspection were to be enforced, and specific services were to be improved.

Another body (the Hospitals Council) proposed that for hospital administration Ulster should constitute a single region under a central hospital board appointed by the Minister. The

[1] H.C. Deb. (N.I.), 25, c. 3191. [2] ibid., 31, c. 1754.

focal point would be the teaching hospitals in Belfast, the rest of the country being divided into catchment areas, each with a hospital able to undertake all but the most difficult and specialized cases. A Committee on Water Supply and Sewerage proposed in effect to extend local authority joint boards throughout the country outside Belfast by the creation of four regional authorities large enough to employ competent technical staff and secure other economies of scale.

In June 1944 the Government took the first and most important step to realize these aims. A new Ministry of Health and Local Government was given all the health functions of Home Affairs and other departments.[1] Free from financial worries and directed by an energetic Minister (Mr. William Grant, a former shipyard worker), the new Department set to work like a new broom to sweep the country clean. In a rapid transformation, effected for the most part by three statutes in 1946 and 1948,[2] the administrative debris of a century or more was cleared away to make room for a new structure.

Two features of this went beyond the proposals outlined above. The Government determined to extirpate tuberculosis by a further application of the principle that underlay the new Ministry. One headquarters free from other distractions was needed to conduct a vigorous onslaught on Koch's bacillus. Therefore in 1946 the Northern Ireland Tuberculosis Authority was created with the threefold duty of discovering cases of tuberculosis, preventing it, and treating persons suffering from it.

In the field of general medical treatment, too, Ministers were able to go farther than the Select Committee. It was impracticable to abolish poor law dispensaries until the British Government had defined their attitude towards Lord Beveridge's proposals for a comprehensive medical service. In 1948, however, Ulster followed the lead of Great Britain. The Northern Ireland General Health Services Board which was created in that year administers general medical, dental, pharmaceutical and eye services which are available for the whole community. The Board consists of laymen and representatives of relevant professions appointed by the Minister.

[1] Ministries Act (N.I.), 1944.

[2] Public Health and Local Government (Administrative Provisions) Act (N.I.), 1946; Public Health (Tuberculosis) Act (N.I.), 1946; Health Services Act (N.I.), 1948.

The hospital system was remodelled on the broad basis of the Hospital Council's proposals. Almost all hospitals were vested in the Northern Ireland Hospitals Authority (also appointed by the Minister), whose functions include hospital, specialist, ambulance, laboratory and blood transfusion services. Local management committees are responsible for day-to-day hospital administration.

Local authorities thus lost their hospitals and their functions of treating and preventing tuberculosis, while the dispensary system, like the rest of the poor law, was swept away. At the same time, the services provided by larger authorities were extended and those of the smaller were restricted. County and county borough councils, acting through statutory committees, were constituted health and welfare authorities, and to the health authorities in the counties were transferred functions formerly shared by county and district councils and boards of guardians. These include personal health services (maternal and child health, home nursing and health visiting, care of patients discharged from hospital, school health, vaccination and immunization) and a number of environmental functions. In each county a medical officer of health was appointed, with a staff (mostly whole-time) of medical and dental officers, health visitors, midwives, home nurses and public health inspectors. The functions left to borough and district councils include refuse collection, housing, water supply and sewerage.

This transformation was remarkably similar to that in England, though not identical. The Tuberculosis Authority was a local invention and there were and are differences in detail. It might have been expected, though, that a region with its own Parliament would have departed more radically from the English pattern. But in Ulster, as in England, it was recognized that all citizens have an equal claim to enjoy good health as far as State action can secure it, and administration was designed to provide higher and more uniform standards in the most economic way. Economy meant spreading over larger areas expanded costs that do not vary with the number of persons served (e.g. the salaries of county medical officers). Moreover, Ulster's local government structure was based on the English pattern, and the province has never been averse from adopting improvements that have proved their worth in other parts of the Kingdom. It was natural that local and independent inquiries should have found that changes made or contemplated in England would be appropriate in Ulster.

Financial considerations strengthened this conformist tendency, and indeed drove it farther than it would otherwise have gone. The post-war principle of parity meant that Ulstermen could enjoy great benefits initiated in London (e.g. dissolution of the poor law, and a comprehensive medical service) at little extra cost because they had no alternative but to pay taxes levied by Westminster; and once their Government had concluded the Social Services Agreement of 1949, they had no option but to keep the scale and standard of health services in general conformity with Britain.[1] But there seems to be no evidence that these restrictions were irksome. On the contrary, they provided means of realizing reforms long advocated by men and women of public spirit.

So much in bare outline for structural changes and their causes. What of effects? Statistics of mortality are the simplest and most general measuring rod, but they do not reflect administrative changes alone. Diminished unemployment, higher incomes, better housing and nutrition, and striking advances in medicine have all helped to prolong life, and it seems certain that the people of Northern Ireland would in any event have enjoyed better health after the war. In 1946 the death-rate had already fallen to 12·5 per 1,000, against an average of 13·8 for the previous ten years. Since, however, the factors we have mentioned were not confined to Ulster, comparative statistics afford some indication of the revolution in her health services. In less than a decade she was able to draw level with England and Wales except only in infant mortality.[2] She was still slightly behind in 1963, but by that time the probability of death at all ages, which used to be a good deal higher than in the rest of the British Isles, was lower than anywhere else.[3] It

[1] H.C. Deb. (N.I.), 31, c. 2231.

[2] Mortality rates were as follows:

	England and Wales		*Northern Ireland*	
	1946	*1954*	*1946*	*1954*
Death-rates*	12·0	11·3	12·5	10·9
Death-rates from tuberculosis*.	0·55	0·18	0·83	0·18
Maternal mortality† . .	1·47	0·7	2·3	0·7
Infant mortality†	43	25	54	33

* per 1,000 population † per 1,000 live births

[3] Death-rates per 1,000 population:

	1961	*1962*	*1963*
England and Wales . .	12·0	11·9	12·2*
Scotland	12·3	12·2	12·6*
Republic of Ireland . .	12·3	12·0	11·9*
Northern Ireland. . .	11·3	10·6	11·0

* provisional

should be mentioned, though, that the incidence and duration of sickness may still be excessive. The Northern Ireland Public Accounts Committee reported in 1964 that the cost per head of drugs and national insurance sickness benefit was about one-third greater than in Britain and the average cost of prescriptions was slightly higher.[1] The exact causes of this have yet to be established.

It would be tedious to catalogue in detail achievements since 1946, remarkable though they are.[2] Diminished mortality attests to the success of the anti-tuberculosis campaign. Indeed, the Tuberculosis Authority worked so vigorously as to undermine its own existence. In 1959 its functions were transferred to the health and welfare authorities and the Hospitals Authority. The latter body, the largest public employer in Ulster, has made substantial progress in modernizing old hospitals and providing new ones. Its building programme is estimated to cost some £66·5 m., of which one-third was spent by 1963, leaving £44 m. for the next ten years.[3] In mental health (also the charge of the Hospitals Authority) Ulster leapt at a bound from darkness into light. Her post-war legislation was well in advance of England's.[4] The medical, dental, pharmaceutical and eye services administered by the General Health Services Board are used by virtually the whole population. Personal health services that remain with local authorities have been quite transformed. Regular collection and disposal of refuse sweeten the countryside as well as the town. The number of joint water boards has risen from two to ten, and a really prodigious expansion of water and sewerage schemes—the necessary basis for industrial development, and therefore essential for economic as well as personal health—is making obsolete the well and the bucket.[5]

Yet this splendid success provoked, rather than disarmed, parliamentary criticism. The pre-war Minister of Home Affairs was rarely attacked on account of health services, whereas post-

[1] P.A.C. 1962–63, H.C. 1613, pp. 14–15, 162–71.

[2] For an authoritative summary see 'Health and Welfare Services in Northern Ireland' in *Ulster Year Book, 1957–59*.

[3] *Report on Health and Local Government Administration*, 1963, Cmd. 474 (1964).

[4] ibid. See pp. 14, 28 of Cmd. 474 for recent developments.

[5] At the end of 1963 the ten joint boards embraced thirty-seven water authorities, and the Ministry was trying to make further amalgamations. H.C. Deb. (N.I.), 55, c. 944.

war Ministers of Health came under sustained and concentrated fire. In some ways this was to be expected: a new department is a target. Back-benchers aimed, however, at two particular points. One was of special interest to Roman Catholics. When the health service began in 1948 the board of management of the Mater Hospital, a large Catholic teaching hospital in Belfast, were unable on conscientious grounds to hand over their buildings and property to the State. In consequence they received no help from public funds. This, it was complained, was unjust. For although the hospital stood outside the State service, it continued to treat patients of all creeds and classes, and the great majority were insured persons who would otherwise have sought admission to State hospitals. In effect, the Mater Hospital at its own expense was helping the Northern Ireland Hospitals Authority to fulfil its statutory responsibilities.[1]

The second and wider point concerned the administrative methods and constitutional status of the Hospitals Authority and the General Health Services Board. They were accused of bureaucracy, lack of co-ordination and general inefficiency, while further complaints arose because the Minister disclaimed responsibility. For it was not the Ministry's statutory duty to provide services, but only to promote the provision of them and secure their effective co-ordination.[2] The Department also possessed specific powers of control (notably over finance and staff), but it did not stand to its offspring as a principal to an agent, as did the Minister of Health in England and the Secretary of State in Scotland. So it was argued that although Parliament supplied virtually all the money for the health services, its control was insufficiently effective because ministerial responsibility was incomplete. When, for example, an M.P. questioned or complained to the Minister about hospital administration, he would be referred to the Authority.

All this induced the Minister in 1954 to appoint three advisers under the chairmanship of Dr. H. G. Tanner[3] to examine inform-

[1] This matter, like others in Northern Ireland that impinge, however remotely, on religion has aroused sharp and passionate dispute. There is therefore no general agreement on what facts are most to the point. See H.C. Deb. (N.I.), 56, cc. 695 et seq. (18 February 1964).

[2] Health Services Act (N.I.), 1948, s. 1.

[3] Dr. Tanner was chairman of the South-Western Regional Hospital Board, Bristol. The other members were Sir George Henderson (sometime Permanent Secretary of the Department of Health for Scotland) and Dr. J. V. S. Mills, a Resident Magistrate for the City of Belfast.

ally the working of the health services. In their Report[1] in 1955 the Tanner Committee reviewed the complex and difficult problem of relations between the Mater Hospital and the State service, and they concluded that a radical solution was impossible while the hospital stood apart. A subvention from public funds was no answer, for the hospital was not providing services on behalf of the Hospitals Authority, and public aid would necessarily mean public control in one form or other, if only to ensure co-ordination with the Authority's hospitals. The Committee did, however, strongly commend a limited form of contractual relationship between the hospital and the Authority, not only for financial reasons, but to diminish the hospital's isolation and re-establish a sense of fellowship in a common cause.[2] This idea came to nothing, and the position of the Mater Hospital remains unchanged.[3]

On the wider issue the Committee put criticism in perspective by reviewing Ulster's progress, and they declared that her record would bear examination against that of any area of Britain. But they advocated administrative and constitutional changes:

> We subscribe to the principle that a service which is financed entirely from voted moneys must be subject finally to parliamentary, and therefore to ministerial, control; and we see no alternative to this which does not infringe constitutional practice and precedent and contain inherent possibilities of friction and confusion. . . . We therefore recommend that the present equivocal status of the Hospitals Authority should be clarified and that the Authority should be placed in the relation to the Ministry of an agent to a principal.[4]

When this was debated in 1955 the Minister (then Dame Dehra Parker) persuaded the Commons not to disturb the *status quo*, saying that she was acutely aware of the dangers of travelling too far along the road of control.[5] Members of the Hospitals Authority (like those of several other *ad hoc* boards in Ulster) are unpaid, and there is obviously some danger that strict parliamentary supervision may deaden initiative and discourage able citizens and those

[1] *Report of the Committee on the Health Services in Northern Ireland*, Cmd. 334 (1955).

[2] ibid., p. 53.

[3] In 1964 the Minister said that the board of management of the Mater Hospital had made it clear that a contractual arrangement would not be acceptable. H.C. Deb. (N.I.), 56, c. 709.

[4] Cmd. 334, p. 30.

[5] H.C. Deb. (N.I.), 39, c. 2252.

with special knowledge from devoting time to public work. On the other hand, in the judgment of the Tanner Committee, the regional hospital boards in Britain, acting within the broad framework of departmental policy, enjoyed much the same freedom as the Hospitals Authority.

So the controversy smouldered. In 1964 it broke into flame following a blunt attack on conditions in the Royal Maternity Hospital, Belfast, by an eminent gynaecologist and M.P. for Queen's University (Mr. H. I. McClure). In a debate on 24 November back-benchers, while paying tribute to the achievements of the Hospitals Authority, renewed the demand to subject it to direct ministerial and parliamentary control. The Minister (Mr. W. J. Morgan), like his predecessor, emphasized the need to secure a balance between freedom and control, pointed out that a mere change in statutory relationships would not solve the real and deep-seated problems of the health service, but expressed his readiness to bring forward proposals for further discussion. The House resolved that the hospital service should be brought more into line with the position in the rest of the United Kingdom and called upon the Government to implement the recommendation of the Tanner Committee as soon as practicable.[1]

[1] H. C. Deb. (N.I.), 58, cc. 810 et seq.

CHAPTER EIGHT

Housing and Planning

HOUSING legislation before 1921 divided Ireland into two worlds—town and country. Rural district councils were empowered by the Irish Labourers Acts to build labourers' cottages but not houses; urban authorities could provide houses for working-men. In Ulster after 1921 this distinction continued to be enshrined in legislation, though the bus and the bicycle were rapidly making it obsolete. The Northern Ireland Labourers Acts extended Exchequer assistance to those rural authorities that provided cottages, while the Housing Acts subsidized and regulated the house-building activities of borough and urban district councils.

This legislation was not only out-moded; it was also in large part ineffective. In housing, as in health services, the pre-war record of local authorities and of the Ministry of Home Affairs was one of failure. Their performance fell far short of public need. This was not apparent at the time, for no attempt was ever made to enumerate dilapidated and overcrowded dwellings. It is certain that a high proportion of houses were not fit to live in, and the first census of 1926 showed that 18 per cent. of the population lived at a density of more than two persons to a room. In contrast to Great Britain, however, no housing survey was undertaken. So the scale of the problem remained concealed until in 1943 the first housing survey showed that some 100,000 new dwellings were urgently needed.

Yet during the whole period from 1919 to 1939 only about 50,000 dwellings of all types were built. This was in marked contrast to England and Wales where, with a population about thirty times larger than in Ulster, the number of houses built between the wars was eighty times greater. In England and Wales, too, local authorities built over a quarter of all houses,[1] whereas in Ulster they constructed only 3,839 houses (about one-twelfth of the total) and 3,669 labourers' cottages.[2]

Why did local authorities do so little? In housing, as in other services, lack of money is largely the answer, but it is not the

[1] C. L. Mowat, *Britain Between the Wars* (London, 1955), p. 458.

[2] *See note* 1 *on page* 148.

whole answer. Many councils were lethargic. Others were too small to make an effective contribution.

Lethargy was most in evidence in rural districts. There, at least, for several years money presented no pressing problem. The details can be relegated to footnotes. Here we need only note that the first Northern Ireland Labourers Act in 1923 offered such generous Exchequer assistance that on average some 3,000 cottages could have been built in the 32 rural districts for little more than a penny rate.[2] The response fell far short of even this modest aim. Between 1923 and 1927 only 21 of the 32 councils framed approved schemes for 1,882 cottages, of which 1,858 were actually built.

In 1927 the Exchequer was obliged to stiffen its borrowing terms. They were not unduly onerous,[3] but only one new scheme (for 20 cottages) was confirmed in the next two years. Derating in 1929, which transferred to the Exchequer most expenditure (including loan charges) in rural districts, together with representa-

---

[1] Dwellings completed, 1919–39:

Houses	
Local authorities	3,839
Private builders with State financial aid	32,644
Private builders without State aid (approx.)	9,000
Cottages	
Rural district councils	3,669
Irish Sailors' and Soldiers' Land Trust	1,251
	50,403

Source: *Ulster Year Book, 1947*, p. 206.

[2] A council could borrow in respect of each cottage up to £350 for 68½ years and repay both principal and interest by an annuity of 3¼ per cent., but the Exchequer contributed 36 per cent. of the loan charges. On a cottage costing £350 the annual loan charge payable by a council was £7 5*s*. 6*d*. The rents charged for new cottages appear to have averaged about 3*s*. a week, or £7 16*s*. a year. On this basis the rent covered the loan charges. Some contribution from the rates was required to cover the cost of maintenance and rent collection and also because building in the twenties was so expensive (the cost of cottages ranged from £370 to £420) that the maximum Government loan of £350 might need to be augmented by money raised at a higher rate of interest. A council might thus have had to find an additional £50 a cottage, say £3 a year. Since, however, the average valuation of the 32 rural districts in 1926 was £81,296 (and the product of a penny rate therefore £339), 100 cottages could have been built in the average district for about a penny rate. (The facts and figures for pre-war years cited here and elsewhere in this chapter are taken, unless otherwise stated, from the *Reports on the Administration of Local Government Services* and *Local Taxation Returns*.)

[3] On a cottage costing £350 the annual loan charge was raised to about £14 6*s*.

tions from labourers needing cottages, spurred some authorities to renewed activity. Fourteen of them were preparing or considering schemes when in 1931 the Government, enforcing every possible economy, suspended the Labourers Acts altogether. They authorized the resumption of building in 1935, raised the maximum Exchequer loan in 1937, and stimulated a spurt of activity which produced another 1,619 cottages in 1938 and 1939.

Such in brief is the story of a lost opportunity. In the whole inter-war period only 3,477 labourers' cottages were completed under legislation passed at Stormont,[1] and most of them were in three counties—Antrim, Down and Londonderry. Not a single cottage was built in Fermanagh.[2] Yet, as we have shown, in the twenties in particular, rural district councils could have transformed the housing situation in their areas at little cost to themselves. True, even the best of their efforts rarely went beyond providing four walls and a roof. In Ulster's countryside adequate sanitation, electricity or gas were conspicuously absent, and 87 per cent. of all dwellings had no running water.[3] By 1939 it must have been evident that the Labourers Acts had had their day.

We turn now to the towns. Here the achievements of local councils can not unfairly be described as derisory. Of 34,312 houses erected between the wars under the Northern Ireland Housing Acts, they provided 2,166. Private builders were responsible for the rest.[4]

This conspicuous failure stemmed from several causes. It was the Government's declared policy to rely mainly on private enterprise.[5] The Housing Acts enabled speculative builders not only to get Exchequer subsidies at the same rate as urban authorities, but also to apply for more financial help both to those bodies and

[1] Of the 3,669 cottages built by rural district councils, 192 were included in schemes approved before 1921.

[2] J. M. Mogey, *Rural Life in Northern Ireland* (London, 1947), p. 34.

[3] *Housing in Northern Ireland*, Cmd. 224 (1944), App. V.

[4] Houses erected with State financial aid, 1919–39:

	*1919–23**	*1924–39*
Local authorities	1,657	2,166
Private persons	498	32,146
	2,155	34,312

* Erected under the Housing (Ireland) Act, 1919 or with the aid of grants from the Unemployment Fund. One local authority built 16 houses without State aid in 1939.

[5] H.C. Deb. (N.I.), 18, c. 78.

to rural district councils, though the latter themselves had no housing powers. Then, too, Exchequer subsidies, which took the form of a lump sum for each house completed within a specified period, were much smaller and subject to more frequent change than in England. The first Northern Ireland Housing Act of 1923 fixed the subsidy at £60. In 1925 it rose to £80 and in 1927 to £100, in both cases for houses finished within six months. Reduced to £50 in 1931 and to £25 in 1932, it was completely withdrawn in 1937.[1] Whereas the maximum sum of £100 ran only from August 1927 to April 1931, the English Housing Act of 1924 gave a subsidy of £9 a year for 40 years, and it was not withdrawn until 1933.

Two further points must be noted. Most urban districts were hardly large enough to subsidize to any appreciable extent their own housing schemes, or even to act as housing authorities on a big scale. Ten of the 32 urban districts in 1928 had a rateable valuation of less than £10,000 and only nine a valuation higher than £20,000. Even the larger of them had little incentive to recruit specialized staff and embark on the long-term business of preparing housing schemes because they did not know whether Exchequer assistance would be forthcoming in the future. The Government, evidently living from hand to mouth, not only changed the amount of subsidy with bewildering frequency, but took powers to pay it for short periods only. To take one example from the consequent jungle of legislation: the Housing Act of 1927 provided for payment of a grant of £100 for each house completed within six months before 1 April 1929, the Act of 1928 extended the time limit to 1 April 1930, and the Act of 1929 extended it for one more year.

For these reasons most urban authorities could not reasonably have been expected to erect many dwellings to let at low rents. Yet it was precisely houses of this sort, and not those built for sale by speculative builders, that were most urgently needed. 'The greatest need at the moment', declared the Select Committee on Rents in 1931, 'is for houses which can be let at low rents, i.e. not exceeding 6*s*. per week.'[2] Houses built for letting commanded rents of 15*s*. a week or more during the period of inflated costs and low subsidies after the First World War. A reduction in the size of subsidized houses and in building costs, together with the larger

[1] Cmd. 224, App. VIII. Subsidies were renewed by the Housing Act (N.I.), 1939, but no houses were built because of the outbreak of war.

[2] *Report from the Select Committee on Rents*, 1931, H.C. 249, p. 21.

Exchequer grant, drove rents down until in the thirties it was possible to get a new house for 8*s.* or 10*s.* a week. Even that was beyond the reach of the many working-men with wages of 30*s.* to 35*s.*[1] As the Ministry of Home Affairs acknowledged in 1938:

> While the subsidy given under the Housing Acts had been successful in getting houses built for people able to pay an economic rent, the problem of providing accommodation for the poorer classes, mostly residing in houses more or less unfit for habitation, remained.[2]

In the fields of planning and slum clearance the pre-war record was even more dismal. In England and Wales local authorities were empowered to control and plan the use of land by various enactments, from the Housing, Town Planning, etc., Act, 1909 to the Town and Country Planning Act, 1932, though this legislation had serious weaknesses.[3] Local authorities in Northern Ireland, however, had no planning powers at all. They were even allowed to consent to the erection and use for human habitation of buildings of a kind not permissible under existing by-laws.[4] So the speculative builder was subject to few restrictions, and ramshackle structures sprang up to mar the beauty of Ulster's coast and countryside.

The Planning and Housing Act (N.I.), 1931, which was based largely on the model of the English Town Planning Act, 1925,[5] eventually authorized local councils to prepare planning schemes for the development of land and the clearance or improvement of slum areas. It also obliged them to make building by-laws. The planning provisions of the Act were permissive and no schemes were ever made. For slum clearance (also permissive) the Government were unable to offer any financial help, though in Britain from 1933 special grants were payable. Indeed, in a circular letter explaining the Act, the Ministry warned local authorities of the 'pressing need for rigid economy in local as well as central administration'.[6] Practically the only outcome of the Act was the framing by twenty-one urban and twenty-eight rural district

[1] H.C. Deb. (N.I.), 18, cc. 78 et seq.

[2] *Report on the Administration of Local Government Services*, 1937–38, Cmd. 200 (1938), p. 55.

[3] *Report of the* [*Scott*] *Committee on Land Utilization in Rural Areas*, U.K. Cmd. 6378 (1942), chap. vi.

[4] Housing (Ireland) Act, 1919, s. 21. This dispensation, intended to last for only three years, was prolonged in Ulster until 31 December 1929.

[5] W. R. Davidge, *Preliminary Report on Reconstruction and Planning* (H.M.S.O., 1944), p. 4.

[6] Circular letter H.G. No. 75 (1931).

councils of building by-laws which the Ministry approved between 1932 and 1938. But by 1932 more than two-thirds of all subsidized houses had already been built.

In housing, as in other services, the war was a catalyst. New building and maintenance virtually stopped, old houses rapidly deteriorated, and air raids destroyed 3,200 dwellings and damaged more than 50,000.[1] The pre-war gap between the supply of modern dwellings and the need for them soon became a gulf.

At the same time, war transformed Ulster's expectations for the future. As explained in Chapter Four, she secured Britain's promise that her claim to parity would be, if not conceded, at least sympathetically considered. A primary purpose of the housing survey conducted by the Ministry of Home Affairs in 1943 was to peg that claim on the indisputable ground of fact. This was not difficult. The survey was based on modest criteria, for 'the adoption of standards approaching modern ideals would have led to the condemnation of a vast proportion of the existing houses in the country'.[2] Even so, it was shown that, of the existing stock of 323,000 dwellings, 229,500 wanted repairs. To meet immediate needs the country required 100,000 new houses (more than double the number built in the twenty years between the wars); and to eliminate overcrowding and slums at least 200,000 would be wanted.[3]

The Ministry of Health and Local Government that was established in 1944 met this challenge with vigour—and with experience harvested from the past. In post-war legislation, beginning with the Housing Act (N.I.) of 1945, four leading principles can be distinguished. First, the artificial distinction between town and country enshrined in the Labourers Acts was abolished. The councils of rural, like those of urban, districts and county boroughs became housing authorities.

In the second place, Parliament at Stormont created a new housing agency. It was clear that many local councils lacked the resources, and that some lacked the energy, to be reliable instruments of rapid improvement. In 1945 the Northern Ireland Housing Trust was given the task of providing houses at the Exchequer's

[1] J. W. Blake, *Northern Ireland in the Second World War* (H.M.S.O., 1956), p. 238.

[2] *Report on Health and Local Government Administration*, 1938–46, Cmd. 258 (1948), p. 265.

[3] Cmd. 224.

expense and managing them when built. The members of the Trust, who serve in a voluntary capacity, are appointed by the Minister and operate under his general control, though they enjoy a sufficient measure of discretion in determining policy to make their effort worth while. The Ministry has power to give formal directions but has never had to exercise it.[1]

Thirdly, private building with State aid took second place to the provision by public authorities of houses to let. A wide variety of subsidies has, indeed, been extended to private persons, including industrialists and farmers, but on less favourable terms than in the public sector.

Finally, both private and public schemes have benefited from State aid infinitely more generous than in Ulster before the war or in England and Wales after it. A few examples will illustrate this. Northern Ireland has been the only part of the United Kingdom to enjoy subsidies for private enterprise building. In the public sector, the standard Exchequer subsidy in England and Wales from 1952 to 1955 on each house built for general need stood at £26 14*s*. a year for 60 years. The Northern Ireland Housing Trust got £56 10*s*. a year for 60 years for each house of 800 square feet. (Local authorities in Ulster are required to pay one-quarter of the total subsidy from the rates.[2]) Whereas in 1952 the economic rent of an average council house was 32*s*. 8*d*. a week, the tenant had to find about 12*s*. Halcyon days ended for a time in 1955. Interest rates rose sharply, subsidies were reduced, and rents were increased. Nevertheless, as the Minister acknowledged, the Treasury gave Ulster very favourable consideration.[3] In England and Wales the general subsidy was cut to £10 in 1956 and then virtually abolished, though there were special payments for slum clearance, overspill and other purposes.[4] In Northern Ireland the general subsidy reached its lowest point of £48 in 1955. Thereafter it was augmented year by year until in 1963 it ranged from £56 to £80 a year (depending on the size of house) for 60 years. Subsidies then reduced rents on average by about 27*s*. a week. At the same time, with the United Kingdom's

[1] P.A.C. 1956–57, H.C. 1310, p. 126; 1961–62, H.C. 1556, p. 183.

[2] The Exchequer contribution could be commuted to a lump sum representing the present value of the annual subsidy over sixty years. Many local authorities chose commutation.

[3] H.C. Deb. (N.I.), 42, c. 898.

[4] The Housing Act, 1961 recast subsidies in England and Wales. These were too complicated to summarize, but they were far lower than in Ulster.

agreement,[1] a new subsidy structure was introduced to offset variations in interest rates. Generous State aid is also available for housing elderly people. Grants to improve existing houses have been payable since 1956, and additional payments for slum clearance were authorized in 1961.[2]

Building operations were handicapped in the immediate post-war period by bad weather and shortage of materials, and at intervals thereafter by shortage of skilled labour and high interest rates. Nevertheless, in the 19 years 1945–63 a total of 112,383 new permanent houses was completed. Local authorities and private enterprise each provided more than one-third and the Housing Trust almost one-quarter.[3] This annual rate of construction of some 5,900 houses compares with the 1919–39 average of 2,270. Nor is increased quantity the only contrast. Standards of building, layout and amenity have been vastly improved. Many sites developed by the Housing Trust in particular are noticeably spacious and pleasing.

When one remembers that in Ulster there was no tradition of public enterprise building on any scale, her achievement must seem creditable. The 1943 target—100,000 new dwellings for immediate needs—had been hit. She has, however, only begun to remedy the long years of neglect. In 1956 local authorities were required to submit schemes of slum clearance. Their surveys, published in 1959, showed that 95,364 houses (about one-quarter of the whole stock of 376,324) were not fit to live in, and 53,722 of these were beyond repair.[4] (The proportion of unfit houses in England and Wales was then about one-twentieth.)[5] In addition Northern Ireland will require another 50,000 dwellings to replace

[1] H.C. Deb. (N.I.), 52, c. 764.

[2] The statistics for Northern Ireland are taken from the *Reports on Health and Local Government Administration*.

[3] New permanent houses completed, 1945–63:

Local authorities	41,813
Northern Ireland Housing Trust	26,490
Housing associations and other agencies	2,890
Private builders with subsidy	35,801
Private builders without subsidy	4,806
Rebuilt war-destroyed houses	583
	112,383

Source: *Northern Ireland Digest of Statistics.*

[4] *Report on Proposals for Dealing with Unfit Houses*, Cmd. 398 (1959).

[5] *Housing in England and Wales*, U.K. Cmd. 1290 (1961), pp. 2–3.

very old ones during the next twenty years.[1] And during that period many more will be wanted for the increasing population.

Planning after 1945 made little progress, though (as mentioned on page 72) the Planning Commission and Planning Advisory Board, which were temporary bodies, made a host of proposals during and after the war. A purely interim measure in 1944, the Planning (Interim Development) Act (N.I.), again based on an earlier English model,[2] brought all land under planning control. Thirty-seven interim development authorities—the councils of counties, county boroughs, boroughs and nearly all urban districts—were authorized to control development pending the coming into operation of planning schemes which they already had power to frame under the Act of 1931.[3] But most of the boroughs and urban districts were too small to employ professional staff; the provincial Exchequer gave no help to meet claims for compensation arising from planning decisions; and local planning lacked co-ordination, largely because the Ministry of Health and Local Government had no comprehensive plan for the whole province. Within the Government itself no department was in a position to take a conspectus of the activities of others that impinged on the use of land.[4]

Even if these problems had been resolutely tackled, and there seems to have been no effort to do this, it is certain that comprehensive planning and redevelopment would have run into difficulties because Stormont's powers were limited in two important respects. (*a*) The Government of Ireland Act (s. 5) prohibited taking any property without compensation. Until 1960 it was not clear whether property was taken whenever permission to develop was denied. If it was, compensation would be so massive as to destroy all hope of planning.[5] (*b*) The constitution absolutely prohibited (even on payment of compensation) the compulsory

[1] Of the stock of houses in Ulster in 1962, 63 per cent. were built before 1919, compared with 50 per cent. in Scotland and 47 per cent. in England and Wales. *Report of the Joint Working Party on the Economy of Northern Ireland*, Cmd. 446 (1962), p. 88.

[2] The Town and Country Planning (Interim Development) Act, 1943. This was swept away by a spate of subsequent legislation. Cf. A. E. Telling, *Planning Law and Procedure* (London, 1963).

[3] Belfast Harbour Commissioners were also a local planning authority.

[4] *Planning Proposals for the Belfast Area*, Cmd. 302 (1952); *Belfast Telegraph*, 25 August 1955, 18 April 1957.

[5] In *Belfast Corporation* v. *O.D. Cars, Ltd.* [1960] A.C. 490 the House of Lords held that restrictions on the user of property in Northern Ireland planning legislation did not necessarily constitute a taking of property.

acquisition of any property belonging to religious denominations or educational institutions except for the purposes of roads, railways and public utilities. The property did not need to be a church or a school; it might be a row of derelict houses or a disused hall, or even a field. This could seriously impede slum clearance and redevelopment.

So for twenty years after the Act of 1944 there was little planning in Northern Ireland. Land use was haphazard; the life of the province drained towards the sprawling and congested Belfast region; roads, houses, factories and other works, both public and private, sprang up in piecemeal fashion; and the superlative countryside suffered from neglect and abuse.

The Government finally tightened their grip. Having secured the United Kingdom's agreement in principle to amend the constitution,[1] in 1960 they invited Sir Robert Matthew to prepare a survey and plan for the Belfast Region. The Matthew Report[2] set before Ulstermen a vision of an environment at once aesthetically satisfying and conducive to sustained industrial growth. Its recommendations included the creation of a new city in co. Armagh, measures to prevent Belfast from encroaching further on the surrounding countryside, planned expansion of other centres, improved amenities and better administrative arrangements.

These ideas, which for Northern Ireland were wholly revolutionary, are evidently to be realized. In 1963 the Government accepted the Report's main proposals, undertook to pay all planning compensation, drew a 'stop-line' round Belfast and announced that the survey would be extended to the rest of the

[1] The Northern Ireland Act, 1962 abolished the restriction at (*a*) above and modified that at (*b*), though only after some controversy. The Bishops of the Roman Catholic church, while recognizing the desirability of housing, slum clearance and development schemes, feared that extended powers might be improperly used. *The Times*, 12 February 1962. The upshot was that Northern Ireland was empowered to control the use of land and, for the purposes of housing, slum clearance, development or redevelopment, to purchase compulsorily land belonging to religious denominations or educational institutions, other than buildings occupied and used exclusively for religious or educational purposes. The Lord Chancellor gave an assurance on behalf of the Northern Ireland Government that every owner of property would be dealt with in a manner no less favourable and on a financial footing no less generous than was the case in Great Britain. Lords Deb., 5 s., 237, c. 383.

[2] *Belfast Regional Survey and Plan 1962*, a Report prepared for the Government of Northern Ireland by Sir Robert H. Matthew (H.M.S.O., 1964). The *Recommendations and Conclusions* were published in 1963 (Cmd. 451).

country.[1] In 1964 they published a first plan for the new city[2] and a White Paper containing proposals for administrative reform.[3] On 1 January 1965 a Ministry of Development was established.[4]

Comprehensive regional planning still lies in the future. It is already clear that fresh minds are at work within the Ministry—and that its path is unlikely to be smooth. The concept and situation of the new city at once aroused some opposition, as did the decision to stop the growth of Belfast, while local authorities disliked the idea of losing their planning powers. In the White Paper noted above, the Government stressed the need for a consistent and impartial planning system answerable to Parliament, for economy in the employment of scarce professional staff, and for localized administration. They suggested that all planning powers and duties should be legally vested in a central planning authority responsible to the Minister and advised by a planning council of experts in various fields, and that the thirty-seven planning authorities should be superseded by ten local development committees which together would cover the whole province and act, under a standing delegation, as executive agents of the central planning authority. These arrangements would differ from constitutional practice in England and Wales, where the Minister to all intents and purposes is the central planning authority,[5] and where also the county and county borough councils are still responsible for local planning. This matter had not been debated at Stormont by the beginning of 1965. The legislation that is ultimately enacted in Northern Ireland could be of interest beyond its own borders.

[1] H.C. Deb. (N.I.), 53, c. 1020; 54, c. 517.

[2] *First Report on the Proposed New City, co. Armagh* (H.M.S.O., 1964).

[3] *The Administration of Town and Country Planning in Northern Ireland*, Cmd. 465 (1964).

[4] The idea of a Ministry of Development probably came from, or at any rate was strengthened by, Scottish experience. The Prime Minister said on 4 November 1964, 'We might benefit from the experience of Scotland, where the Scottish Development Department has given a major boost to physical development'. H.C. Deb. (N.I.), 58, c. 351.

[5] Telling, op. cit., p. 12. The Barlow and Scott Reports recommended a central planning authority for England and Wales.

CHAPTER NINE

Social Security

SOCIAL security services in Ireland before 1921 comprised two elements. The first, the poor law, was the product of an age when horizons were narrow. The machinery of unions, workhouses, boards of guardians and local rating devised in England in 1834 was extended to Ireland in 1838. The second marked the beginning of an era of State provision. Old age pensions dating from 1908, and unemployment insurance from 1911, provided some support from central funds for the aged and for certain classes of manual workers. Both elements were so similar to those in Great Britain that they require no detailed description.

We must, however, refer briefly to the more conspicuous defects of the Irish poor law, which was preserved in Ulster until 1948, though it stood in even greater need of improvement than its counterpart in England. An exhaustive inquiry in 1906 by the Vice-Regal Commission on Poor Law Reform[1] and a Report on Ireland in 1909 by the Royal Commission on the Poor Laws[2] adduced good reasons for reforming both institutional relief within the workhouse and relief outside it.

Institutional relief was relatively expensive. In the province of Ulster in 1904 it cost £183,846, but almost half of this (£79,141) went on salaries and rations of officers and upkeep of buildings. The cost per inmate per week averaged 7*s.* 3*d.* whereas three-quarters of all persons on outdoor relief were kept alive on 2*s.* 6*d.* a week or less. Workhouses, originally designed for up to a thousand paupers, or more in large cities, generally housed only a fraction of that number. In the second half of the nineteenth century the population of Ireland had fallen, living standards had risen, and guardians interpreted liberally their very restricted

[1] *Report of the Vice-Regal Commission on Poor Law Reform in Ireland,* U.K. Cd. 3202 (1906); *Appendix to Report,* U.K. Cd. 3203 (1906); *Minutes of Evidence,* U.K. Cd. 3204 (1906).

[2] *Royal Commission on the Poor Laws: Report on Ireland,* U.K. Cd. 4630 (1909).

[3] The statistics for the period in question are reproduced or compiled from U.K. Cd. 3203.

statutory powers to grant out-relief.[1] In Ulster on 11 March 1905 the average workhouse population outside Belfast numbered no more than 173. Hence, establishment charges were disproportionate.

At the same time, institutional relief was unjust. We do not mean that it was ungenerous or that the destitute were treated differently from other people. The point is that inmates of workhouses had nothing in common save the fact of their destitution. The able-bodied were in a minority. The majority included the sick, aged and infirm, illegitimate infants and their mothers, epileptics and the insane. Since lunatic asylums were overcrowded, the mentally deranged and defective were often kept out of sight—and out of mind—behind the massive stone walls of the workhouse. On 11 March 1905 in Ballymena (co. Antrim) workhouse, 154 of the 401 inmates were classified as insane. Of the 3,819 paupers in the Belfast workhouse, 3,068 were aged and infirm or sick, 174 insane or epileptic, and 330 mothers and children. Indoor relief did not discriminate finely enough between human beings whose needs, by the standards of any civilized society, merited distinctive treatment.

Outdoor relief, by contrast, wanted uniformity. Paupers living at home were treated very differently from each other, but often for no good reason. The amount awarded by guardians was determined as much by the wealth or poverty of a union as by the recipient's needs, and unions where poverty was greatest necessarily lacked the resources to relieve it.

For these and other reasons the majority of the Royal Commission, following closely the recommendations of the Vice-Regal Commission, proposed to make committees of county and county borough councils responsible for poor relief and to abolish boards of guardians and general workhouses. Their inmates were to be housed in distinctive fashion—aged and infirm in almshouses, lunatics in asylums, able-bodied vagrants in labour houses and children in private homes. But the British Government were not prepared to break up the poor law in England, let alone in Ireland, though in 1916 in the interests of economy they authorized the concentration of paupers in fewer workhouses.[2]

[1] For evidence of the trend towards outdoor relief see *Royal Commission on the Financial Relations between Great Britain and Ireland, Minutes of Evidence*, vol. i, U.K. C. 7720–I (1895), pp. 77 et seq.; vol. ii, U.K. C. 7720–II (1895), App. IV A; U.K. Cd. 3202, pp. 65–66.

[2] Local Government (Emergency Provisions) Act, 1916, s. 23 (4).

So Ministers in Northern Ireland took up their offices with some awareness of the poor law's defects and, as we have seen, with high hopes of eradicating them. The Commission appointed by the Minister of Home Affairs in 1924 gave point to both knowledge and ambition. On 29 March 1924 the workhouse population in Ulster of 4,784 included 2,789 sick, 1,281 aged and infirm, 308 children under 15, and 200 lunatics, idiots and epileptics.[1] Although two of the twenty-seven workhouses had been entirely closed and only the sick remained in nine others, indoor relief was still comparatively extravagant. In 1924 it cost £93,944 to maintain a daily average of 4,851 paupers in workhouses, but only £35,834 to keep 4,906 on out-relief. Salaries and rations of officers absorbed £62,083.[2] The Commission advocated substantially the same sort of changes as earlier inquiries. To secure greater economy and uniformity they proposed to dispense with unions and boards of guardians and make counties units of administration and areas of charge. Workhouses were to be abolished and their inmates given treatment proper to their condition.

This Report, like its predecessors, was pigeon-holed. After the Commission had finished their labours in 1927, the Government could not and local authorities would not leap into the dark. The local Exchequer was bound by the terms of the Colwyn Report. Local councils feared that radical reform would cost more in rates than it would save. So boards of guardians (abolished in England in 1929) continued in Ulster to administer mixed workhouses and to pay to paupers outside them a pittance that varied from union to union as well as from case to case.

There were, however, two changes of importance between the wars. One of these simply reflected the policy of Whitehall. Ulster not only maintained the schemes of unemployment insurance and non-contributory pensions which she inherited in 1921. She followed Britain's lead in improving them, notably by extending the scope of insurance and by introducing contributory pensions in 1925 and unemployment assistance in 1934. Since these and related measures were essentially the same as in Britain, it is unnecessary to explain their provisions.[3] The more interesting ques-

[1] *Report of Departmental Commission on Local Government Administration in Northern Ireland*, Cmd. 73 (1927), p. 73.

[2] ibid., p. 74.

[3] For a short survey see D. C. Marsh, *National Insurance and Assistance in Great Britain* (London, 1950).

tion for the student of parliamentary devolution is why Ulster kept in step at all when she was legally free to go her own way.

Part of the answer lies in the financial arrangements described earlier. Ulster was precluded by the terms of the Colwyn Report from securing better services than Britain. That was first made clear during the debate on the Widows' and Orphans' Old Age Contributory Pensions Bill in 1925. The Minister of Labour resisted demands that the scheme, like that of 1908, should be non-contributory because expenditure that had no parallel in Britain could not be found at the expense of the imperial contribution.[1] Thereafter, the Unemployment Insurance Agreements and less formal arrangements with the Treasury set further limits to the extent to which Ministers could respond to local opinion. There were, for example, demands by local authorities that the provincial Exchequer should relieve them of the burden of unemployment relief. In Belfast poor relief expenditure soared from £98,265 in 1923–24 to £331,494 (more than one-third of all rate revenue) in 1933–34; poverty and misery sharpened social tension to such a point that rioting began and a curfew was imposed;[2] and the Belfast Board of Guardians proposed to stop special outdoor relief and throw the onus of supporting able-bodied unemployed on to the Government.[3] Ministers were obliged to resist this until legislation at Westminster enabled them to break new ground. The Unemployment Act (N.I.), 1934 created an Unemployment Assistance Board to pay money to many of the unemployed who had no right to insurance benefit.[4]

Finance was essentially, however, a limiting factor rather than the master of policy. Since Northern Ireland was relatively poor, it was hardly realistic for local M.P.s to press for faster progress than in other parts of the United Kingdom, and they became more conscious of this after 1925 as the imperial contribution dwindled; but they were quite free to abandon insurance schemes or put them on a less favourable basis. That, however, was what the Northern Ireland Government were resolved to avoid. As early as 1922, before committing themselves to any financial agreements at

[1] H.C. Deb. (N.I.), 6, c. 1199.

[2] *Belfast News-Letter*, 11–13 October 1932.

[3] The facts and figures relating to poor relief are taken from the *Reports on the Administration of Local Government Services* and *Local Taxation Returns*.

[4] Unemployment assistance, which did not come fully into operation until 1 April 1937, covered all persons aged 16–65 whose normal occupation was insurable under the Northern Ireland Contributory Pensions Acts.

all, Ministers determined to keep in step with Great Britain.[1] The arguments were overwhelming. Cash social services had been the same as on the mainland since their inception. To have impaired them would have affronted established expectations the more sharply because the slightest reduction in money payments is measurable. That this would weaken the Unionist Party and strengthen its rivals was the least important consideration. In 1922 opposition parties had already dished themselves by abstention, and they stood no chance whatever of gaining power thereafter. Yet, in the long term, uniformity with Britain was essential to unionism in both the party and non-party sense, for Ulster was determined to remain an integral part of the United Kingdom. The Minister of Labour declared in 1934:

> We are citizens and taxpayers of one United Kingdom, and we are determined to maintain the heritage of uniform social standards which the Imperial Parliament passed on to us.[2]

In the terms of this statement were implicit reasons for policy. It is doubtful if Ulstermen would have been willing to pay common taxes and make an imperial contribution if the cash services they were accustomed to enjoy before 1921 were eroded. Common citizenship meant that they could move to the mainland whenever they wished, and they might well have done so in large numbers had the advantages of migration been conspicuous. That could have reduced the dimensions of the unemployment problem, but local industries would have found it hard to retain skilled workmen and attract specialized labour from England and Scotland. Further, once Ulster had initiated lower scales of cash payments, it would have been difficult for her leaders to argue convincingly for the abolition of the differential or against its extension to other fields. Finally (as a Committee pointed out in 1922), a different scheme of unemployment insurance would have been inconvenient in view of the constant flow of labour between Great Britain and Northern Ireland.[3]

The province's leaders thus had some choice. On the one hand, they could allow insurance schemes to deteriorate sharply, provoke resentment among their followers about the finance of Home Rule, precipitate conflict with Britain, and create admini-

[1] See above, p. 50.

[2] H.C. Deb. (N.I.), 16, c. 1900.

[3] *Final Report of Committee of Enquiry on Unemployment Insurance and Employment Exchanges*, Cmd. 11 (1922).

strative difficulties. Or they could conclude financial agreements and sacrifice part of the local autonomy that Ulstermen had never greatly valued. Their resolution to reject the first course made the second inescapable, and the decision became more irreversible with time because financial benefits created and strengthened expectations among the electorate.

None of these considerations applied to other social services. Financed in large part by local rates and administered by local authorities, they had never been uniform with similar services in Britain, and variations in their quality were less perceptible than changes in money payments. It was politically practicable to allow them to stagnate or even to grow worse. So the poor law remained unreformed.

One of its principles, however, was turned inside out by local initiative. Institutional relief, instead of being the legal rule, became the exception. The average daily number on poor relief rose from 9,741 in 1922 to 35,908 (almost 3 per cent. of the population) in 1934. Pauperism on this scale was felt to deserve better treatment than the breaking up of family life entailed by incarceration in the workhouse.[1] Perhaps of greater importance, since social divisions inhibited compassion, was the fact that institutional relief was so expensive. Boards of guardians, who in the twenties were able to keep single persons at home for as little as 2*s*. 6*d*. a week,[2] continued to close workhouses wherever this was possible.[3] The desire to economize, reinforced in many cases by humanitarian feeling, provided an uncommonly strong motive for extending out-relief to all healthy paupers.

To do this within the four corners of the law was, however, impossible. The Irish poor law was rooted in the principle that only the workhouse gave a sufficient test of destitution. Guardians had no general power to grant out-relief save in time of exceptional distress, and then only with the Ministry's consent and if the county agreed to bear half the cost;[4] but county councils did not administer the poor law and were reluctant to assess all their ratepayers for the benefit of particular areas.[5] Thus, guardians had

[1] See e.g H.C. Deb. (N.I.), 9, c. 2424.

[2] Cmd. 73, p. 91.

[3] Of the twenty-seven workhouses, one was wholly closed by 1938 and fourteen were closed for the able-bodied.

[4] Local Government (Ireland) Act, 1898, s. 13.

[5] *Report on the Administration of Local Government Services*, 1928–29, Cmd. 110 (1929), p. 50; H.C. Deb. (N.I.), 9, c. 2422.

either to send paupers to the workhouse or make unlawful payments.[1] They took the latter course. All boards of guardians were breaking the law by 1937.[2] In that year they were given wide powers to grant outdoor relief and were indemnified in respect of unlawful payments made during the past three years.[3]

The changes we have outlined were of importance not only in themselves, but because they prepared the ground for willing acceptance of later reforms initiated in Great Britain. As the 'step-by-step' policy in State services was extended and out-relief became more general, the latter's inadequacy and lack of uniformity were sharply exposed. The number of persons covered by State schemes rose from 302,063 in 1922 to 468,643 in 1938.[4] While the Ministry of Labour prescribed rates of cash payments throughout the country, boards of guardians in different unions paid sums that by contrast were both small and arbitrary. The legal expansion of out-relief meant, too, that the workhouse lost its *raison d'être*. Originally designed to give work to the destitute, it was now little more than a refuge for those who by reason of age, sickness or mental defect could not help themselves.[5]

For social as well as financial reasons, Ulster had therefore

[1] The Poor Relief (Exceptional Distress) Act (N.I.), 1928, s. 1 (1), (3) empowered guardians with the Ministry's consent to grant special outdoor relief, but its whole cost was to fall on the union or the district electoral division in which there was exceptional distress. This literally retrograde measure (divisional rating was abolished in 1898) meant that the heaviest burden would fall on areas least able to afford it, and few boards of guardians availed themselves of the power.

[2] The Minister of Home Affairs said in April 1937, 'So far as I am aware all boards of guardians in Northern Ireland do in fact make provision for relieving deserving destitute able-bodied persons outside the workhouse, although at the moment this is not strictly legal.' H.C. Deb. (N.I.), 19, cc. 1052, 1968.

[3] Poor Relief (Amendment) Act (N.I.), 1937, ss. 1, 4.

[4] These statistics are for persons covered by unemployment insurance and pensions schemes and in receipt of unemployment assistance. *Ulster Year Books*, 1922, p. xiv; 1947, p. xlviii.

[5] The following table shows the average population of workhouses on the last Saturday in March in the three years 1936–38:

Sick in workhouse hospitals and infirmaries	3,497
Aged and infirm	1,006
Children under 15	240
Lunatics, idiots and epileptics	165
Mothers having infant children	63
All other classes	138

One of the Nuffield Trust surveyors (page 72 above) said the conditions in which many of these people lived were disgraceful for a civilized society. Old people, perpetually fed on soup and porridge, were crowded together in bare wards that sometimes lacked even chairs and tables.

everything to gain by recasting her social security system on similar lines to those introduced by the British Labour Party after 1945. The poor law, more than century old, disappeared and boards of guardians were abolished. National insurance, industrial injuries insurance, family allowances, national assistance, non-contributory old age pensions and welfare services provided by local authorities were all built on the British model. We have seen that national insurance and industrial injuries insurance operate as virtually a single system in Britain and Ulster. Administrative arrangements for local welfare services are slightly different,[1] and Northern Ireland did not bind herself to keep exactly in step in national assistance, family allowances and non-contributory pensions. The Social Services Agreement of 1949 obliges her to maintain these services only in general parity.

Nobody outside government service can say how much latitude this confers on Ulster, but it is clear that it does confer some. That was shown in 1956, when the provincial Government proposed to alter rates of family allowances so as to give more money to small families and less to bigger ones, most of which happen to be Roman Catholic. This aroused widespread criticism, both because it could give substance to charges of religious discrimination, and also because a departure of this sort from British policy could have undesirable repercussions. Ulster Unionist M.P.s at Westminster told Lord Brookeborough, the Prime Minister, that there was likely to be formidable opposition in England.[2] The plan was abandoned in favour of maintaining absolute uniformity, and this has been observed ever since.

This was the first time since 1921 that any government had suggested in public that Northern Ireland should diverge from British practice in social security. The strength of the opposition, together with the fact that Ulstermen have always acquiesced in their leaders' other policies, tend to show that in this field the ordinary man is even more firmly wedded to 'step-by-step' than his Government.

[1] For details see *Ulster Year Books*. Recent developments in local welfare services are described in the *Report on Health and Local Government Administration*, 1963, Cmd. 474 (1964), chap. iv.

[2] *Belfast Telegraph*, 29 May, 12 and 23 June 1956.

PART FOUR

CHAPTER TEN

Parliamentary Devolution

WE began this study by showing that devolution was a necessary evil. Had it not been for the Irish question, no government would have created subordinate parliaments anywhere in the United Kingdom. Home Rulers often held out before Scotland and Wales the prospect of self-government, but when in power they never satisfied Nationalist aspirations; and eminent Unionists, Lord Carson among them, argued that the attempt to build a non-federal half-way house between union and separation was bound to fail.

Today Lord Carson's statue stands at the approach to the Parliament Buildings at Stormont. And Ulster has not merely survived as a political unit. Her relations with Britain have been singularly free from friction. Whether we can conclude from this that devolution would be equally practicable in Scotland and Wales, where there is still some demand for it, is a question that must be examined in this chapter.

It will, however, be better to begin by considering the value of Home Rule in Ulster; for what is practicable in politics depends in large part on the value people attach to the courses that are open to them. We have seen that in 1921 Northern Ireland was given the choice of accepting Home Rule (and, with it, partition) or of joining a united Ireland; and in later years she could have pressed for independence within the Commonwealth or for reversion to direct government from London. Of these, only the first and last are relevant to our theme. Is devolution preferable to government from Whitehall?

Now, in Ulster's case it seems that Home Rule has two special advantages. Since distance and expense separate her from the mainland, she probably gains more from local institutions than would small areas in Britain. Ministers and M.P.s are easily accessible to constituents; businessmen and interest groups of all kinds can press their cases on the spot; witnesses can appear before parliamentary committees with little inconvenience; and members and officials of local authorities have developed close and easy relations with government departments. As the Nugent Committee on the Finances of Local Authorities observed in 1957:

> This interaction between the government on the one hand and the local authorities on the other has led naturally to the formation of close personal relationships. Local councils look to central departments for help and guidance on points of difficulty, whilst the departments in their turn seek advice in local government circles as to the probable effect of new proposals. Local government deputations to Ministries are a common occurrence, readily sought and readily received; sometimes they are undertaken to settle a disagreement or to ventilate a grievance, but more often to plan together for the attainment of some common aim. Again, it is by no means unusual for a Ministry official to attend a council or committee meeting. Council members and officers of central and local government are generally known to one another, so that negotiations within the strictest official setting are conducted as between persons with official responsibilities rather than between impersonal offices. Thus it is that we may well be witnessing the evolution of a new pattern of relationships between the local bodies and government departments peculiar perhaps to Northern Ireland, but none the less adapted to our special needs.[1]

In general the whole political and administrative process is more intimate than it would be if control were remote. Against this it can be urged that intimacy may not be of equal value in all fields of public activity. Impartiality, the greatest political virtue, tends to increase with distance. So while the point must not be overlooked, in the final reckoning we must not put too much weight on it.

The second special advantage is related to Ulster's social divisions. Intolerance and hatred were once endemic, not only or even mainly because of tension between Protestants and Catholics, but because Nationalists hoped and Unionists feared that violence would break the British connexion. Today these emotions have lost their edge. A spirit of indifference, if not yet of toleration, is abroad.

This transformation is attributable, not merely to the passage of time (which may inflict new wounds as fast as old ones heal), but to growing consciousness among Irishmen of the fact that

[1] *Report of the Committee on the Finances of Local Authorities*, Cmd. 369 (1957), p. 73.

force is neither necessary to maintain the *status quo* nor likely to end it. Parliament at Stormont has always reflected the determination of most people to stay in the United Kingdom. Any lingering fears that a bargain struck in London might lead to their incorporation in a Roman Catholic republic were laid to rest by the Ireland Act, 1949. As long as that Act remains on the statute book and the electorate continues to return a majority pledged to maintain the Union, Ulster can count with absolute confidence on remaining part of the United Kingdom. To supporters of the régime, therefore, it gradually became obvious that reprisals against sporadic outrages were pointless. To its opponents, who profess to desire the unity of Ireland and the co-operation of all her people, it became equally obvious that bloodshed must frustrate their own purposes. Home Rule at least enabled both sides to live together in peace, and without that there can be no progress of any kind.

Not that the situation in Ulster is ideal. Single-party government and all it implies is distasteful to liberal-minded men, and privacy in public finance is a formidable hindrance to the development of informed democracy. It has, indeed, been argued that the transfer to London of Ulster's affairs would weaken Unionist domination, make government more open, and heal social divisions more rapidly because Westminster would be more willing than Stormont to redress Nationalist grievances. That, however, seems too simple a prescription for a deep-seated malady. The most resolute discrimination by both communities is practised by private persons rather than public bodies; it is widely, if not openly, justified as necessary to preserve fundamental values; and one party has been in power since 1921 simply because Nationalists repudiated a constitution that perpetuates partition. By changing their attitude they could gradually make party politics less rigid and partiality less defensible. The decision by the Nationalist Party in 1965 to accept the role of official Opposition at Stormont could have a profound effect on Ulster politics. As long as Ireland remains divided, however, partition will be a grievance, though under the Government of Ireland Act it could have been ended by the Irish people themselves. But Dublin and Belfast have never sought to reverse their original decision not to unite, and this has made it as plain as can be that partition is sustained, not by British bayonets, but by the will of Irishmen themselves. The United Kingdom would not only obscure this fact if she were to resume direct responsibility for law and order in Ulster. She could easily revive hopes and fears of ending partition and exacerbate the attitudes of which single-party government is no more than a symptom. She would, too, revive the Irish question in British politics and inflict on Westminster debates on matters that have generated incessant and bitter controversy at Stormont.

The merits of parliamentary devolution as a general reform have always turned mainly on two points. First, it would relieve congestion at Westminster. This was a live question a generation and more ago, but it has lost much of its urgency because the House of Commons has transformed its procedure. Governments have taken most of the time of the House, debate is frequently cut short, the committee system has been extended, questions to Ministers are rationed, and delegated legislation is more common. True, time is still a scarce commodity, and it would be somewhat less scarce if purely regional affairs were hived off, but the gain would be trivial compared with that which followed the exclusion of Irish business.

The second point is that devolution is a method of securing regional self-government without fundamental reconstruction of the constitution. With the passage of time, it can fairly be argued, this has become more rather than less urgent. The vast expansion of centralized State activity has weakened local initiative, and the very effectiveness of procedural reforms has left the House of Commons with limited opportunities for reviewing matters of special concern to particular areas. Regional government, together with regional elections and political parties, would help to reverse these trends and give local people greater freedom and independence in the management of their own affairs.

This, then, is the crux of the matter, and we must not lose sight of it. For if we are to draw useful conclusions from Northern Ireland's experience, we must begin with a clear idea of what to look for. Proponents of Home Rule are apt to point to the extent to which Ulster differs from Britain in policy and administration and to conclude that devolution is justified on this ground. Diversity rather than independence is made the touchstone. This is to confuse the accidental with the essential. Although Ireland had no parliament in the nineteenth century, she probably differed from Britain to a greater extent than Northern Ireland does now.[1] Besides, the example of Scotland (to which we shall presently

[1] Much legislation passed at Westminster applied to Ireland alone, for example in respect of education and technical instruction, public health, poor

turn) shows that even today a local legislature is not necessary to secure variety. Parliamentary devolution is to be distinguished from other forms of decentralization because it provides for a regional executive which is accountable, not to some outside body, but to a regionally elected legislature whose discretion within a defined field is unlimited.

The Government of Ireland Act was obviously intended to secure this. Ministers in Northern Ireland were to be responsible to a Parliament that was free to legislate on all matters not withheld from it. Subject only to this (and to the United Kingdom's overriding supremacy), Ulstermen through their representatives had complete liberty to make whatever changes they desired, whereas the people of Ireland before 1920 could do no more than try to influence Westminster, Whitehall and Dublin Castle. We have seen, however, that regional autonomy has in part become a fiction. The problem is, therefore, to try to determine how much of the substance, as distinct from the trappings, of independence still remains.

In forming a judgment on this point it must be noted in the first place that Ulster need not seek Britain's agreement in matters that are free from financial implications. Many of these are far from trivial. By a free vote in October 1962 the Commons at Stormont retained capital punishment and did not adopt the distinction between capital and non-capital murder which Westminster embodied in the Homicide Act, 1957.[1] The system and procedure of the inferior courts in Northern Ireland are unique in material respects. Legislation to improve the standard of agricultural produce is distinctive. Such highly controversial questions as the management of schools, religious instruction and methods of appointing teachers have been resolved by local debate. There is plural voting in elections; the local government franchise, tied for the most part to ownership or occupancy of property, is more restricted than in England; and constituency boundaries are not subject to adjustment by an impartial body. In these and other respects Northern Ireland differs from any part of Great Britain.[2]

---

relief and local government, agriculture, rating and valuation, elections and public order. The existence of a separate Irish Office under the Chief Secretary also meant that administrative measures often differed considerably from those in England.

[1] H.C. Deb. (N.I.), 55, cc. 535 et seq.

[2] The list can be extended by referring to the *Ulster Year Book* and other works noted on p. 19 above.

But (to repeat) it is not the differences that are relevant; if it were, their value would come into question. Our concern is with self-government, not good government, and there can be no doubt that Stormont has been wholly free to go its own way.

In the second place, however, governments can do relatively few things without money. 'Finance', as Mr. J. M. Andrews once observed, 'governs nearly everything we do.'[1] Financial relations have certainly developed in a manner that has greatly diminished Stormont's autonomy. Its powers in taxation are now very slight indeed. We have seen that transferred taxes as a proportion of tax revenue have fallen from an average of 17·9 per cent. in the ten years 1929–38 to 5·9 per cent. in 1962–63, and even in this limited field Ulster is bound to observe parity. While this does not mean that every local tax must be levied at the same rate as in Britain, free trade with the more prosperous mainland sets sharp limits to divergence. On the revenue side the local Budget is now so dominated by decisions taken in London that few people in Northern Ireland would notice any difference if all taxes were imposed there.

In expenditure, however, Ulster's leaders have more freedom. They must 'clear the rails with the Treasury',[2] but Treasury control appears to be applied with every consideration—and it is essentially negative. Local institutions provide seedbeds for initiative which may be pruned but is never stifled. Nor do Ministers need to rely solely on the Treasury's goodwill. The Home Secretary, always a member of the British Cabinet, watches Ulster's interests. The Joint Exchequer Board, composed of a chairman appointed by the Crown and one member each from the Treasury and the Ministry of Finance, can be a buffer between London and Belfast. The Ministry of Finance itself stands between the Treasury and the spending departments in Ulster, so that the latter are probably not conscious of Treasury control at all. The terms inserted in the post-war financial agreements—parity, general parity and general conformity—give deliberate scope for variation because they prescribe general standards for comparing the services to which they apply with similar services in Britain; and when submitting Budget proposals for discussion with the Treasury, it is open to the Ministry of Finance to make proposals for diverging from parity.

The trouble with these arrangements is that they appear to give more freedom to the provincial Government than to local people.

[1] H.C. Deb. (N.I.), 28, c. 77.

[2] The phrase was used by the Minister of Finance in 1949. ibid., 33, c. 1988.

Knowledge of what can be done is essential to liberty of action; but nobody, it seems, outside a narrow circle of Ministers and civil servants can forecast whether departures from British practice are likely to be feasible in any particular case. Discussions between the Treasury and the Ministry of Finance, like the proceedings of the Cabinet and the Joint Exchequer Board, are shielded from public scrutiny. This situation is in sharp contrast to that provided for by the constitution, whose published rules were designed to give freedom to the provincial Parliament by enabling its members to know in advance what they were and were not permitted to do. Judged by the intentions of its creators, it seems clear that devolution has failed.

The failure would be more obvious, and more serious, if Stormont were to insist on some innovation which the Treasury (or the Joint Exchequer Board) were not prepared to sanction. That, however, has never occurred. On the one hand, party ties are tightly drawn. No party with policies different from those of Ulster Unionism stands any chance of victory at the polls, and though Ministers are sensitive to back-bench parliamentary opinion, there is little danger of radical changes being pressed against their advice. On the other hand, financial arrangements are flexible. Ulster is neither expected nor obliged to imitate England exactly, and her leaders have been able to devise methods of overcoming problems that reflect the needs and desires of local people. What this means in concrete terms is sufficiently illustrated in earlier chapters. The Housing Trust was the outcome of the failure of local authorities to build houses on the necessary scale before the war and of the need to provide them quickly and in large numbers after it. The Tuberculosis Authority, though transient, was a unique device to meet a special problem. The health service is modelled on, but is by no means an exact replica of, the British service. Educational policy is the product of compromises arrived at by debate at Stormont and by consultations between Ministers and interested bodies. Agriculture, land drainage, the fire service, public transport and other services have been shaped by local conditions.

While, therefore, Ulstermen do not in practice enjoy the freedom to control their own affairs that is still enshrined in the constitution, they do have a government which they can influence. And their government can not only initiate proposals and amend them in the light of local discussion; it can concentrate its whole attention on them and if necessary exert pressure to obtain Treasury approval. In these respects it seems clear that Ulster is at least better off than any part of England.

Whether she is very much better off than Scotland, though, is not quite so clear. The Scots were always more successful than the Welsh and (until recent times) the Irish in resisting the assimilation of their institutions to those in England. Their legal system was preserved by the Union of 1707, and since the creation in 1885 of the Scottish Office arrangements have been evolved to give more weight to Scottish opinion and to ensure that Scottish problems are accorded distinctive treatment.

Scotland has her own Ministers headed by the Secretary of State; she has separate administrative machinery at Dover House in Whitehall and at St. Andrew's House in Edinburgh; many of her Estimates, including those for law and order, health and welfare, agriculture and fisheries, housing, education, roads and grants to local authorities,[1] are distinct from those for England and Wales; and legislation relating to Scotland alone is embodied in separate Scottish Bills or in special provisions inserted in Bills affecting the United Kingdom or Great Britain as a whole. Moreover, although Scotland has no parliament, she enjoys at Westminster a limited measure of devolution. Certain Bills, Estimates and motions applying only to Scotland may be remitted to the Scottish Grand Committee, and the committee stage of any Bill whose provisions relate exclusively to Scotland may be referred to the Scottish Standing Committee.[2] By these means the Scots have been able to influence the formulation and execution of policy and to diverge from the English in many ways. As Sir David Milne has written, 'There has been a definite and increasing tendency to assign to a Scottish Minister matters in which there is a distinctive Scottish tradition or body of law or where Scottish

[1] These and other functions are the responsibility, under the Secretary of State, of the Department of Agriculture and Fisheries for Scotland, the Scottish Development Department, the Scottish Education Department and the Scottish Home and Health Department.

[2] See *Report of Royal Commission on Scottish Affairs, 1952–54*, U.K. Cmd. 9212 (1954); Sir David Milne, *The Scottish Office* (London, 1957); Lord Campion, *An Introduction to the Procedure of the House of Commons* (London, 1958), pp. 211, 241–3; J. H. Burns, 'The Scottish Committees of the House of Commons', *Political Studies*, vol. viii (1960), pp. 272 ff.; J. P. Mackintosh, 'Regional Administration: has it worked in Scotland?', *Public Administration*, vol. 42 (1964), pp. 253 ff.

conditions are notably different from those in England and Wales.'[1]

Thus, while Scotland resembles Northern Ireland in that she is not independent, she also resembles her in that she is not obliged to copy England.

It can be argued that the Scottish model is a poor alternative to that in Ulster. The Secretary of State and other Scottish Ministers are not responsible to a separate parliament. The duties of those Ministers are restricted: many services which in Ulster come under local departments are in Scotland the responsibility of central departments such as the Board of Trade and the Ministry of Labour, though they maintain separate headquarters north of the Border. The Scottish Committees at Westminster are not really comparable to the Parliament of Northern Ireland. Their scope is narrower, the time of their members is limited, matters may but need not be referred to them, and they include a sufficient number of non-Scottish members to ensure a majority for the party in power. It may be claimed, therefore, that through their own Parliament and the Ministers accountable to it, Ulstermen can exert much more influence than Scotsmen on matters that closely concern them.

On the other hand, Scotland is probably in a better position than Ulster, not only to press her special interests at the highest levels, but also to share in the shaping of policy that affects both her and every other part of the United Kingdom. Ulster's Ministers make frequent visits to London, but their influence can hardly be other than intermittent and indirect. The Secretary of State for Scotland, by contrast, is always a member of the Cabinet.

> South of the Border, he has his share in the collective responsibility of all members of the Government for its decisions and actions; north of the Border, not only is he the Scottish equivalent of a number of English Ministers but he is regarded as 'Scotland's Minister', who must see that the Cabinet are made aware of the impact on Scotland of whatever they are discussing, and will indeed be failing in his duty if he does not do so.[2]

Then, too, Scotland's representation at Westminster in proportion to population is larger than Ulster's, presumably because the latter has a Parliament of her own; and far from its being a drawback, it may be a positive asset that the scope of the executive in

[1] op. cit., p. 21. [2] Sir David Milne, op. cit., p. 3.

Scotland is more restricted. The Board of Trade and other economic departments are at least wholly responsible for Scotland's welfare. In Ulster, by contrast, Stormont has formal responsibility for employment and economic matters but little real power, while Westminster has power but no formal responsibility. The Scottish Council (Development and Industry) emphasized to the Royal Commission on Scottish Affairs that

the experience of the Council and of its predecessors over a long period of years, in work which has necessitated close contact with all Departments of Government, leaves it in no doubt that more would be lost than gained by disassociating Scotland from the major United Kingdom Departments.[1]

Where the balance of advantage lies as between the Scottish and Ulster models must evidently be a matter for informed judgment. The majority of people in both countries seem content with what they have, and this probably reflects the fact that neither is conspicuously better off. So far as Scotland is concerned, the Royal Commission concluded:

The existing legislative and administrative arrangements in Northern Ireland have come into being as a result of historical causes peculiar to that country. After considering the evidence which we received from Government Departments and others in Northern Ireland we are of opinion that these arrangements, however well adapted to conditions there, would not further the special needs and interests of Scotland. In Scotland devolution has taken an indigenous, but different, form due to the preservation following the Treaty of Union of her native institutions founded on her distinctive legal and ecclesiastical systems, and now exemplified by Scotland's direct representation in the Cabinet. While there may be support for the adoption of a form of devolution more readily apparent, we feel that this would inevitably reduce the prestige and standing of Scotland and her representation in Parliament at Westminster, and would thereby weaken her voice in British and world affairs.[2]

To sum up so far. We have suggested that Home Rule in Ulster has special merits which are the product, not of devolution as such, but of its application to a geographically remote and politically abnormal area. Whether it would be of much value as a general reform is by no means certain. Regional institutions have made it possible for people in Northern Ireland to escape complete centralization and uniformity and to exert more influence on their

[1] op. cit., p. 43. [2] op. cit., p. 53.

affairs than they would secure as members of a wholly undifferentiated political unit, but there are other ways of securing these benefits. What is certain is that Ulster's experience does little to encourage the belief that the creation of regional parliaments will safeguard that measure of independence which parliamentary devolution is designed to secure.

This conclusion may mean, not that independence is unattainable, but that Ulster has not chosen to attain it. Stormont has acquiesced in agreements that have limited its powers. It might equally well have rejected them.

What if it had done so? It is plain enough that Ulster is relatively poor. Without Britain's assistance after 1921 she would probably have been obliged to abandon unemployment insurance and would possibly have been unable to finance derating. After the war there could have been no question of keeping pace with Britain in social services and industrial and agricultural development. The price of independence—that is, of keeping expenditure within the bounds of ordinary revenue—would have been abysmally low standards.

That is not all. Northern Ireland, like Ireland as a whole, has always been a high-cost area. She has no large home market nor abundant supplies of materials and fuel to offset her remoteness from overseas markets and supplies. Unlike Southern Ireland, however, Ulster is an integral part of the closely-knit common market of the United Kingdom. As we have noted at different points in this study, the extent to which she can control her economic life is extremely restricted. She can neither protect her industries against external competition nor conclude trade agreements with overseas countries nor shield herself from the impact of United Kingdom taxation, interest rates, purchase tax regulations and the host of other fiscal and economic measures devised in London. Without Britain's agreement she can do practically nothing to encourage enterprise by remission of taxation and other financial inducements. Indeed, her people's lives and fortunes are so closely tied to Britain's that it is not generally in her interest to impose any taxes at all. Nor, on the other hand, can she expect market pressures to drive down wage rates appreciably, for they are largely determined by national agreements; and men, as well as money and commodities, can flow freely across the Irish Sea.[1] Yet Britain is at the same time the principal market for her exports

[1] The Safeguarding of Employment Act (N.I.), 1947 now limits the flow of labour into Northern Ireland.

and her strong competitor both at home and, as in the case of shipbuilding and many other industries employing skilled labour, abroad. In brief, although Ulster enjoys slighter natural advantages than Britain, she is held firmly in Britain's economic orbit.

If therefore she was not to compete on hopelessly unequal terms, she had to secure for farmers, industrialists and workers conditions at least as favourable as—and, if possible, more favourable than—those in Britain. She had literally no choice but to adopt derating, to accept agricultural subsidies, to maintain unemployment insurance and to keep pace with social improvement and educational advance. True, had she failed, labour would have had a stronger incentive to migrate; but deliberately to maintain squalid conditions in order to diminish unemployment is to use a very blunt instrument. There is an abundance of labour in Ulster, but not of skilled labour. It is doubtful if local industries could have survived if craftsmen had been able to secure for themselves and their families markedly better conditions across the water. So the penalty of independence and nonconformity would have been, not merely relative squalor and ignorance, but in all probability a declining level of economic activity, dwindling revenue, drastic cuts in public expenditure and ultimately a state bordering on economic and social decay.

Analysis on these lines alone does not, however, catch the full subtlety of Ulster's predicament. It was shown in the first chapter that in 1921 she was heir to the contradictions inherent in Britain's attempt to build a half-way house. In order to preserve the unity of the realm and secure an Irish contribution to common services, British politicians restricted severely the Irish Parliaments' powers to tax. At the same time they decided that Southern (and equally Northern) Ireland should not enjoy Home Rule at Britain's expense; or, what comes to the same thing, that they should be no less independent in fact than they were in law. This determined the form of Ulster's public accounts and the division of powers between her and the United Kingdom. She was to be a distinct and self-sufficient fiscal unit. Distinct, because the revenue deemed to be due from reserved taxes, together with that collected by herself, was segregated. Self-sufficient, because from that revenue she was in general required to defray the whole cost of all services on her territory and to contribute to common services from which she was presumed to benefit. Thus, whereas for the purpose of taxation and general financial and economic policy Ulstermen were treated for the most part like other individual citizens, for the purpose of expenditure they were regarded as inhabitants of an area whose government was expected to finance the widest possible range of services with whatever revenue was left after they had made an imperial contribution.

Now, if they had been determined to make Home Rule a reality and live within their own income, or what counted as such, it seems that they would have been impelled to move from their half-way house to a completely separate dwelling. For two reasons. First, it was purely a matter of chance whether revenue would cover expenditure. No government could have operated in such conditions. Secondly, we have seen that independence would have condemned her people, not only to inferior services, but to a hopeless and unequal struggle. Compelled to pay virtually uniform taxes and share other common burdens but denied an equal share in common benefits, they would have become acutely aware that devolution was in fact, if not in intention, an organized method of discrimination. If her people had been forced, or had freely chosen, to be financially self-sufficient, they would it seems have had no alternative but to try to enlarge their fiscal and economic powers and, in particular, to repudiate the obligation to make an imperial contribution and get control of taxation and the host of factors that governed its yield and their economic life. Failure would have meant chronic conflict with Britain; success, a measure of independence similar to that enjoyed by Southern Ireland. In either event devolution could hardly have survived.

'Devolution', said the Minister of Finance on 15 March 1960, 'is a difficult art to practise.'[1] That Ulster has been able to practise it without apparent difficulty is due to a conjuncture of circumstances. Her people share with those in Great Britain ideals and loyalties that lie deeper than words. On a more tangible level it has been in Britain's interest that the settlement chosen by Irishmen themselves should not be disturbed. Successive governments, both Conservative and Labour, have obviously gone very much out of their way to help the province overcome her difficulties.

Ulster, for her part, has been fortunate in her leaders. Lord Craigavon, Mr. J. M. Andrews, Lord Brookeborough and their colleagues steadfastly pursued two dominant aims—to maintain

[1] H.C. Deb. (N.I.), 46, c. 844.

their country as an integral part of the United Kingdom and make life for all citizens better and more gracious—and they have allowed nothing to deflect them. Not that they have been indifferent about preserving the freedom of the provincial Parliament—on the contrary, in his submissions to the Colwyn Committee the first Minister of Finance tried to secure the maximum autonomy—but their overriding objective has always been, not independence, but improvement, and they have been willing to sacrifice the one to the other.

The sacrifice has not been agonizing. Ministers have often freely chosen to follow the British pattern. True, in many cases agreements have left them little choice. They could not have had a different system of old age pensions or unemployment insurance or a very different sort of health service. This, so far as one can see, has been no cause for regret. Ulster's administrative structure was similar to Britain's in 1921; subsequent problems have been similar in character; and it was natural that they should frequently have been overcome by similar action. It is radical nonconformity, not general conformity, that requires explanation. Legislative plagiarism (to use a term of Professor McCracken's) has not been confined to Northern Ireland. Even in the Irish Republic, where native culture and traditions nourish a distinctive political style, the Oireachtas (Parliament) has found it convenient on many occasions to follow Britain's lead.[1]

This approach in Ulster undoubtedly reflects the views of the majority. It is true that they are not well informed about agreements concluded on their behalf, but it seems certain that they would not feel keenly frustrated if they knew more about them. Self-government has never ranked high in their scale of values. The Protestant Ulsterman originally accepted Home Rule because it was the only practicable method, not of securing freedom from British domination, but of retaining British citizenship. His attitude is not wholly negative though. Inquiries by persons not in government (for example, those into the health services in 1927 and 1944 and into education in 1923) have found that many reforms already made in England would be appropriate, and in at least one case (the Government's proposal in 1956 to change family allowances) public opinion demanded absolute uniformity. In general it seems true to say that the citizen has not merely tolerated the

[1] J. L. McCracken, *Representative Government in Ireland* (London, 1958), p. 176.

actions of his leaders; he has encouraged them to hitch their wagon more firmly to the British star.

Yet the position of Ministers has not always been free from difficulty. They must satisfy the demands of legislators and their constituents without imperilling good relations with Britain. The friction implicit in this situation has come nearest to being explicit in the field of rating and taxation. The Ulsterman has a keen eye for his material interests. More than most people, he wants the best services at the lowest cost to himself; and he is especially liable to argue that rates and taxes should be lower than in Britain, first because his country is poorer, and secondly because the form of Ulster's public accounts has encouraged the delusion that he, alone among British citizens, must always and in all circumstances contribute to imperial services. Although Ministers point out that 'we are taxed as individuals and not as a country,'[1] they encountered strong resistance whenever they implemented Britain's requests to increase rates and taxes.

The resistance was strongest in the thirties, when poverty and squalor were widespread and nobody could foresee that relatively small financial burdens would eventually bring infinitely greater benefits in parity of services. It is true that Lord Craigavon, with remarkable prescience, always acted on the assumption that this would be so, but he could not know the future, and not all his followers shared his faith. Had Stormont not been controlled by a party committed to Craigavon's support, it is more than doubtful whether it would have accepted increased taxation. In that event, relations with Britain would have taken a very different course. As the Minister of Finance said in 1934, they had either to impose the education levy or upset their whole relations with the Imperial Government. It is probable, too, that Ulster would not have got help to improve her services. 'We can always have parity', said Mr. J. M. Andrews in 1945, 'as long as we pay our share of parity.' Now, we have given reasons for holding that improvement has been necessary to make devolution work. Stormont's rejection of parity in taxation would certainly have meant conflict with Britain; and it could easily have begun a train of events ending in the breakdown of a scheme of self-government which was incoherent as long as the United Kingdom taxed Ulstermen as individuals but treated them for the purpose of expenditure as residents of a distinct and self-sufficient financial unit.

[1] H.C. Deb. (N.I.), 27, c. 1288.

There has, however, never been any risk of this. Nationalism, the most powerful force making for political independence, has aimed, not to preserve and extend Stormont's powers, but to destroy them. This constant threat gave the Unionist Party unusual solidarity and endowed its leaders with exceptional authority. In effect, for more than forty years every general election and every critical parliamentary division, whether on taxation or any other subject, have been plebiscites on whether the Union should be maintained. Party cohesion was of first importance, both for this purpose and also for ensuring the smooth working, if not the survival, of devolution.

Northern Ireland has therefore evaded rather than refuted the Unionist thesis that Home Rule is impracticable. That thesis rested on the natural assumption that a regional legislature would insist on making full use of its powers. Ulster preferred close co-operation with Britain. She has been able and willing to pay the price, in part because of the quality of her leaders, in part because her people did not want self-government, and in part because they were deeply divided.

We may now turn to the question with which we began. Would the system that was introduced in 1921 work equally well in Scotland and Wales?

There can be little doubt about the answer. *Per capita* expenditure on local services in Scotland and Wales is higher than in England but *per capita* incomes are lower.[1] If, therefore, those countries were required to live within their own revenue, they would be confronted with similar problems to those that beset Ulster after she was established. They, however, are free from tensions that produce monolithic parties, and they are equally free from the danger that Home Rule would be imposed on them. Self-government for them would be the outcome of an insistent demand. The stronger that demand—the more vehement the desire for some measure of independence—the less likely it is that Scottish and Welsh political parties would be content with devolution on the Ulster model.

Would they need to follow that model? It seems clear enough that extensive powers to tax could not be transferred to regional parliaments. The considerations that induced the United Kingdom

[1] See U.K. Cmd. 9212, chap. iii and App. V for comparisons between Scotland and England and Wales, and E. Nevin (ed.), *The Social Accounts of the Welsh Economy, 1948 to 1956* (University of Wales Press, Cardiff, 1957) for comparisons between Wales and the rest of the United Kingdom.

to limit Ireland's powers are still relevant; and in the modern world all central governments, especially those of countries like the United Kingdom which are highly dependent on overseas trade, must retain their fiscal and economic powers if they are to steer between the shoals of slump and unemployment and the rapids of boom and external deficit. Moreover, the proportion of the Budget devoted to defence and other national services is now so great that Westminster could not afford to remit to subordinate parliaments the power to levy and appropriate to their own use any of the more productive taxes.

In other respects, though, it would be feasible to depart from the Ulster model. That model incorporated a division of powers on the broad principle that the United Kingdom retained only 'imperial' services, essential to safeguard national unity. Today, for reasons that require no examination, it would be desirable to centralize such other matters as industrial and agricultural development, employment policy, national insurance and assistance, railways and arterial roads. If, however, the line were drawn, not between 'imperial' and residual services, but simply between those which for one reason or another were charged either on central or regional Votes, there would be no point in requiring Scotland and Wales to make an imperial contribution, and little point in trying to segregate the revenue attributable to them. Many of the difficulties we have analysed would not then arise. It can be argued, therefore, that a workable scheme could be produced on the lines proposed by the Conference on Devolution in 1920.[1] The United Kingdom would impose most taxes, finance all national services, and grant to Scotland and Wales sufficient money to make good the deficit between their expenditure on regional services and whatever revenue was produced locally.

A plan of this sort would not be simple. Any system of grants designed to give regional parliaments wide freedom to spend while preserving the national government's control of taxation and its duty to check waste and extravagance, would be complicated and no doubt controversial. The standard of regional services and the severity of regional taxes as well as local rates would at once come into question. So would the cost of paying for more politicians and civil servants and their accommodation. It might well be hard to find able men and women willing to serve in parliaments with restricted financial powers, and a modern democracy can

[1] See p. 10 above.

imperil its foundations by injecting into public life large doses of mediocrity.

Other problems would probably be more formidable. It would be difficult for a parliament responsible for both United Kingdom and English affairs to include Scottish and Welsh representatives, but it could certainly not exclude them. In his account of the Irish Home Rule Bill of 1893 Morley wrote:

> Exclusion [of Irish members], along with the exaction of revenue from Ireland by the Parliament at Westminster was taxation without representation. Inclusion for all purposes was to allow the Irish to meddle in our affairs, while we were no longer to meddle in theirs. Inclusion for limited purposes still left them invested with the power of turning out a British government by a vote against it on an imperial question.[1]

This has never been of importance in Ulster's case. Her M.P.s number only twelve.[2] In Great Britain, however, Home Rule would, it appears, mean a parliament, not only for Scotland and for Wales, but for England (whether she wanted one or not) and for the United Kingdom as a whole.

This raises a further point. Proponents of parliamentary devolution do not merely desire variety (which, as Scotland has shown, can quite well be secured by other means) but some measure of independence. Most of the revenue of regional parliaments would, however, be controlled by a legislature in which England, the more populous and wealthy partner, would predominate. In order to temper that predominance there might well be pressure to create institutional restraints so as to transform the British constitution into one more akin to that of a federal State. In two of his more polemical works A. V. Dicey condemned Home Rule for Ireland as being a leap in the dark and a fool's paradise. Regional self-government in Britain would certainly be the one if not the other.

Our review has centred upon the relations between the central governments in Great Britain and Northern Ireland. Hopes are

[1] J. Morley, *The Life of William Ewart Gladstone* (London, 1903), vol. iii, p. 498.

[2] Virtually all of Ulster's M.P.s have always been allied to the Conservative Party. Had they formed a distinct party their position would have been more anomalous, especially on those occasions when a difference of twenty-four votes could change the outcome of a parliamentary division and precipitate a general election.

often held out that regional government would encourage experiment and allow more freedom at every level of administration; and Home Rule in Ulster could be of substantial value if it had produced reforms that might be studied with profit in other parts of the United Kingdom. However, although Stormont has made vast improvements in public services, it seems fair to say that it has not on the whole been a pioneer in matters of political organization that engage attention on the mainland. There has been no occasion for this in certain directions because some problems in Britain (e.g. those of the great conurbations) do not arise at all in Ulster.[1] In most other respects local administration has developed on much the same lines as in England and Wales.

This generalization can be sufficiently illustrated by a brief survey of three problems that do arise in both Britain and Ulster. The first of these concerns the freedom of local government. A common complaint nowadays is that central control is excessive. If democracy is to be firmly rooted, it is argued, local authorities should be accountable to the citizens who elect them, not to government departments. In Northern Ireland, however, the trend has been to make local councils instruments of general improvement. They are not, indeed, mere agents of the regional government. Within the framework of general policy they have a wide field of executive action in which they can move freely and independently, and the Ministry is accustomed to guide rather than to direct.[2] In addition, as noted above, consultation with government departments is easy and informal, and frustration arising from delay and impersonal relations is minimal. Local autonomy is certainly wider than in Ireland before 1920 (when government was highly centralized and corruption among local authorities was not uncommon), but it is narrower than in England. Forms of ministerial control are similar—inspection, loan sanction, audit and surcharge, default powers, approval of schemes, control of officers and so on—and supervision of this sort is if anything closer than in England. The existence within a small area of government departments seems to strengthen rather than weaken

[1] The Belfast region is the nearest approach to a conurbation. Stormont has more than once rejected proposals to extend the City boundary, and the aim of present policy is to restrict the growth of Belfast and encourage development in other areas.

[2] Cmd. 369, p. 73.

the tendency to interfere in local administration.[1] In financial matters we have already seen that the scope for independent action by local councils is extremely restricted.[2]

The second problem concerns areas and functions of small county districts. Proposals for reform arouse resentment, for Lilliputian authorities may be deeply rooted in a local community. There can, however, be no doubt that many districts throughout the United Kingdom need enlarging to enable the council to employ adequately qualified staff and discharge efficiently a range of functions sufficiently wide to make membership attractive to able citizens. In recent years Great Britain has moved rather hesitantly in this direction. Since 1958 it has been the duty of county councils in England and Wales to review county districts.[3] In the case of Scotland the Government in 1963 suggested amalgamating burghs and contiguous districts to form new sorts of authorities with populations of at least 40,000.[4] Ulster has a plethora of small councils, but the provincial Government have made no proposals at all. The question is even more difficult than in Britain because boundary changes could transform the political complexion of some councils which are now controlled by Unionists or Nationalists.

Finally, there is the problem of regional government. In Britain many *ad hoc* bodies (e.g. regional hospital boards) have been set up to discharge functions that need areas larger than those of any local authority. Regional administration already exists. A case can be made for creating elective regional councils to be responsible for all or most regional functions.[5] Compendious authorities of this sort could also continue to provide, under democratic control, services which many counties and county boroughs lack the resources to develop, such as further education and special schools, fire services, police, water supply and main roads.

[1] Until 1962 health and welfare authorities could not appoint even junior clerical staff without Ministry approval. *Report on Health and Local Government Administration*, 1963, Cmd. 474 (1964), p. 100. The Ministry of Education supervises local education authorities more closely than is the case in England. P.A.C. 1961–62, H.C. 1556, p. 114.

[2] Above, p. 95.

[3] Local Government Act, 1958, s. 28. County reviews begin after the Local Government Commissions for England and for Wales have reviewed the areas of counties.

[4] *The Modernization of Local Government in Scotland*, U.K. Cmnd. 2067 (1963). The Labour Government have dropped these proposals, which aroused strong opposition. *The Times*, 6 March 1965.

[5] For a discussion see *Public Administration*, vol. 42, Autumn 1964.

This question does not arise in the same form in Ulster. For one thing, the Government of Northern Ireland is not a local authority.[1] For another, Ulster may be described as a natural region. She has less need than Britain to concern herself with the difficulty of devising regions that are optimum areas for different services and in which citizens are conscious of sharing common interests. Nevertheless, there are similarities. The provincial Government have assigned many functions to special bodies rather than to local authorities or departments directly responsible to Parliament. These functions (mentioned on page 25) include the police, fire service, hospitals and general health services, electricity, public transport, housing and youth employment. In favour of such *ad hoc* authorities it is argued that their members and officials may be experts or may become such by specializing in a limited field; they have more time to think about long-term objectives; their work gains impetus because they are responsible for a particular task; they may be more efficient than a body that is constantly supervised by elected persons; and in some cases those who actually operate a service can be represented on the authority that runs it. For example, at least half of the members of the General Health Services Board represent the professions concerned. On the other hand, *ad hoc* bodies make co-ordination difficult and they are less likely than democratic institutions to do what people want or to stimulate popular discussion and promote political education.[2]

In this field, therefore, Ulster's experience does little more than show—what is already common knowledge—that no solution is ideal. The special bodies she has created have without doubt served her well. Their enterprise has transformed materail conditions of life since the war. But the student of comparative administration hardly needs to look across the Irish Sea to discover the virtues of *ad hoc* authorities, though he might learn something from the Royal Ulster Constabulary, which appears to be an

[1] The difference turns on powers and organization. The subordinate Parliament has statutory authority to do what is not forbidden, whereas a local authority can in general do only what is permitted. In local government, also, there is no distinction between executive and legislature. The council frames local policy and supervises administration through officers whom it employs and who are directly accountable to the council and its committees.

[2] These points were made in 1953 by the then Permanent Secretary, Ministry of Health and Local Government, Northern Ireland. See L. G. P. Freer, 'Recent Tendencies in Northern Ireland Administration', in D. G. Neill (ed.), *Devolution of Government* (London, 1953).

outstanding example of efficient police organization on a regional basis. The rate of crime detection in Northern Ireland is the highest in the United Kingdom.[1] For the rest, Ulster would be of greater interest as an administrative experiment if all regional services were under the direct control of one compendious authority, the regional Government. There has never been any demand for this, though it was mooted in 1964 when the House of Commons at Stormont decided that the Hospitals Authority should be the Ministry's agent. It is interesting to note, incidentally, that the experiment of freeing the Authority from detailed parliamentary control—a conspicuous departure from British practice—was not acceptable to local opinion. The whole argument for more democratic control does, indeed, appear to be unusually strong in Ulster today. Since 1921 her people have made remarkable progress, often against heavy odds. What seems to be most needed at the present stage of her evolution is further improvement, not only in the material sense, but in the qualities of mind and spirit that make a civilized community.

[1] *Belfast Telegraph*, 11 January 1965.

APPENDIX ONE

Irish Nationalists and Home Rule Finance

WE suggested in Chapter One that none of the Liberal Home Rule Bills would have worked in Ireland. Fully to substantiate this would entail a detailed analysis of the financial provisions of those Bills, an exact account of Nationalist reactions to those provisions, and an examination of Irish revenue and expenditure. A study of that sort would be out of place in this book. The statements that follow are, however, sufficient to show that the more prominent Irish leaders were well aware that the Irish people would not accept a legislature with the very restricted financial powers that Liberal governments were prepared to concede.

It is common knowledge that in 1886 Gladstone encountered difficulties because of the attitude of Parnell, who is recorded as having said, 'An Irish custom-house is really of more importance to Ireland than an Irish parliament.'[1] In his speech in the Commons on 8 April 1886 Parnell declared his intention to oppose very strongly the financial provisions of the Bill in Committee, and Morley has given his view that it was 'not at all improbable' that the Irish would have rejected the Bill on financial grounds had it gone forward into Committee.[2]

In 1893 Irish Nationalists spurned the finance of the Bill, and John Redmond declared on the third reading:

> As this Bill now stands, I maintain that no man in his senses can any longer regard it either as a full, a final or a satisfactory settlement of the Irish nationalist question. The word 'provisional' has, so to speak, been stamped in red ink across every page of this Bill. ... With regard to the financial part of the Bill, if in every other detail the Bill were satisfactory, that part of the Bill is so grave and faulty that it would be impossible for me to allow the third reading to go without uttering a protest and making it clear that my vote cannot be held as approving that part of the scheme. It is not merely that Nationalists regard the financial clauses as ungenerous ... it is the practical ground that they believe it to be impossible to govern Ireland successfully under these financial clauses.[3]

[1] Joan Haslip, *Parnell* (London, 1936), p. 304.
[2] Morley, op. cit., vol. iii, p. 306.
[3] 16 Parl. Deb., 4 s., 1504–7.

In 1912 the finance of the Bill was condemned outright by the General Council of Irish County Councils and by Irish Nationalists in the Commons. Redmond, bent on keeping his party together but equally anxious not to hinder the passage of a measure that under the Parliament Act would become law despite the Lords' veto, said:

It does not give us that complete and immediate control over all our finances that if circumstances had permitted I would have been glad to see in the Bill. . . . Admittedly it is a provisional settlement. . . . When the time for revision does come . . . we will be entitled to complete power for Ireland over the whole of our financial system.[1]

Finally, at the Irish Convention in 1917 Irish Nationalists insisted:

The taxing power so deeply affects the welfare and prosperity of the people, the dignity of parliament, and the wise and economical administration of the government, that no part of it could be placed under external control without perpetuating friction with Great Britain and discontent in Ireland. . . . Self-government does not exist where those nominally entrusted with affairs of government have not control of fiscal and economic policy. . . . No finality could be looked for in such an arrangement, not even a temporary satisfaction.[2]

[1] 46 H.C. Deb., 5 s., 2330; see also cc. 83 et seq.

[2] *Report of the Proceedings of the Irish Convention*, U.K. Cd. 9019 (1918), pp. 38, 67.

APPENDIX TWO

Revenue and Expenditure, 1923–39

(Selected Years)

Revenue

£ million

Years ended 31 Mar.	*Transferred*			*Reserved*		*From U.K. Exchequer (b)*	*Total*
	Tax	*Non-tax*	*Other (a)*	*Tax*	*Non-tax*		
1923	1·1	0·8	†	11·0	0·8	†	13·8
1924	1·1	0·8	†	9·3	0·8	†	12·0
1925	1·4	0·8	†	8·0	0·8	†	11·1
1927	1·3	1·0	†	7·0	0·8	0·9	11·1
1930	1·5	0·9	†	7·1	0·9	0·3	10·8
1931	1·6	0·9	0·4	7·5	0·9	0·5	11·8
1932	1·6	1·0	0·2	7·5	0·9	0·2	11·3
1933	1·5	0·9	0·3	7·9	1·0	†	11·6
1936	1·8	1·1	0·3	8·1	1·1	0·8	13·2
1939	1·7	1·1	0·2	10·3	1·2	1·8	16·2

Expenditure

£ *million*

Years ended 31 Mar.	Imperial contribution	Reserved Services	Transferred Services									Total
			Consolidated Fund (c)	Supply							Total Transferred	
				State insurance &c. (d)	Pensions	Grants to local authorities		Education (f)	Other	Total Supply		
						Derating (e)	Other					
1923	6·7	1·9	0·3	0·4	1·1	0·2	0·3	1·5	1·3	4·8	5·0	13·7
1924	4·5	1·7	0·4	0·4	1·1	0·3	0·2	1·8	1·9	5·6	5·9	12·1
1925	3·2	1·7	0·5	0·4	1·1	0·1	0·2	1·8	1·7	5·4	5·9	10·7
1927	1·4	1·7	0·7	1·8	1·3	0·1	0·3	1·8	1·9	7·2	7·9	11·0
1930	0·9	1·8	0·9	1·3	1·5	0·6	0·2	1·9	1·7	7·2	8·0	10·7
1931	0·5	1·8	0·8	2·0	1·7	1·0	0·4	1·9	1·6	8·7	9·5	11·8
1932	0·3	1·7	0·9	1·9	1·7	1·0	0·4	1·9	1·5	8·4	9·3	11·3
1933	‡	1·7	1·0	2·2	1·7	1·0	0·4	1·9	1·5	8·7	9·7	11·5
1936	0·4	1·9	1·1	2·9	1·8	1·1	0·4	1·9	1·7	9·7	10·9	13·2
1939	1·3	2·1	1·3	4·0	1·9	1·0	0·4	2·2	2·0	11·5	12·8	16·2

Sources: *Ulster Year Books*; Finance and Appropriation and Consolidated Fund Services Accounts.

Notes. † signifies nil. ‡ signifies less than £100,000. (*a*) Includes education levy and transfers from special Funds. (*b*) Payments under Unemployment Insurance Agreements. Other U.K. payments and certain self-balancing items are excluded. (*c*) Issues increased mainly on account of the Road Fund (financed by motor taxes) and loans to promote employment. (*d*) Includes unemployment assistance and employment services. (*e*) Before 1930, grants to relieve agricultural rates. (*f*) Includes grants to local education authorities. Discrepancies in totals are caused by rounding up the figures.

APPENDIX THREE

Unemployment Insurance 1926–35

Statement showing effect of Reinsurance Agreement

Years ended 31 Mar.		General population	Insured population	Insured population proportion of general population	Exchequer payments to Unemployment Funds and Transitional payments	Exchequer payments: Per head of general population	Exchequer payments: Per head of insured population	Equalization payment in respect of period (included in col. 6)	Payments by British Exchequer to N.I. Exchequer
		000	000	Per cent.	£	£ s. d.	£ s. d.	£	£
1926	G.B.	43,783	11,500	26·26	6,832,027	0 3 1	0 11 10		706,069
	N.I.	1,257	266	21·16	1,164,599	0 18 6	4 7 7	1,046,794	
1927	G.B.	43,964	11,650	26·50	10,837,821	0 4 11	0 18 7		879,591
	N.I.	1,254	263	20·97	1,515,371	1 4 2	5 15 3	1,308,256	
1932	G.B.	44,831	12,360	27·57	49,612,532	1 2 2	4 0 3		165,437
	N.I.	1,251	270	21·58	1,611,167	1 5 9	5 19 4	736,386	
1933	G.B.	45,084	12,400	27·50	79,331,282	1 15 2	6 7 11		Nil
	N.I.	1,262	265	21·00	1,901,903	1 10 2	7 3 6	508,319	
1934	G.B.	45,262	12,473	27·55	71,931,770	1 11 9	5 15 4		Nil
	N.I.	1,271	263	20·69	1,879,336	1 9 7	7 2 11	463,450	
1935	G.B.	45,446	12,540	27·59	66,850,000	1 9 5	5 6 7		Nil
	N.I.	1,280	268	20·94	1,864,000	1 9 2	6 19 1	664,211	

Source: P.A.C. 1933–34, H.C. 348, Appendix B. We have omitted 1928–31.
The 1926 year began on 1 October 1925.

Index